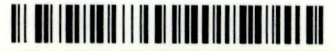

IMAGES
of America

ITALIANS OF
SAN JOAQUIN COUNTY

Local Italian Newspaper. Flavio Flavius began publishing this weekly newspaper in late 1913. *Il Sole* (the *Sun*), "San Joaquin Valley's Messenger," was one of the first in California to print in both English and Italian and had a large circulation throughout the Central Valley and Sierra Foothills. The paper stopped its circulation in 1957. This issue from July 1939 features the Italian Gardeners. (Courtesy of historian Bennie Filippini, Italian Gardeners Society.)

On the Cover: A group of Italians enjoy a meal of fruit and wine under a full arbor of grapevines during the fall of 1912. Italian immigrants who made their permanent home in San Joaquin County helped to develop the area's unique cultural, economic, and agricultural identity. (Courtesy of the Bank of Stockton Historical Photograph Collection.)

IMAGES
of America

ITALIANS OF
SAN JOAQUIN COUNTY

Pacific Italian Alliance
and Ralph A. Clark

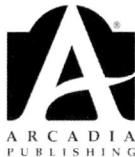

ARCADIA
PUBLISHING

Published by Arcadia Publishing
Charleston, South Carolina

Printed in the United States of America

Library of Congress Control Number: 2014935117

For all general information, please contact Arcadia Publishing:
Telephone 843-853-2070
Fax 843-853-0044
E-mail sales@arcadiapublishing.com
For customer service and orders:
Toll-Free 1-888-313-2665

Visit us on the Internet at www.arcadiapublishing.com

To Italians of San Joaquin County who came before us, and to those who come after us, for through them, history is made and remembered.

CONTENTS

ACKNOWLEDGMENTS

The greatest appreciation must go to the many families and individuals who shared their personal history with us as we gathered the material for this enormous project. Without their generosity and photographs, this book would not have been possible. I have met and interviewed the descendants of our Italian pioneers and have spent many splendid hours looking through fantastic photographs and enjoying some of the finest meals and hospitality I have ever experienced. One thing is for certain: There is no such thing as the cliché of a starving writer when working on a book about Italians. For all of that and more, I offer my deepest and most heartfelt thanks.

Thanks go to the board of directors of the Pacific Italian Alliance for allowing this book to move forward: William Trezza, Gary S. Giovanetti, Jim Falcone, Brian Martucci, Dan Caminata, Robert Benedetti, John Dentoni, Kathy Lagorio Janssen, Carla Donaldson, Giulio Ongaro, Claudia Pruett, Judy Cerri Rodriguez, Toni Sannella, and Michelle Mazzilli. Many thanks go to Andrea Songey-Neff, the driving force behind this project, who dealt gracefully with the challenges I threw at her.

A special thanks goes to the representatives of the local institutions keeping Italian culture alive: Ralph Lucchetti and Cathy Manassero of the Italian School and Bennie Filippini of the Italian Gardeners Society. A personal thank-you goes to my wife, Sarah, for enduring my absence while I was writing this book.

Lastly, a thank-you goes to the keepers of history: Tod Ruhstaller of the Haggin Museum, for use of its collection and access to the popular 2002 exhibit From Italy to California: La Nostra Strada; William Maxwell of the Bank of Stockton Archives, for the continued support; David Stuart and Leigh Johnson of the San Joaquin County Historical Society and Museum, for always being generous with their time; the staff of the Holt-Atherton Department of Special Collections at the University of the Pacific; and finally, the Italian American Studies Association and Italian Historical Society of America.

This book represents a small piece of our fascinating local Italian heritage, and we hope it inspires more exploration of local history. *Grazie mille!*

INTRODUCTION

The Italian experience in San Joaquin County begins, as so many California stories do, with the discovery of gold on the American River in 1848. Prior to that time, during the 1830s, Italian fishing boats in search of better fishing waters were slowly working their way up from Peruvian harbors in South America to the California coast. Interestingly, these sailors mainly came from the coast of northwest Italy, an area that, with its active fishing culture, would play an important role in later immigration. With news of the gold strike reaching around the world, a small number of Italians who were able to make the trip came for the adventure and the chance to strike it rich.

It is important to remember the Italy of this time was in a full-blown state of civil war between independent regions and territories (often controlled by other competing European nations or interests), each with its own traditions, dialects, customs, and behaviors, and no real national identity. A person's loyalty was often to his or her own geographic area—a phenomenon known as *regionalismo* (regionalism)—rather than to a wider Italian culture or identity. The Italian unification, or Risorgimento, would not be completed until 1871 (according to some scholars), and this historical backdrop provided the fuel for the massive amounts of immigrants that came to the United States from Italy. The regions of northwestern Italy were hardly an idyllic paradise. Years of strife in the early 19th century had created a series of economic hardships for the people of the region. Fewer than five percent of the population owned land, and there were very few opportunities available. Constant political strife, war, cultivation practices, and overpopulation had made the land barren, and the topsoil had almost completely eroded away.

The epicenter of emigration in Italy was the region of Liguria, located along Italy's northwest coast, which features a very impressive and dramatic landscape of lofty mountains, hills, and steep cliffs that plunge into the western Mediterranean. It would be this area, and its capital city of Genova (the local Italian spellings for Genoa and Genoese—Genova and Genovese—are employed throughout this book), that would send the vast majority of its sons and daughters to California. Genova is Italy's largest seaport and the birthplace of Christopher Columbus, and it has a deep and impressive history and culture. The second important center of emigration was the region of Tuscany, the birthplace of the Renaissance, which was renowned for its beautiful landscapes, traditions, and culture. By 1860, the largest number of Italian immigrants in the United States lived in California (with 80 percent of them being Northern Italian), and as late as 1890, there were more Italians in the Pacific states than in New England.

Immigration continued to increase considerably from the years 1880 to 1921 in a second wave of migration that brought a significant number of Italians to San Joaquin County. With the similarity in climate and the abundance of opportunity, the immigrants excelled. Aiding the Northern Italians was the fact that many were skilled laborers and brought with them knowledge of masonry, business, mining, finance, irrigation, and agriculture—talents perfect for building a new community. As the arrivals settled locally, they sent back for other family or friends and provided passage and employment once they established themselves. Natives of certain villages or towns lived near one another in the new country as they had in the old country. This village clustering, known as *campanilismo*, helped new arrivals deal with the culture change and the ethnic melting pot that was early California. They were able to assimilate much more quickly in California than elsewhere because of a relative lack of prejudice toward them and a hard-earned economic mobility. Various immigrants rose in status, becoming known as the *prominenti*—not just in the Italian community but in the wider community as well—and serving as pillars of the community, the state, and the nation.

Nowhere was the Italian presence felt more strongly than in the field of agriculture. Italian farmers had quickly planted varietal gardens of fruit and vegetables on the alluvial plains near rivers that other farmers could not use for the grain and wheat crops popular in the early days. These fertile plots were so prominent amongst the immigrants that they became collectively known as the "Italian Garden" lands. Growers would harvest and take their produce to cities and towns and sell from the backs of their wagons and trucks. The establishment of the Italian Gardeners Society in 1902 as a mutual aid society to help provide for farmers in the community who needed health and death benefits solidified the deep connection to their new homeland. It would be the Italian Gardeners who would establish the San Joaquin Marketing Association and build the Growers Market after selling in the streets was banned. The Italian Gardeners Society celebrated its 112th anniversary in 2014. The entire California wine industry owes its success to Italian immigrants and the hard work of the Mondavi, Gallo, Franzia, and Indelicato families, all pioneering winemakers.

Along with the immigrants came the traditions, entertainment, and customs that reminded them of the home they had left and connected them to their community. They formed groups and clubs, such as the Central California School of Italian Language and Culture, which offers classes for the descendants of those who settled here. They joined fraternal and business organizations and established musical bands and other entertainment groups. They excelled in sports and made homemade wine, sausage, and pasta, and they helped build churches, schools, and hospitals. Their community was always growing, adapting, and shaping the wider society with their traditions.

Unfortunately, by the end of the 20th century, connections to Italy had become distant, artifacts and histories had been lost, and apathy toward Italian culture was a concern. A push began for a new Italian organization, and among the first to support the idea were Faliero "Luke" Lucaccini and Frank Garavano. Their interest coincided with the arrival of Joseph Subbiondo and Robert Benedetti at the University of the Pacific. In 1991—joined by Joan Cortopassi and her husband, Dino—Lucaccini, Garavano, Subbiondo, and Benedetti proposed the formation of the Pacific Italian Alliance. Its mission would be to "bring the best that Italy has to offer to all generations." Their proposal was quickly embraced by George and Evelyn Lagorio and Dean and Kathy Janssen. Kathy Janssen agreed to become the organization's first president. Membership is open to all who love Italy. In 2011, the alliance marked 20 years as a driving force among Italian Americans in San Joaquin County.

This book and the photographs within it present only a small part of the vast history of the Italian immigrants that came to California and specifically to San Joaquin County. We have attempted to offer a wide representation of the community throughout the years to give the reader an understanding of its deep roots and the profound effect these people had on the area in which we live. We hope this inspires more people to explore their own family histories and the history of the wider community. We also hope more people will become involved in the organizations and groups that promote and protect the traditions, history, and culture of those who came before us and upon whose shoulders we stand.

One

THE IMMIGRANTS

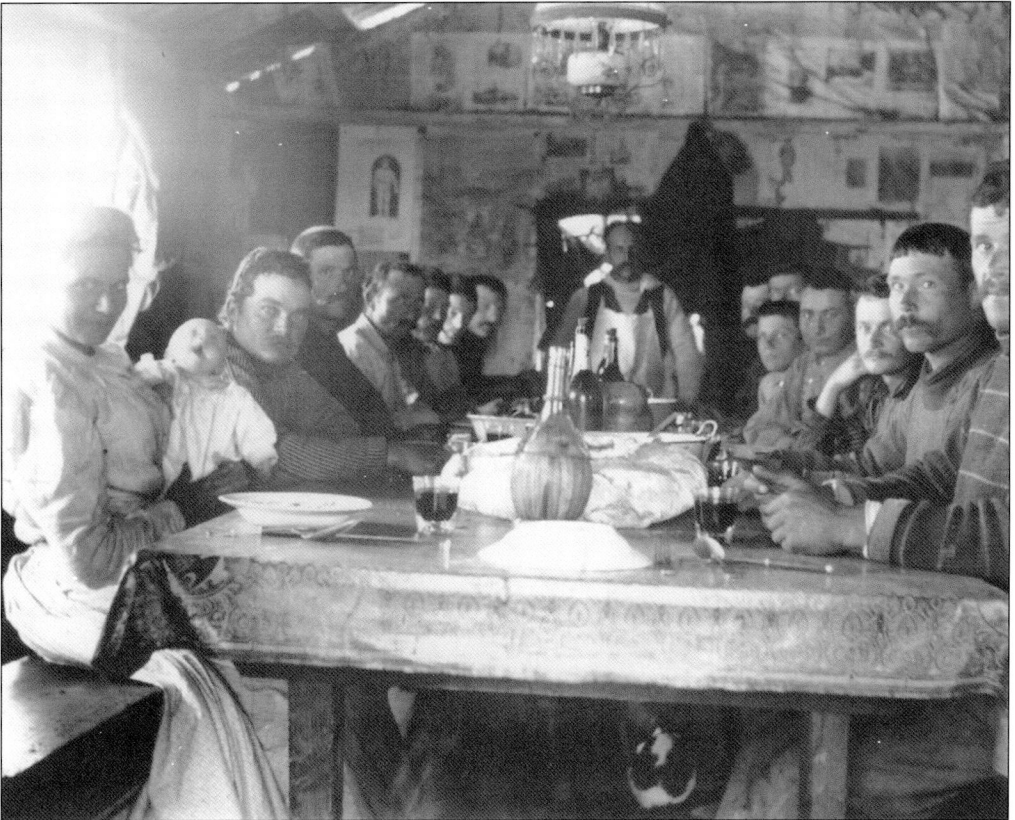

A WORKERS' DINNER. When new immigrants arrived, they often found work on farms and ranches owned or managed by other, already-arrived Italians who had sponsored their entry. The owners' wives would often cook large amounts of food for the various field-workers employed by the farm or ranch, as seen here in this undated photograph. (Courtesy of the San Joaquin County Historical Society.)

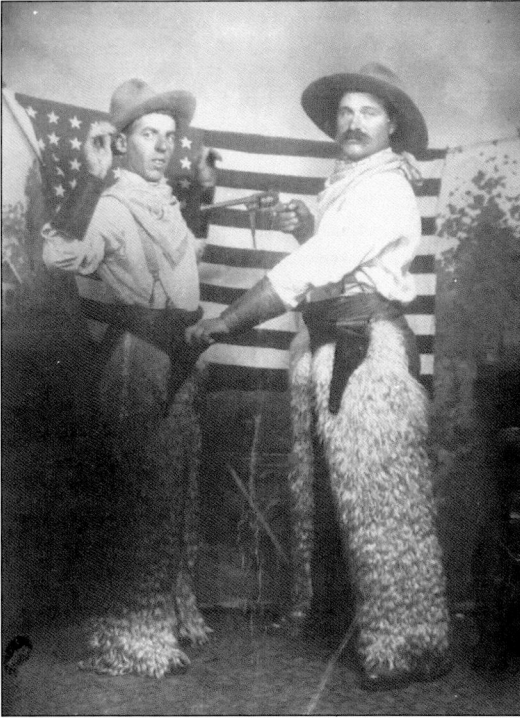

THE WILD WEST. Giacomo Canclini (right) "sticks up" an unidentified man while both are dressed as cowboys to comically show Italian relatives what life was like in the Wild West. Giacomo came to California in 1913 to work, save money, and then send for the rest of the family. After some time in the Eureka area, he settled in Oakdale and started a dairy. (Courtesy of the Canclini family.)

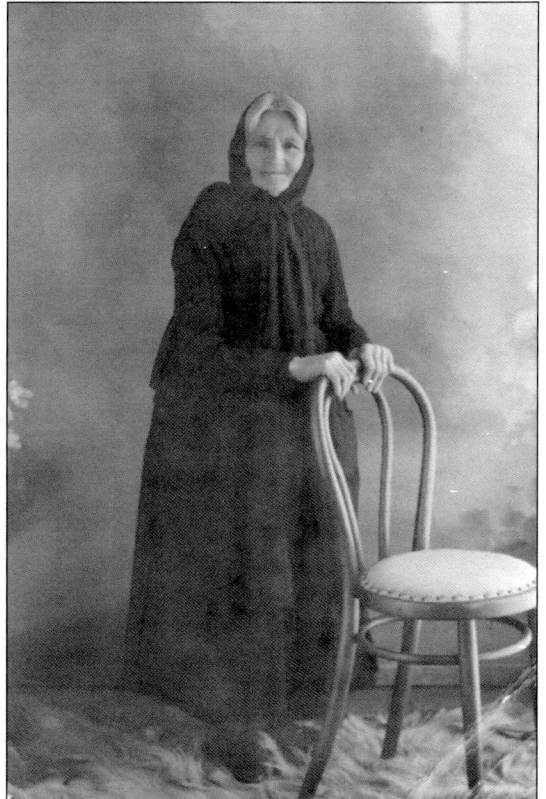

ITALIAN MOTHER. This woman, identified only as Frank Vezzani's immigrant mother, displays the traditional clothing of the Italian working class in a studio portrait taken in Stockton. Immigrants would often save for a few years to bring the rest of their family to the United States. (Courtesy of the San Joaquin County Historical Society.)

10

PRATO FAMILY IN ITALY. Domenico Prato (seated) poses with his unidentified daughter (second from left) and granddaughter Assunta Sivori (far left) in this photograph taken around the 1890s. Another granddaughter, Eugenia "Genni" Prato, stands at right. Eugenia would eventually immigrate to the United States and marry Giuseppi Lagorio in the Stockton area. (Courtesy of the Sanguinetti/Prato family.)

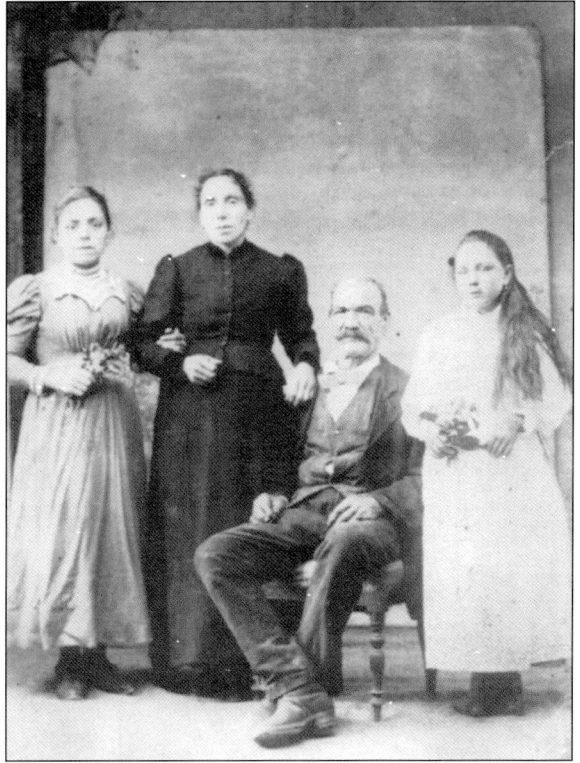

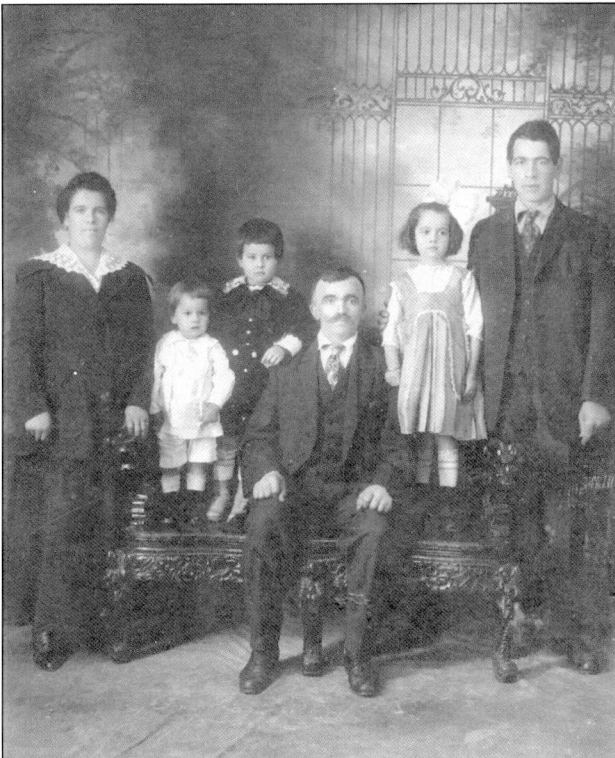

BASSO FAMILY PORTRAIT. From left to right are Lorraine, Mary, John, Art, Camilla, and Louie. The Bassos were Genovese cousins to the Forenti family and helped them eventually make the move from San Francisco to Stockton. Extended families often relied on each other when relocating and when looking for new opportunities. (Courtesy of the estate of Rose Forenti Derivi.)

11

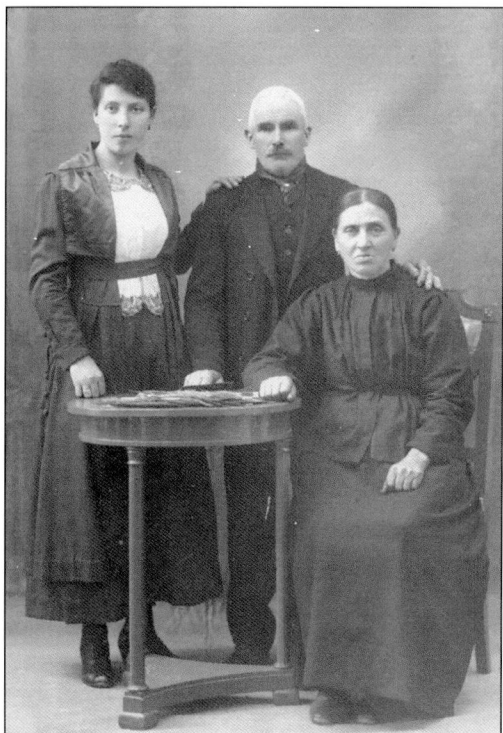

THE BASALTO FAMILY. The Basaltos, pictured at left around 1910 in Italy, were natives of the city of Genova in the Liguria region. Louisa (left) poses with her parents, Constantino and Maria (Sturla) Basalto shortly before immigrating to San Francisco. Louisa married Giacomo "Jack" Podesta of Stockton in January 1912. The couple eventually bought a 33-acre ranch on Duncan Road in Linden together with Louisa's brother Antonio "Tony" Basalto, seen below in an early-1920s studio portrait taken in Stockton. Tony immigrated at 20 years old in 1912 and moved in with his sister and her husband. During a visit to Italy in the early 1920s, Tony, a naturalized American citizen, was conscripted to serve in the Italian military. He returned to Italy again in 1929 in search of a wife. (Both, courtesy of the Basalto family.)

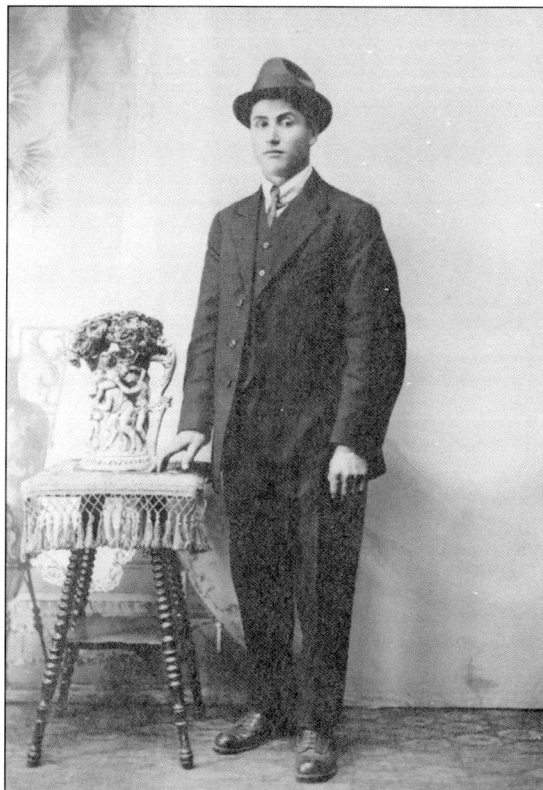

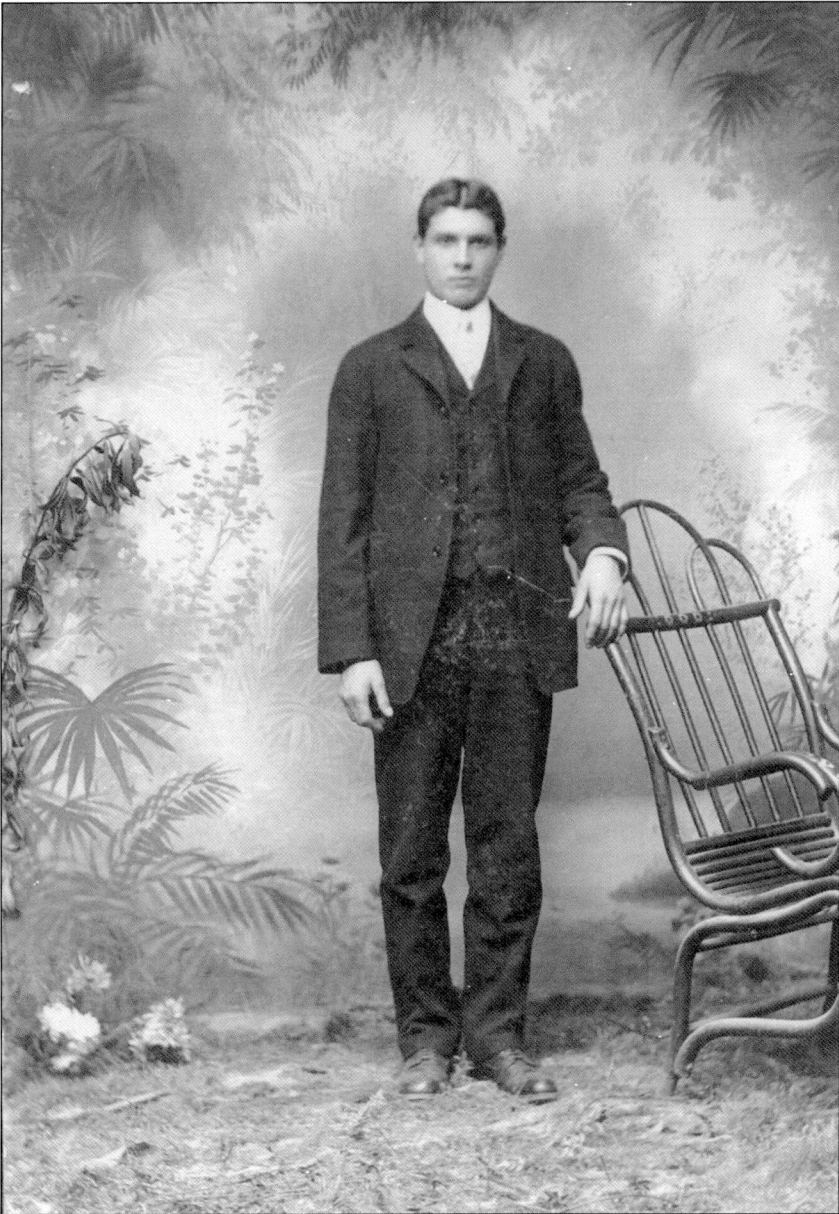

NICOLA "NICK" OLIVIERI. Nick was born in 1886 in Castiglione Chiavarese and immigrated to the United States in 1904 at age 18 with only $20 in his pocket. He left to avoid the military draft and to join his brother Pietro, who had previously settled in Sonora in Calaveras County (where this picture was taken). The brothers eventually partnered in the Europa Hotel in Sonora. After Pietro died of Spanish Influenza, Nick sold out to his sister-in-law and started farming in Columbia. In 1920, while visiting friends (the Martini family) in Linden, he partnered with Luigi Martini, Pippo Martini, and Giuseppe "Joe" Podesta in 80 acres of prime farmland. After a few years, the partners split up, leaving Nick with his own 20-acre portion. In the late 1920s, he bought a tractor and planted peaches and cherries. Nick married Amelia Zappettini, had two children—Guido and Lucia—and remained a farmer for 68 years until his death in 1988 at 102 years old. (Courtesy of Lucia Olivieri-Grillo.)

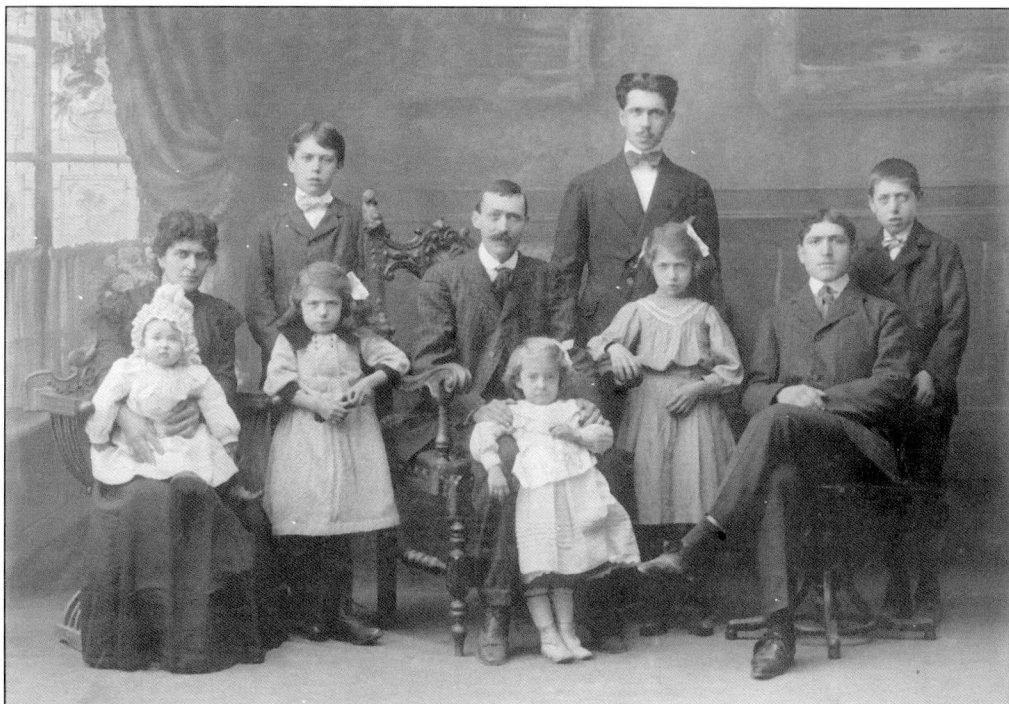

ZAPPETTINI FAMILY, C. 1915. The Zappettini family members pictured here are, from left to right, Victoria (mother), Aurelia (in Victoria's lap), Antonio (behind), Amelia, Camillo (father), Teresa, Narciso (behind), Rina, Giuseppe "Zap," and Angelo. Amelia and Zap settled in California, while Aurelia and Rina became nuns in Italy. Antonio married and remained in Genova, Narciso settled in Lavagna with his wife, and Angelo married and stayed in Castiglione. (Courtesy of Lucia Olivieri-Grillo.)

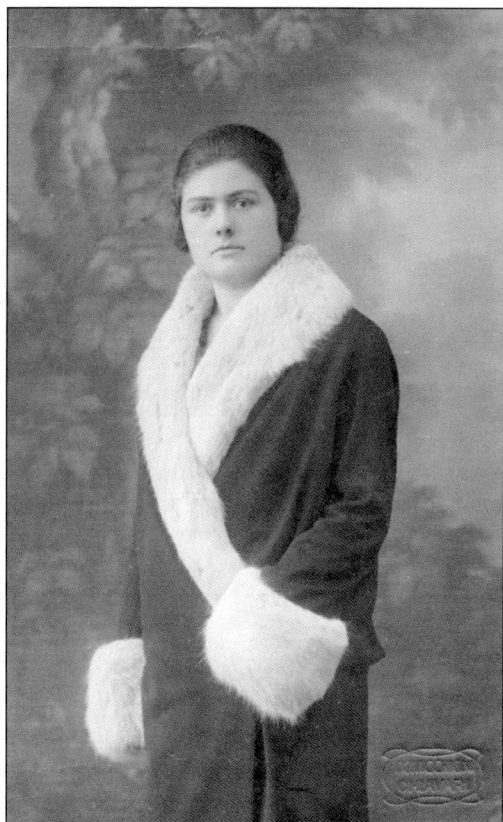

MARIA AMELIA ZAPPETTINI. This photograph of Amelia was taken in her late teens in Italy. She was a younger sister of Giuseppe Zappettini, who owned a market in Stockton. She met Nick Olivieri while he was visiting his family in Castiglione in late 1933. They were married in the church across the street from Amelia's home in Italy on January 29, 1934. (Courtesy of Lucia Olivieri-Grillo.)

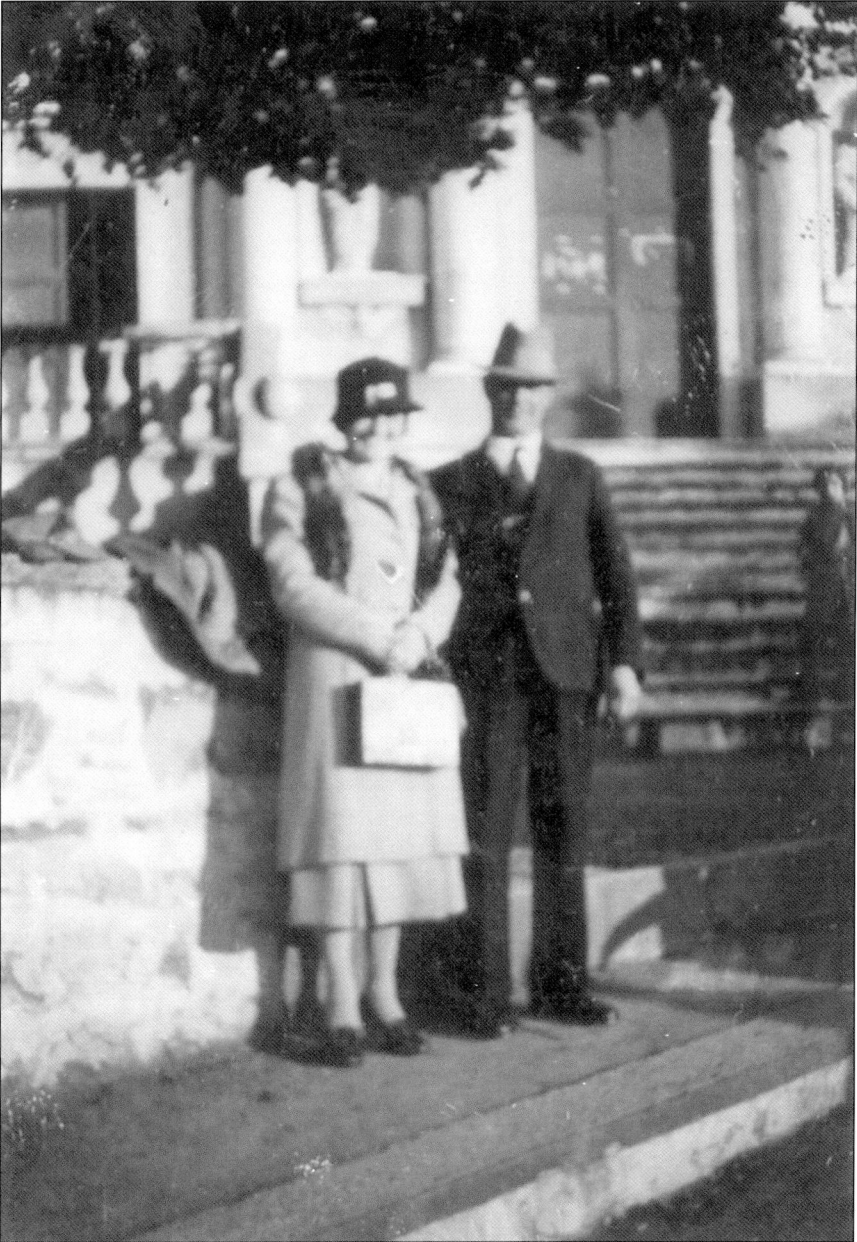

COMING HOME. While Nick and Amelia were visiting his mother in Missano, the *Carabinieri* (Italian police) came to the door after intercepting a telegram that read, *"ciliege rosse"* ("cherries turning red"). The police, perhaps thinking it was some sort of Communist code, tried to get Nick to surrender his passport. The year was 1934, and fascism was rising in Italy. Nick, as an American citizen, loudly refused and said, "If you want my passport you will have to kill me for it!" He explained he was a cherry farmer in California and had instructed his ranch hand to send him a message when the cherries were ripening so he would know when to come home. The authorities did not believe him and swore they would be back. The couple quickly made plans to return to their new lives in America. In this photograph, they are outside the church in their hometown of Castiglione. (Courtesy of Lucia Olivieri-Grillo.)

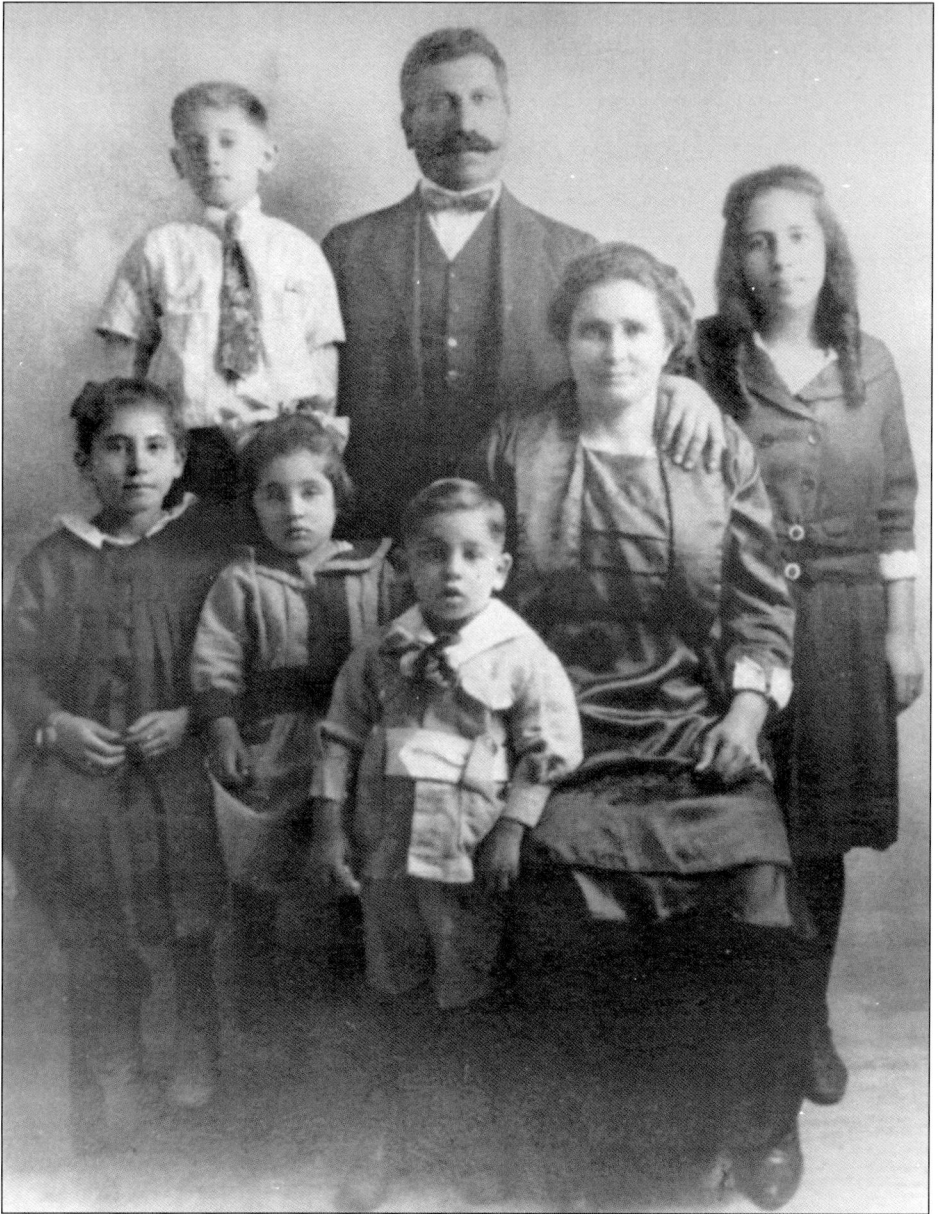

MAZZILLI FAMILY, C. 1920. Antonio (center) and Maria Mazzilli (seated) were married in Basilicata, Italy (near Naples), on August 14, 1902. Antonio immigrated to Stockton and found work with the Southern Pacific Railroad as a boilermaker. After establishing himself, he purchased a home at 326 South Union Street in Stockton, which became the center of the Mazzilli family for two generations. Antonio returned to Italy to collect his family, which at that time consisted of his wife and children: Jimmy (standing next to his father), Carmela (standing at far right), and, from left to right in front, Roxanne, Josephine, and John Anthony. Two more children, Vincent James and Donald, are not pictured. The Mazzilli family maintained many Italian traditions, such as canning fruit and vegetables; making homemade ravioli, prosciutto, and wine; and producing many loaves of freshly baked bread in the outdoor Italian oven built at their home. (Courtesy of the Mazzilli family.)

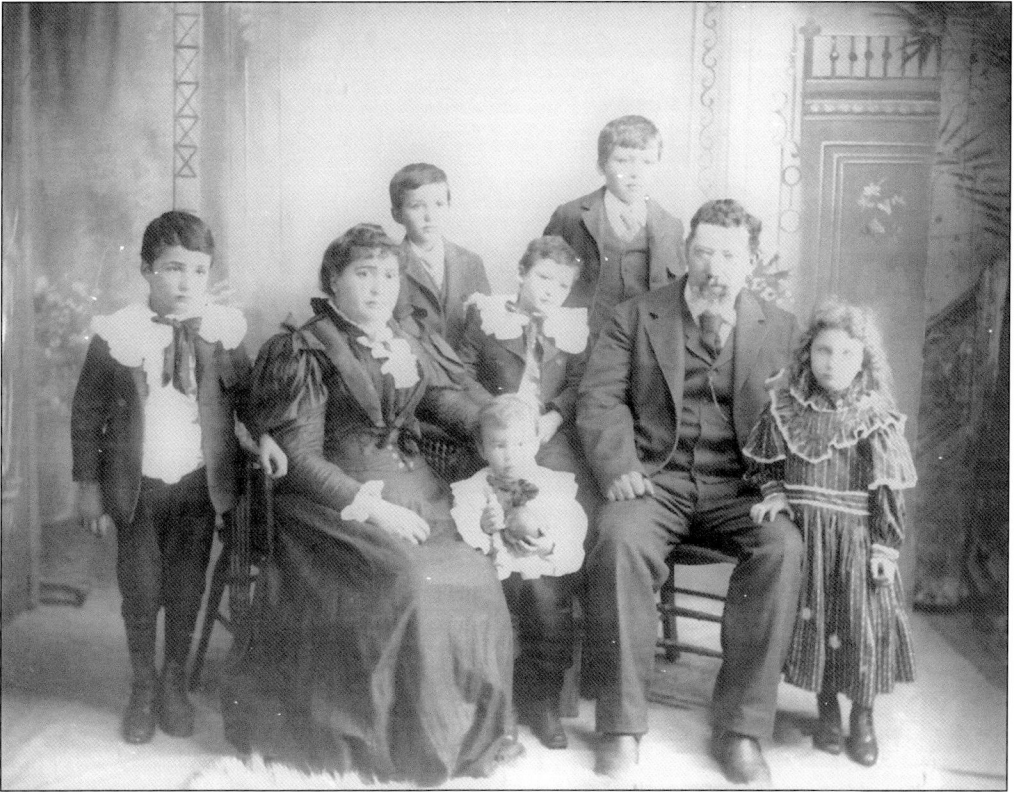

DePauli Family. Juseppi "Joseph" DePauli (the adult seated on right), known affectionately as "Old Joe," was an early pioneer of the county. He had an Italian garden on the Lee tract in Lodi, which later became a residential area. He also operated a peddling wagon for many years and established a strong reputation as a fair and honest businessman. Joseph's wife, Elizabeth (seated at left), and children, (from left to right) David, William, Fred (small child), Joseph, Lawrence, and Marie, pose for this family portrait that was taken sometime around the turn of the century. Joseph and Elizabeth (also seen at right) were married June 5, 1883, and were both natives of Genova, Italy. Joseph was orphaned at 14 and was penniless on arrival in the United States, but he quickly became a successful member of the community. (Both, courtesy of the DePauli family collection.)

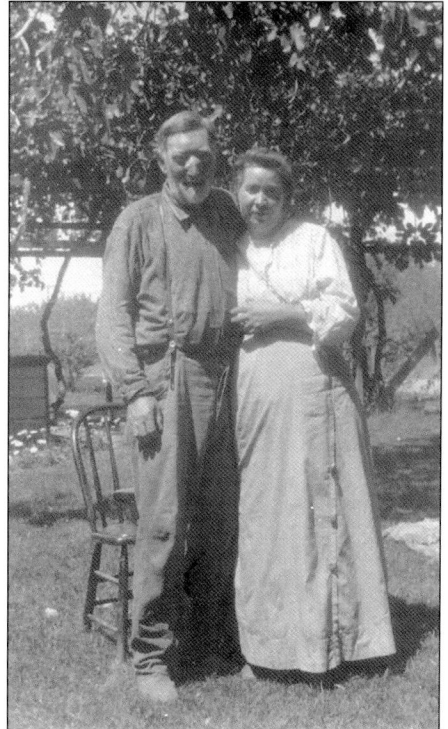

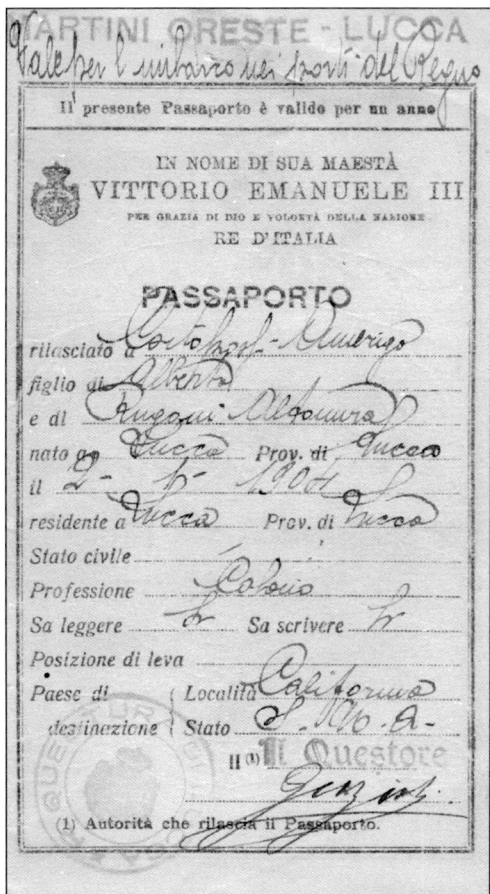

Il presente Passaporto è valido per un anno

IN NOME DI SUA MAESTÀ

VITTORIO EMANUELE III

PER GRAZIA DI DIO E VOLONTÀ DELLA NAZIONE

RE D'ITALIA

PASSAPORTO

rilasciato a

figlio di

e di

nato a ___ Prov. di

il

residente a ___ Prov. di

Stato civile

Professione

Sa leggere ___ Sa scrivere

Posizione di leva

Paese di (Località
destinazione (Stato

Il Questore

(1) Autorità che rilascia il Passaporto.

AMERIGO CORTOPASSI. A native of Lucca, Amerigo Cortopassi (his passport is seen at left) came to California in 1921 during what was the last rush of immigration from Italy because of the passage of the Emergency Quota Act, which set limits on immigration quotas based on ethnic origin. The steamer *Argentina* (pictured below), sailing from Naples, brought Amerigo to New York in 1921 before his 18th birthday and compulsive military service in Italy. The immigration quotas in the United States caused a ticket rush, leaving only first class available. Amerigo's mother, Artemesia, used savings earned from their small farm (acquired by his grandfather) to buy first-class passage. Amerigo traveled by rail to Stockton, where he met cousins Gigi and Giorgio Rugani, who sponsored him and his brother Vittorio. (Left, courtesy of Dino and Joan Cortopassi; below, Richard Faber Collection.)

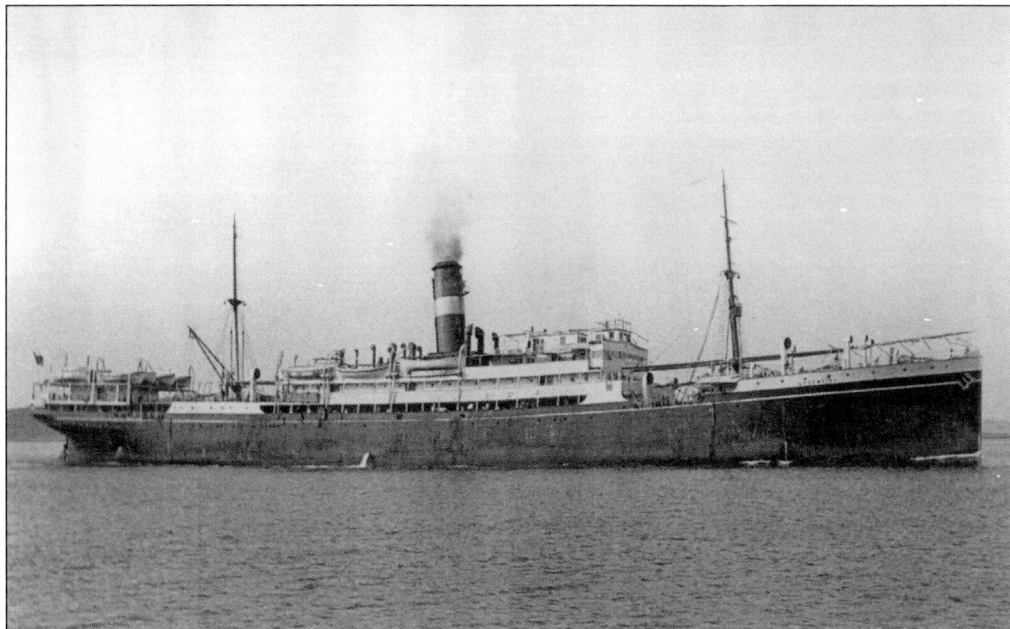

LUCCHETTI FAMILY. Giovanni Lucchetti and Elisa Ginocchio were married on December 3, 1908, in Comuneglia, Italy. Elisa was a first-generation American born in Dayton, Nevada, in 1875, but after the silver mines played out, her family returned home. Giovanni immigrated at 23 years old but returned home, where he met Elisa. They both returned to America in 1908 and settled in Stockton. (Courtesy of the Lucchetti family.)

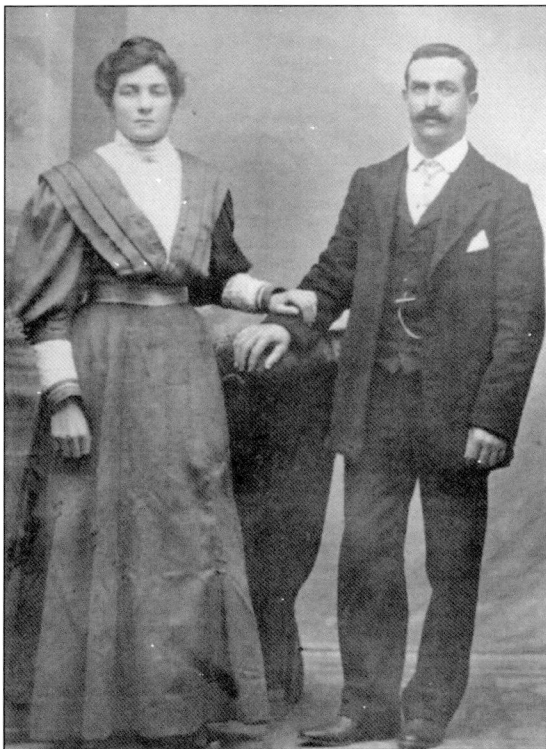

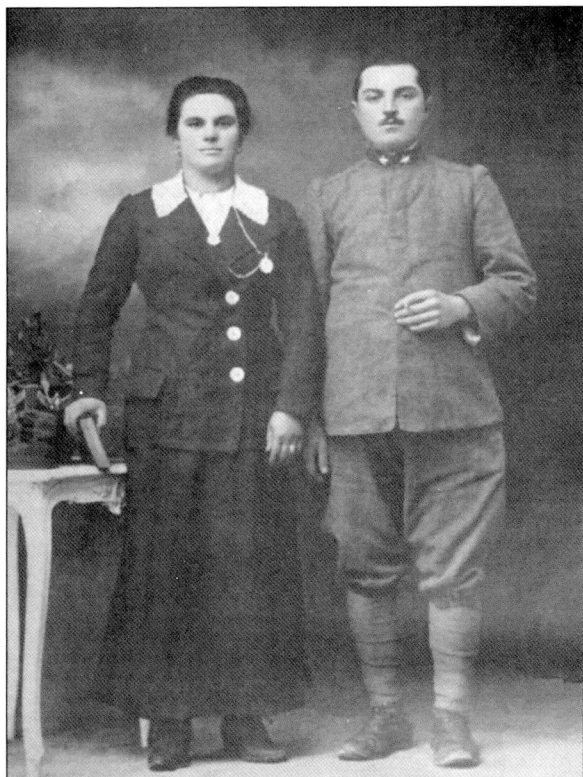

PONSI FAMILY. Ermenegildo and Assunta Ponsi pose for their wedding photograph in 1914. After suffering through the horrors of World War I as a soldier, Ermenegildo left Italy in late 1919 to make a better life in America. It took him seven years of hard work to finally bring his wife, who had unknowingly been pregnant when he left, and daughter Cristina to America in 1927. (Courtesy of the Lucchetti family.)

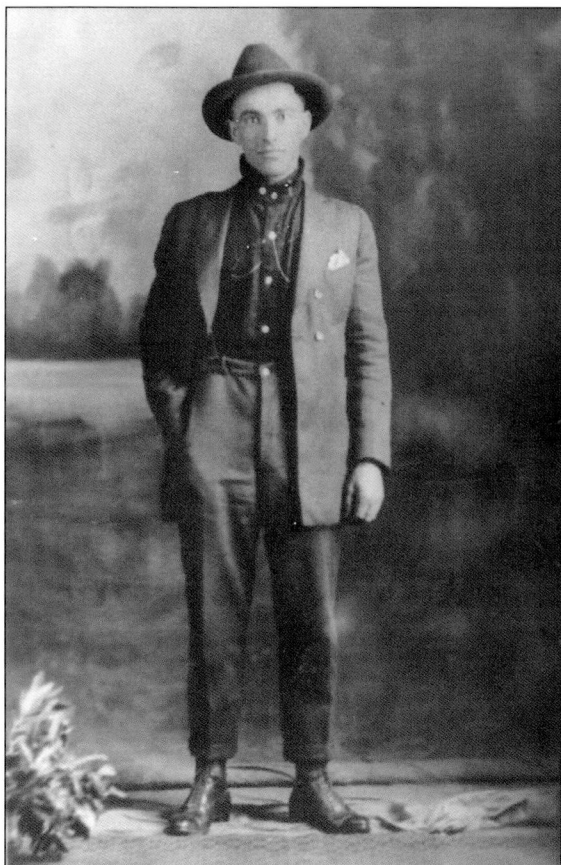

ANTHONY "TONY" BACIGALUPI. Tony came to the United States with his parents at three years old in 1899. He grew up to be a successful businessman, establishing the Stockton Bicycle Supply at the age of 20 in 1919. He was the first Schwinn dealer in Northern California and sold all manner of bicycles, tricycles, and toys. His store was located at 739 East Main Street. (Courtesy of Diana M. Lowery.)

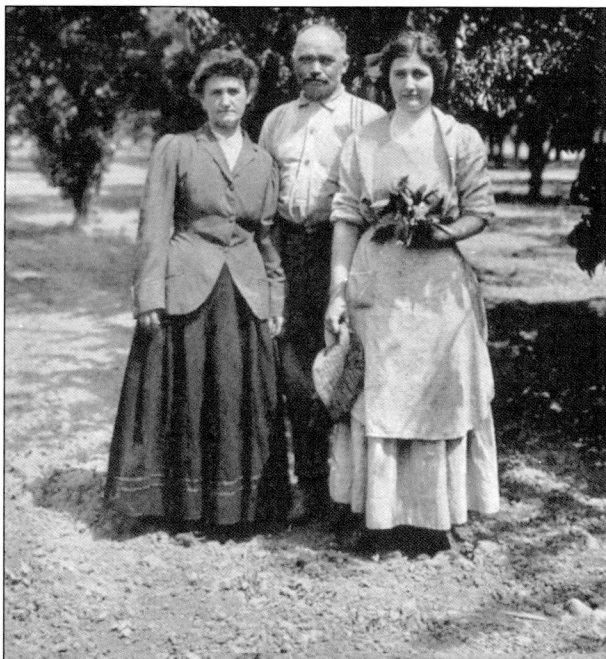

LAGORIO FAMILY. With an important familial name in the Italian American community, immigrant Luigi Lagorio came to San Joaquin County from Reppia, Italy, and settled on 25 acres on the Upper Sacramento Road, which he developed into an orchard. Luigi and wife, Theresa, had six children, Della, Angelo, Leonora, Louis, Amerigo, and Raymond. Many descendants of this family still live in the county. (Courtesy of the Haggin Museum.)

Two

A NEW COMMUNITY

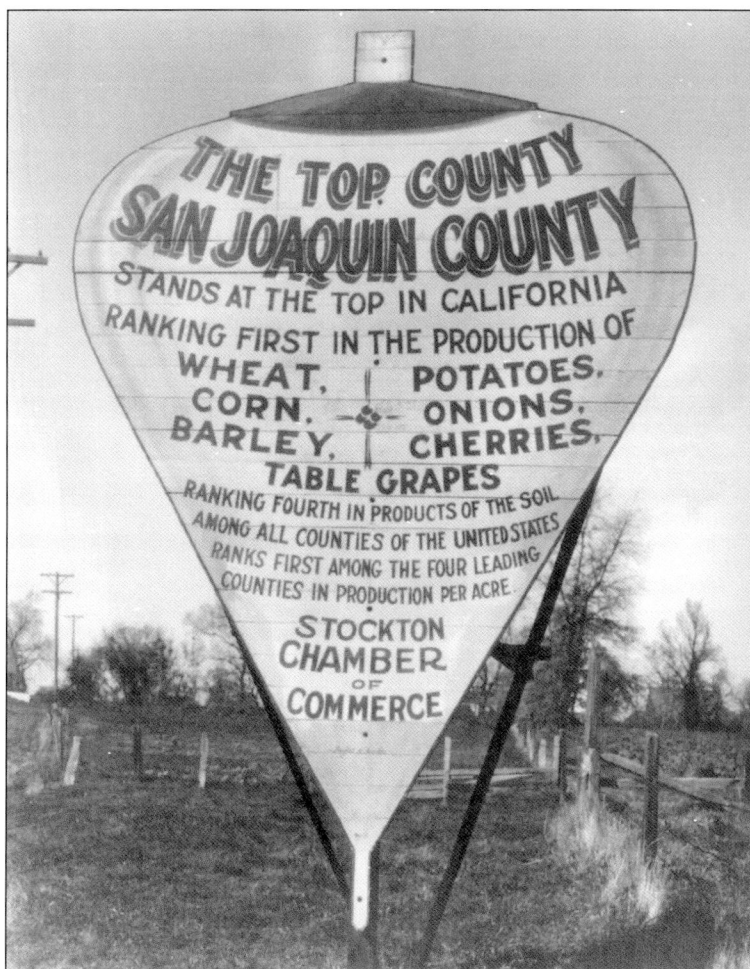

SAN JOAQUIN COUNTY. Named after the father of the Virgin Mary, St. Joachim, San Joaquin County was one of the original counties created upon statehood in 1850. The county seat, Stockton, served as a main port and supply station during the Gold Rush. The county became and remains an agricultural powerhouse, as evidenced by this chamber of commerce road sign. (Courtesy of Historic San Joaquin County.)

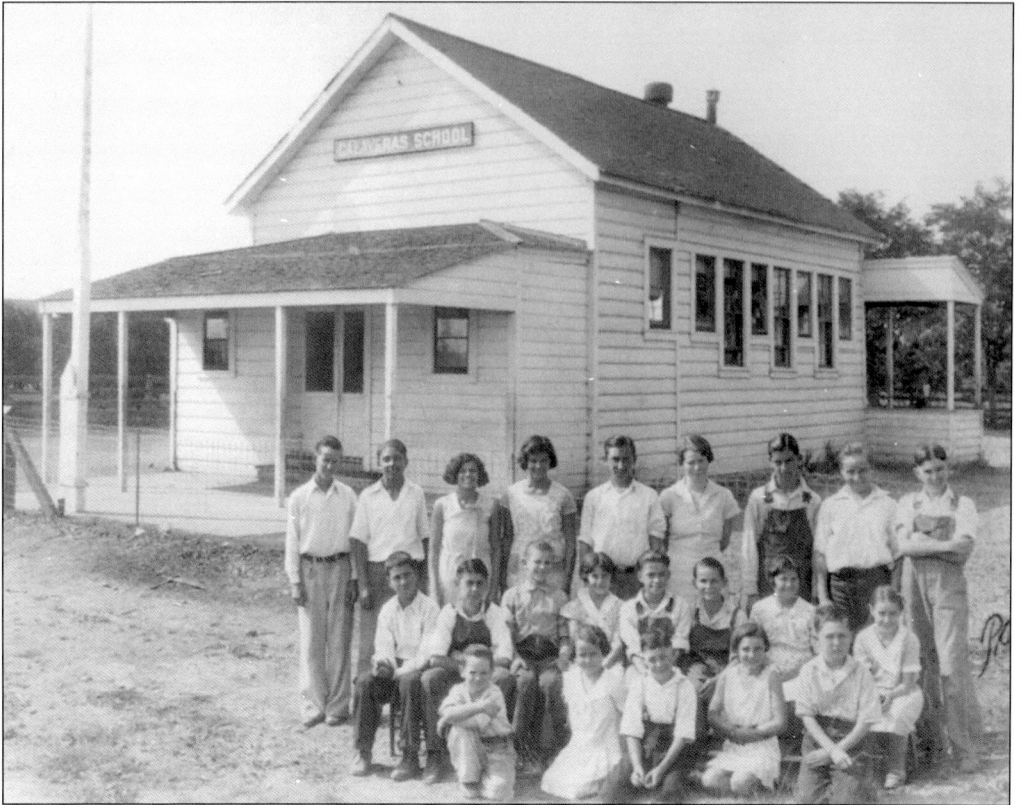

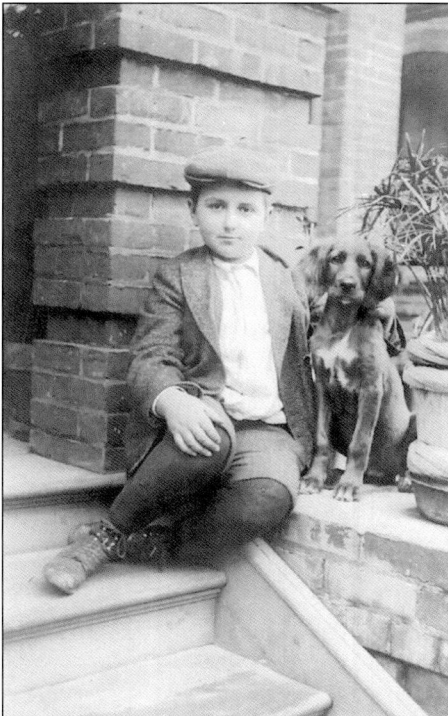

CALAVERAS SCHOOL. One of the country's last one-room schoolhouses when it closed in 1959, the Calaveras School, located at the intersection of Eight Mile and Lockeford Roads, served the rural children of the farms and ranches that surrounded it. In 1928, all the children except for two were Italian American. (Courtesy of the Bank of Stockton Historical Photograph Collection.)

A BOY AND HIS DOG. Gaetano Macchiavello sits on the steps of his home at Commerce and Washington Streets in Stockton with his dog. Gaetano was the grandson of notable pioneer Gaetano Alegretti (see pages 62 and 121), who came to California in 1859 and was one of the first Italians to settle in Stockton. (Courtesy of the Bank of Stockton Historical Photograph Collection.)

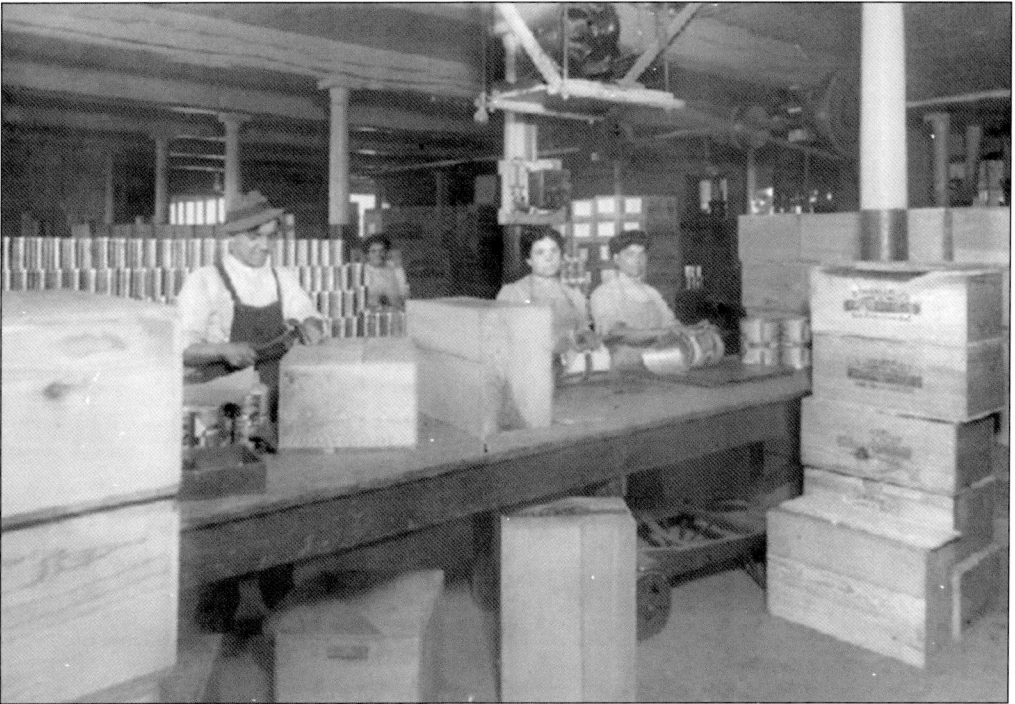

GHIRARDELLI CHOCOLATE. Domenico Ghirardelli was born in Rapallo, Italy (in Liguria), and became an apprentice to a candymaker. During the Gold Rush, he settled in Stockton, selling supplies and confections to the miners. In 1851, his Stockton shop burned, and he relocated to San Francisco and became highly successful shipping chocolate products from his warehouse (shown here in the late 19th century). (Author's Collection.)

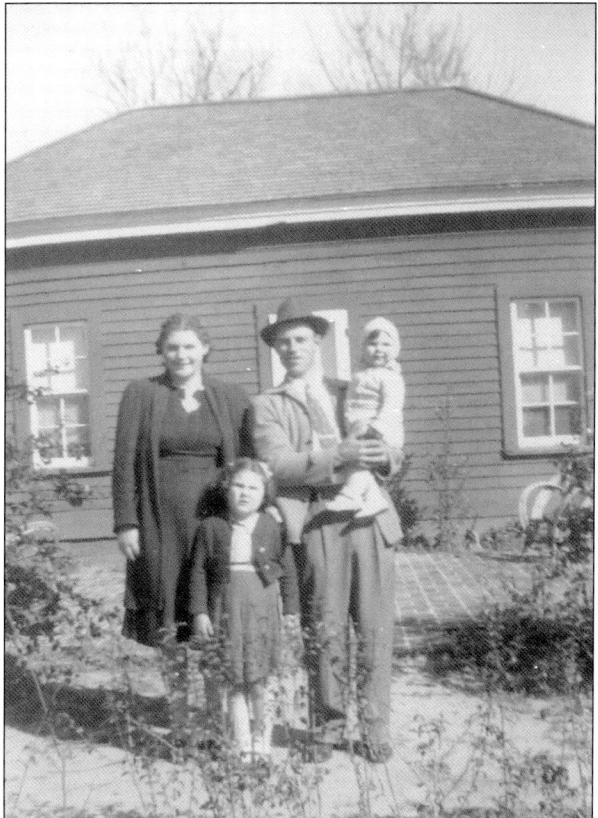

RANCH FOREMAN. Pictured are Lydia and Dave "Sesto" Canclini, their daughter Janice, and son David in front of the Weber cottage in 1941 or 1942. Dave worked on the family ranch until starting in the building trade. A few days of work for Helen Weber Kennedy (granddaughter of Stockton's founder, Charles Weber) turned into a 50-year career as foreman of the Weber Ranch. (Courtesy of the Canclini family.)

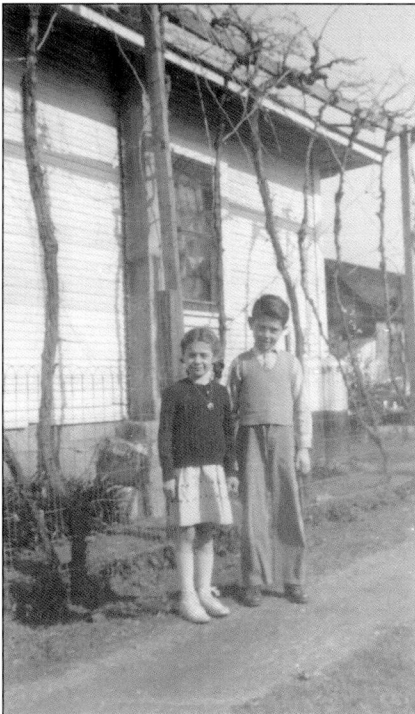

NATURALIZATION PAPERS. In Italy, Amelia Olivieri went to school until the fourth grade. While growing up, Amelia did household work, embroidery, knitting, and crochet and eventually worked in her uncle's leather shop, stitching and designing shoes. When she arrived here, she went back to school to study English and passed her citizenship test with flying colors. She officially became a US citizen on February 15, 1944. (Courtesy of Lucia Olivieri-Grillo.)

GUIDO AND LUCIA OLIVIERI. The Olivieris had two children—Guido (born May 1938) and Lucia (born February 1940), seen here in 1946. Guido wears a vest, and Lucia, a sweater made by their mother. Contrary to the custom, Nick stressed the need for education for both his children. Guido unfortunately passed away at age 38, and Lucia became an educator and eventually came home to manage the ranch. (Courtesy of Lucia Olivieri-Grillo.)

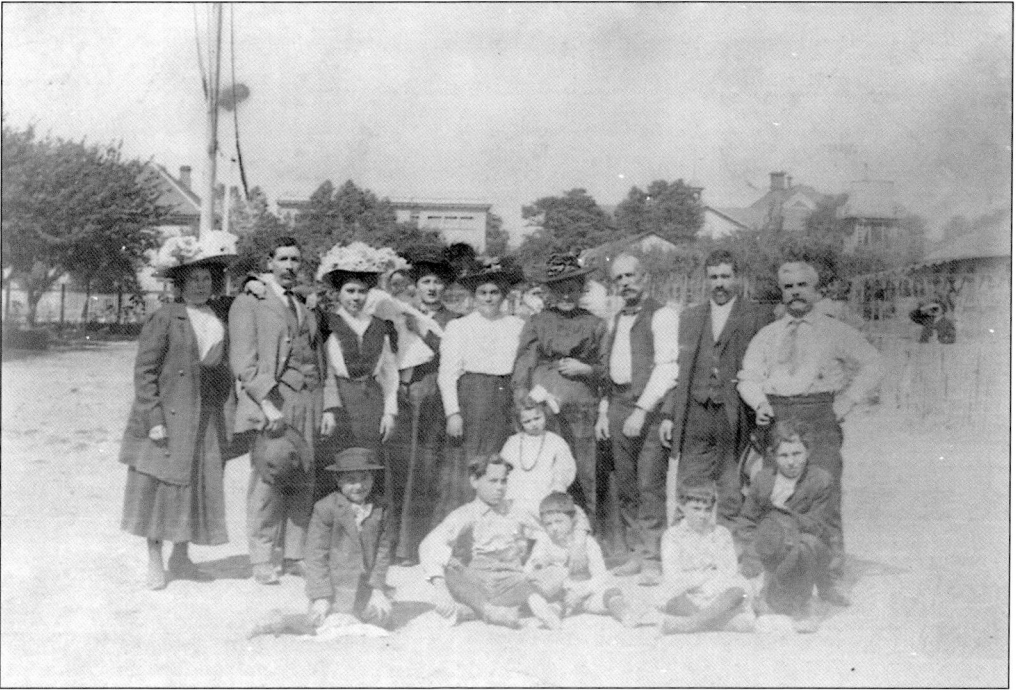

GALLI FAMILY GATHERING. Husband and wife Gerolamo Galli (man on far right) and Maria (woman in the white shirt in center) pose with daughter Anita Galli Canale (second woman from left, with large hat) and the rest of their unidentified relations, possibly after they first arrived in the United States from Italy. Extended family often relied on each other to get new arrivals established here. (Courtesy of the DalPorto/Galli family.)

DALPORTO'S CAR. Emil DalPorto takes his twin sisters, Lina (left) and Yolanda, for a spin in his new Ford Touring Model T in 1918. The twins returned to Italy in 1920 and came back to the United States after World War II. Yolanda settled in Stockton and married Alessandro Bertocchini, while Lina settled in New York. (Courtesy of the DalPorto/Galli family.)

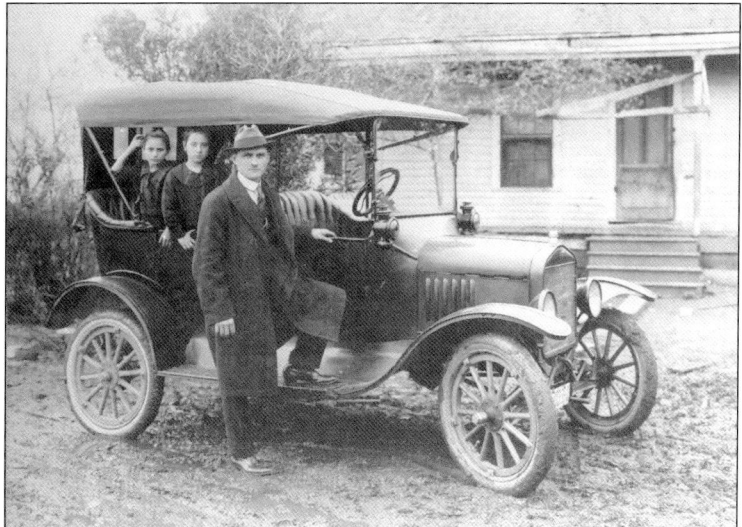

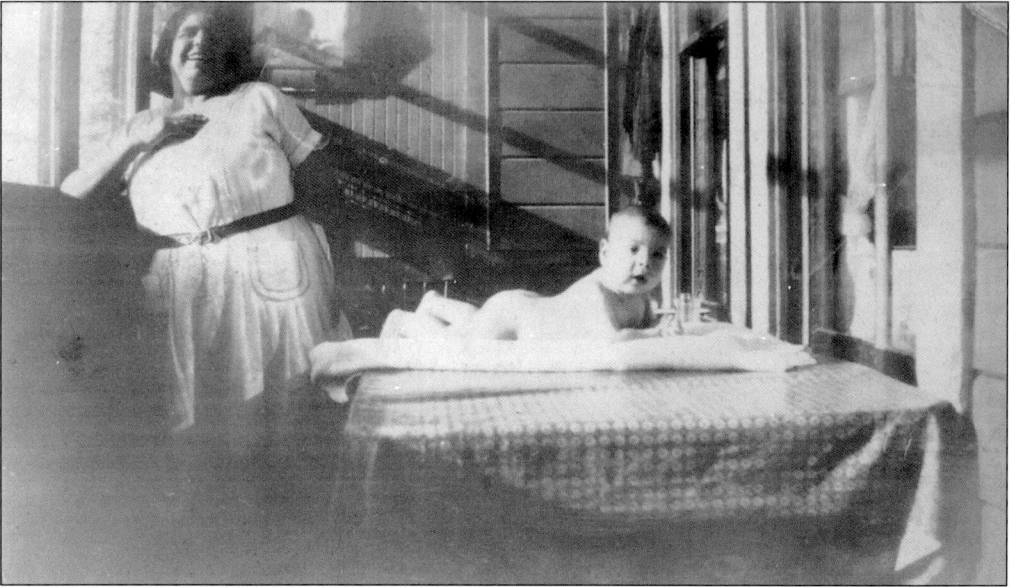

MOTHER'S PRIDE AND JOY. Giuseppina DelCorso flashes a beaming smile as her newborn baby, Raymond DelCorso, dries on the table after a bath at the DelCorso home on Harrison Street in Stockton in 1932. Raymond was the seventh child and the first boy for the DelCorso family. (Courtesy of Angie Gerlomes Nunes.)

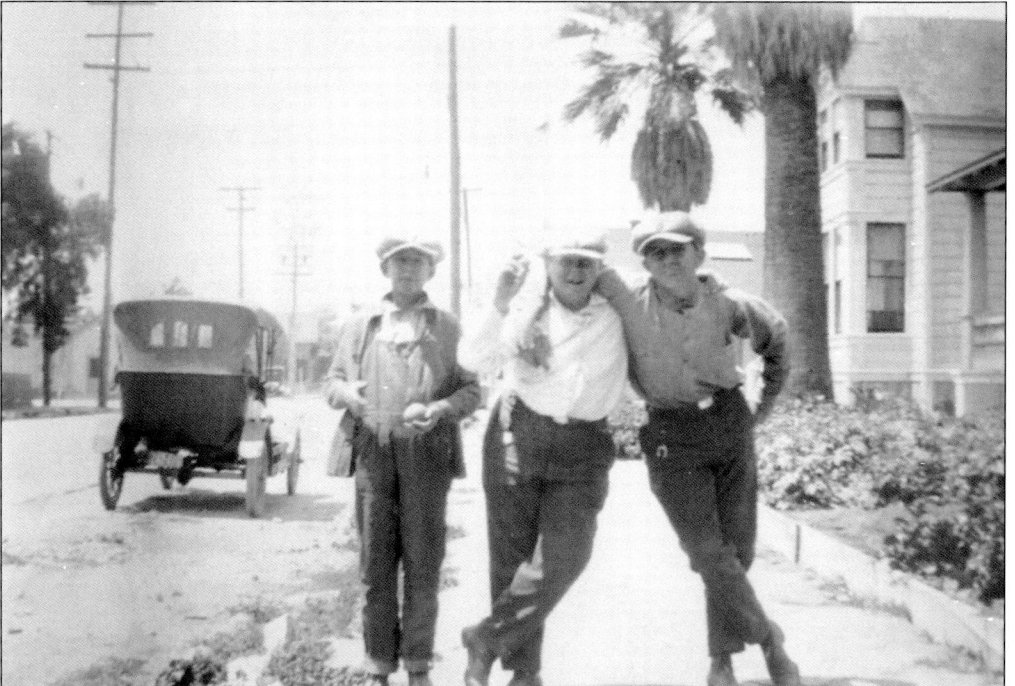

STOCKTON PALS. This photograph shows best friends Michael Angelo Sanguinetti (left), an unidentified boy, and Francis John Sanguinetti (right) hanging out on an unidentified street in Stockton in the 1920s. (Courtesy of the Sanguinetti/Prato family.)

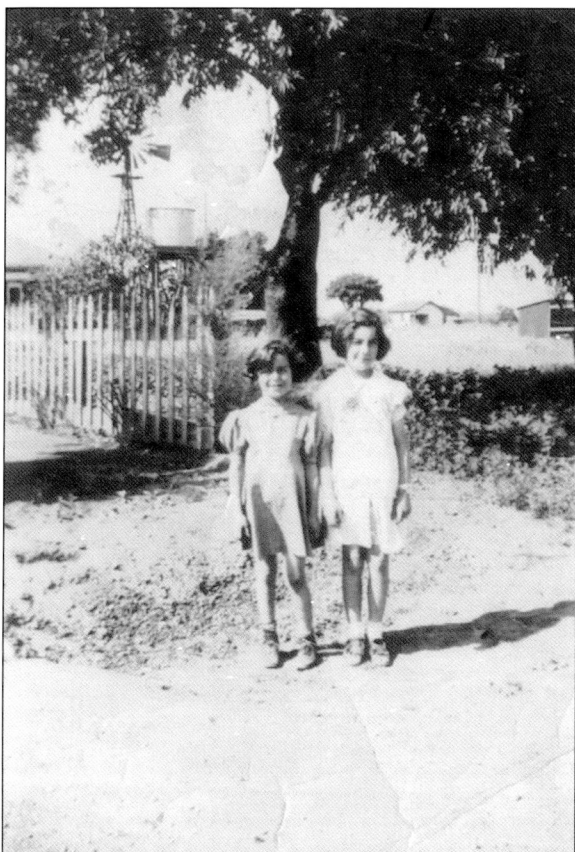

NEIGHBORHOOD FRIENDS. At right, June Schenone (Gerlomes) (left) and May Traverso (Logan) pose in front of June's house on Curtis Street (today's Knoles Way) in China Town in about 1935. China Town was bordered by Alpine, Fulton, El Dorado, and Sutter Streets in Stockton and had nothing to do with the Chinese; rather, it was heavily populated by Genovese immigrants, and everyone knew each other and everyone's business. After a local couple congratulated a surprised friend who lived outside the neighborhood on the pregnancy of his wife, he told them to go back to "Charla-town" to get any information needed. Amongst the local immigrants, *charla* loosely translates as a gossipy know-it-all. Over time, "Charla-town" became "China Town." Below, in an image dating ten years after the one at right, May Passadore (Cima) (left) and June ride bikes on the corner of Grove and Sutter Streets. (Both, courtesy of the Schenone family.)

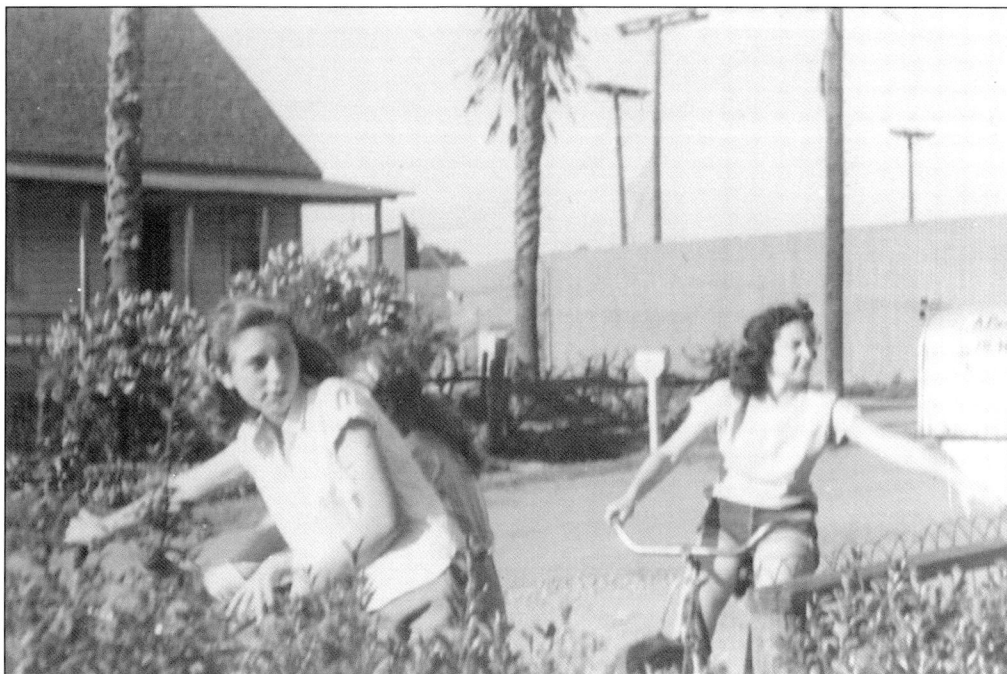

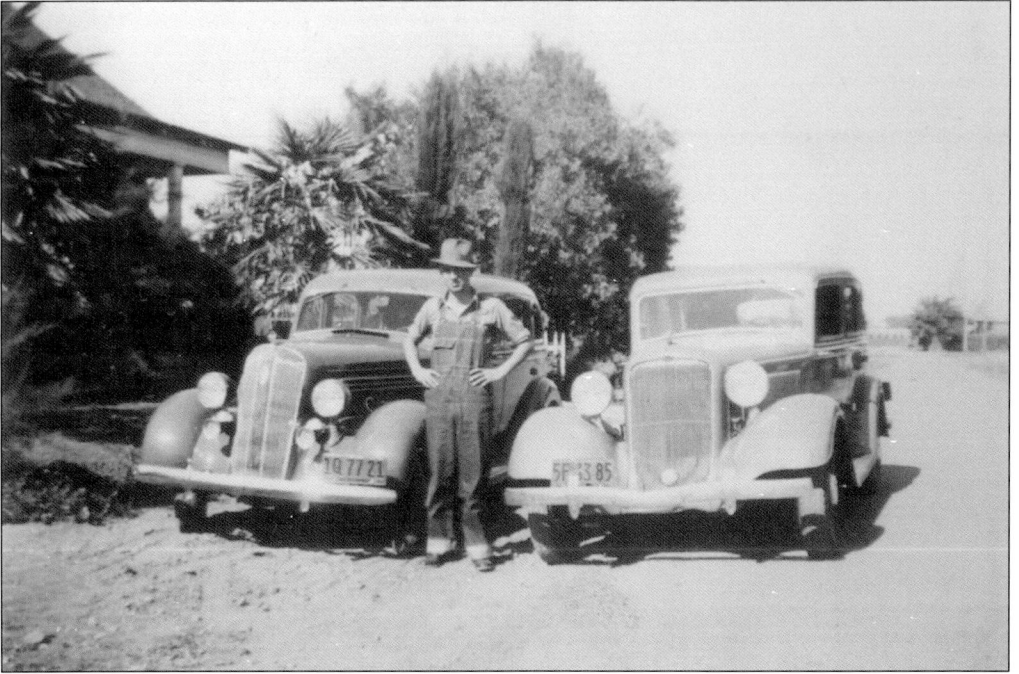

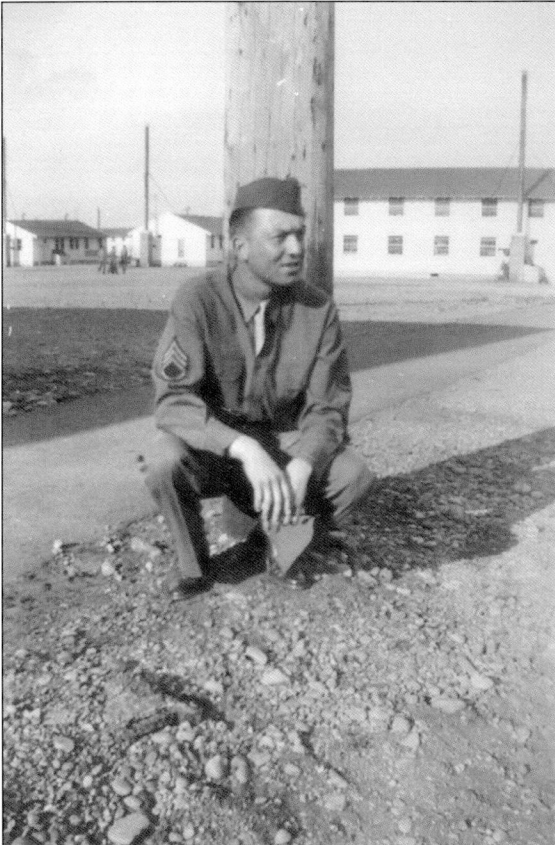

SCHENONE HOME. Pictured on the left in the image above, William "Willie" Schenone (June's brother) poses in front of the family home on Curtis Street (now Knoles Way) in Stockton's China Town sometime in 1935. Buying cars was an important milestone in the lives of most families during this time, so many photographs were taken with hard-earned and cherished automobiles. Willie would later join the Army and be stationed at Camp Roberts near Paso Robles in California. The photograph to the left was taken sometime in 1941 on the base. (Both, courtesy of the Schenone family.)

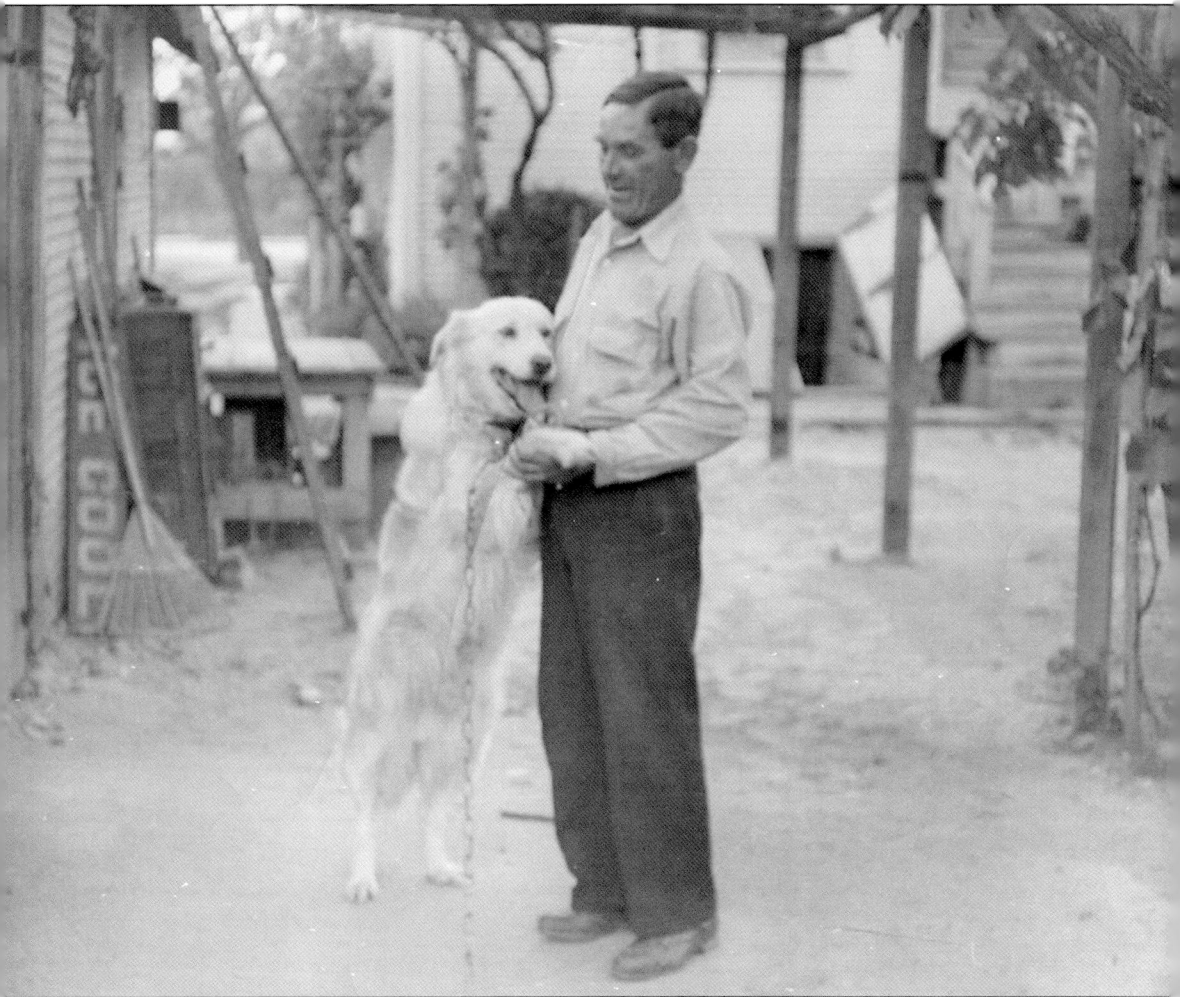

FORENTI FAMILY. Giovanni Forenti and his dog play in the backyard of their home on 1130 South Madison Street in Stockton. Forenti was given up at birth and raised by nuns in an orphanage in Liguria. He would eventually meet his future wife, Mary Bissi, in Genova before deciding to leave for America. Mary, a housekeeper, cook, and babysitter for a wealthy Genovese doctor, followed him later by scrimping and saving for passage after her uncles took the inheritance left to her by her father, a miner in Argentina. The family was living in the Oakland area when Giovanni bought a share in Oakland Scavengers, which hauled away garbage and refuse. This in turn led him to move the family to Stockton and start a new scavenger operation that, years later, was eventually sold to Waste Management. The house on Madison Street served as a lively headquarters for their large family of six children—Bill, John, Rose, twins Julie and Mary, and lastly, Edna. (Courtesy of the estate of Rose Forenti Derivi.)

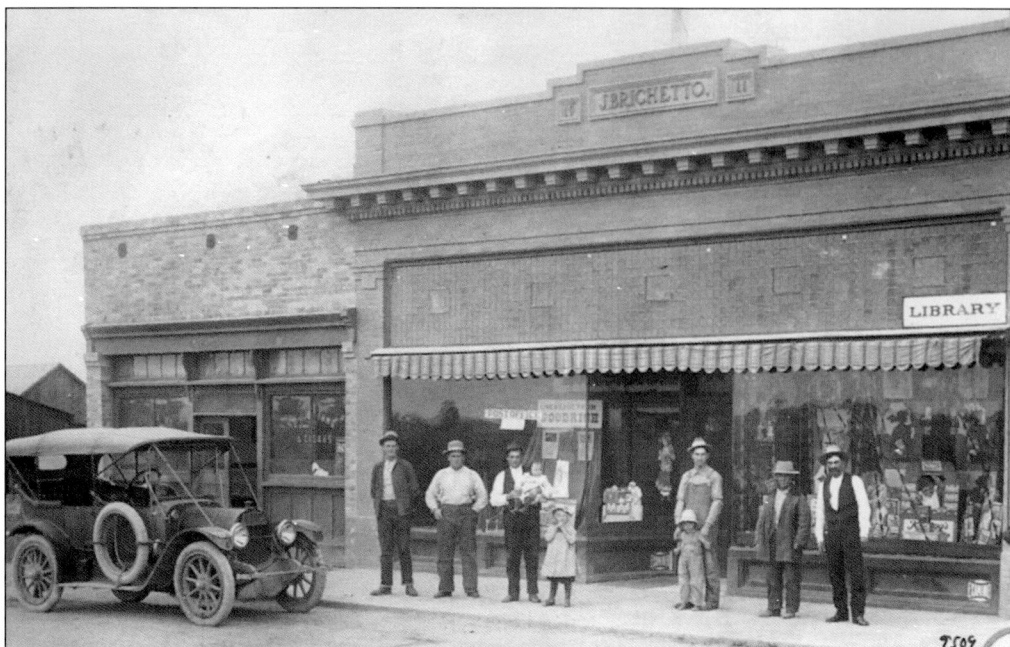

BRICHETTO GENERAL STORE. Giuseppi "John" N. Brichetto built this brick edifice in 1911 to house his father's general store, which had opened in 1872. It served as the library and post office for the small community of Banta, located between Manteca and Tracy. The prosperous Brichetto family farmed significant acreage on the county's west side and were involved in local banking interests. (Courtesy of the Bank of Stockton Historical Photograph Collection.)

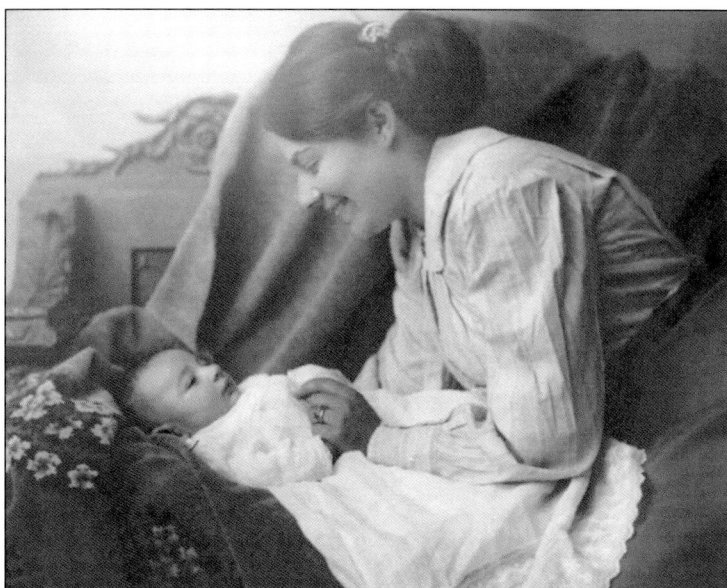

A MOTHER'S LOVE. Mollie Brichetto Raspo holds her son Frank in this c. 1910 photograph. Mollie was the second daughter of Giuseppi N. Brichetto, the founder of the Banta general store. She married Joseph J. Raspo, a native of Saluzzo, Piemonte, Italy, in 1911 and had three children. (Courtesy of the Bank of Stockton Historical Photograph Collection.)

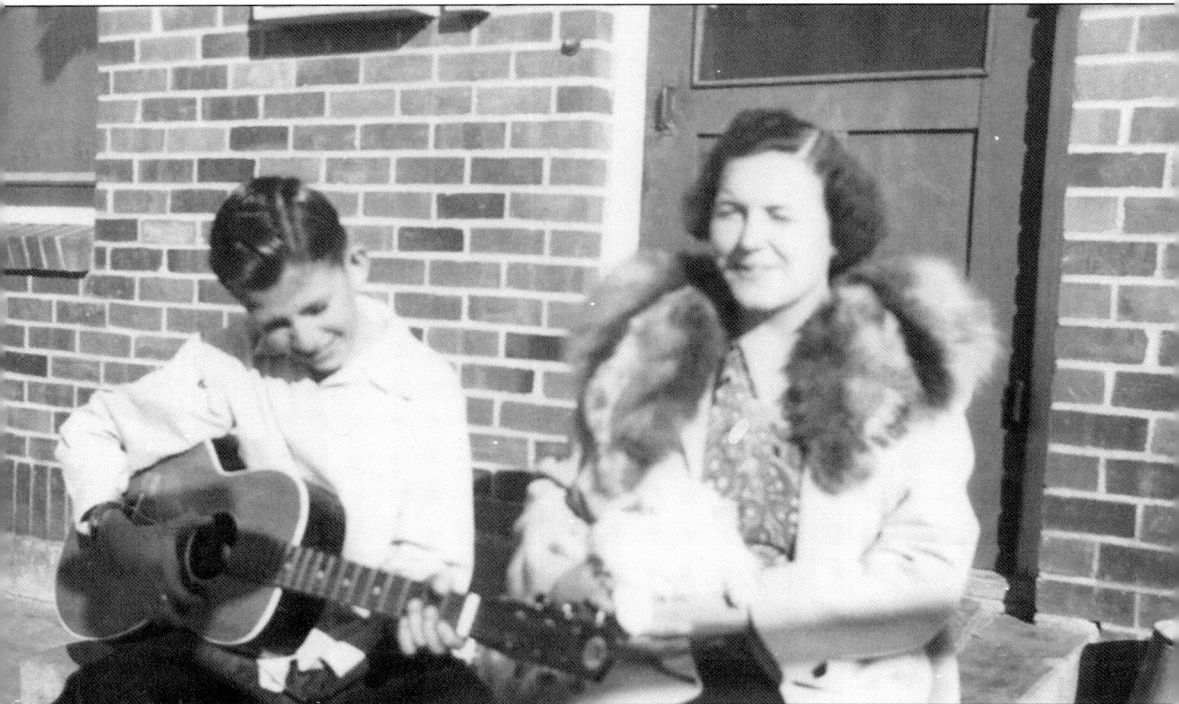

GIULIA AND JOHN BASALTO, 1945. During a 1929 visit to Italy in the hopes of finding a wife, Tony Basalto met Giulia "Lena" Bellagamba while she was washing the windows of a jewelry store in Chiavari, Liguria. They married and settled on his ranch in Linden. As he was a naturalized citizen, they did not have to return through Ellis Island. They took a train and arrived in Stockton on Halloween, and friends gave the couple a reception at the Delphi School on Jack Tone Road that night. They had two sons—Fred (not pictured) and John, seen here with his mother on the front porch of their Garden Street home in Stockton. Unfortunately for Giulia, John never learned how to play that guitar. The Basaltos bought out the Podestas' interest in the ranch in the early 1930s and continued to run it for another 15 years. They sold the ranch in the mid-1940s and moved to Stockton, investing in apartment buildings and other real estate. Giulia worked in area canneries for many years. (Courtesy of the Basalto family.)

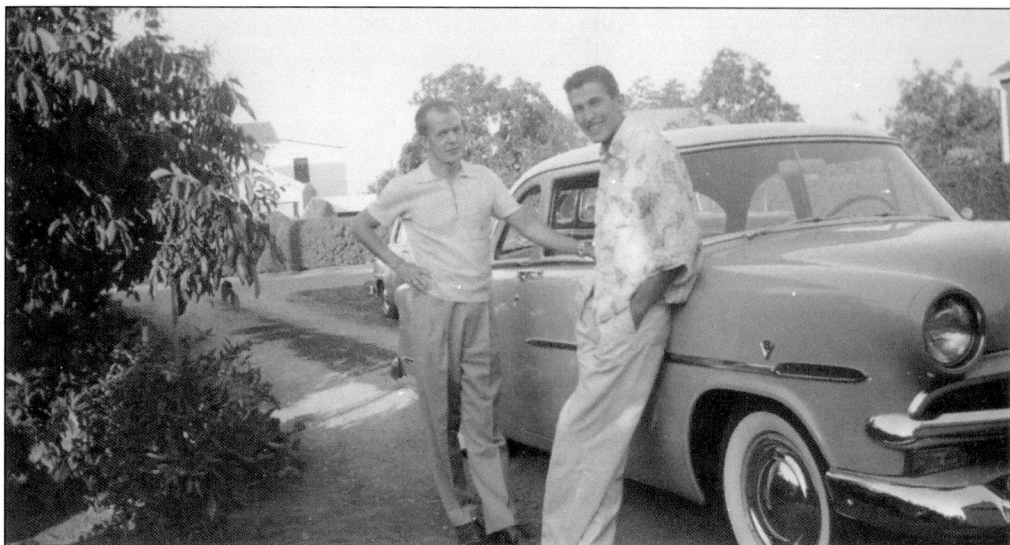

THE BASALTO BROTHERS. Fred (left) and John pose with John's 1955 Ford in Stockton. Fred graduated from the University of California, Berkeley, the first family member to attend college, and worked as a career administrator with the Richmond Unified School District in Contra Costa County. John worked over 45 years with the Marley Cooling Tower Company in Stockton, retiring as an inspector. (Courtesy of the Basalto family.)

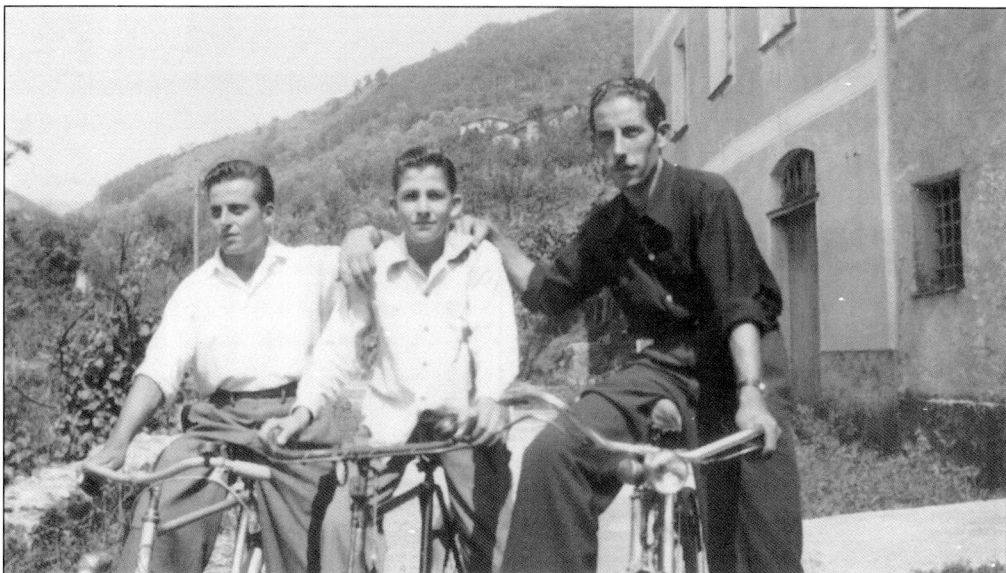

BASALTO FAMILY TRIP, 1948. Here, 15-year-old John Basalto (center) rides bicycles with a couple of his unidentified Italian cousins during a two-month family trip to Italy. John wrote a diary of the trip, documenting their trek across the United States by train and past European landmarks by sea. The family arrived in their ancestral home of Genova on the Fourth of July. (Courtesy of the Basalto family.)

AVANSINO SCAVENGER WAGON. When they arrived, many Italians took what were considered undesirable jobs, including that of scavenger or garbageman (or *spazzini*). Spazzini established their own clientele and routes and would take garbage and refuse away when needed. In this image, Giacomo Avansino holds the lines of his horse-drawn scavenger wagon sometime around the turn of the century. (Courtesy of Dino and Joan Cortopassi.)

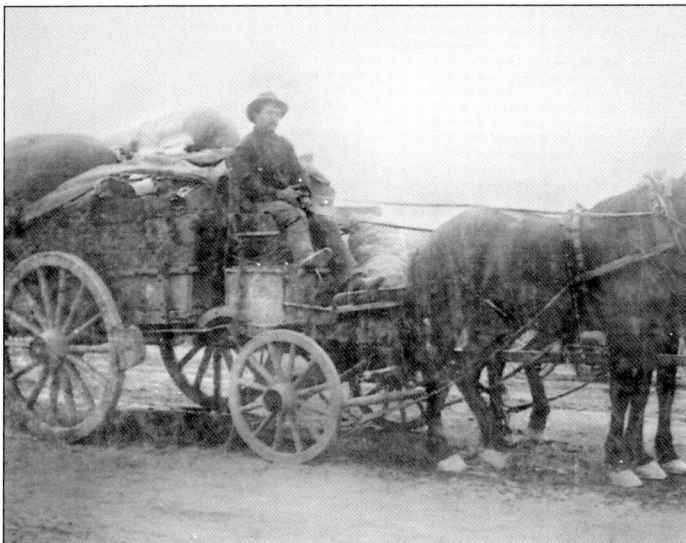

CERTIFICATE OF CITIZENSHIP. Amerigo Cortopassi received American citizenship on December 20, 1938. Citizenship was important to the community and was an accomplishment for Amerigo. His journey from a sharecropping *contadino* (meaning "farmer/worker of the soil") family in Lucca to becoming a land-owning productive citizen of San Joaquin County is a perfect example of the American dream. (Courtesy of Dino and Joan Cortopassi.)

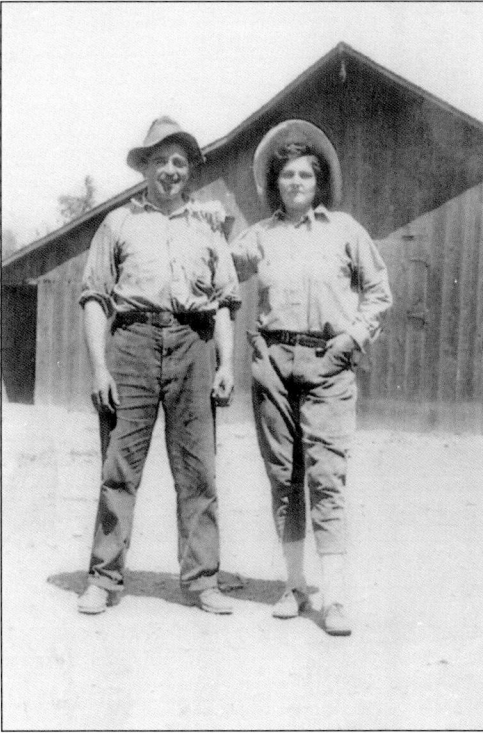

RANCH COUSINS. Mario Trucco and Teresa Avansino pose during work on the Avansino ranch in Linden. Teresa was an excellent student and loved learning, but she was forced by her father to quit school at 16 (state law mandated school until that age). After marrying Amerigo Cortopassi in 1934, she became the full-time cook and part-time bookkeeper at Lucky Ranch. (Courtesy of Dino and Joan Cortopassi.)

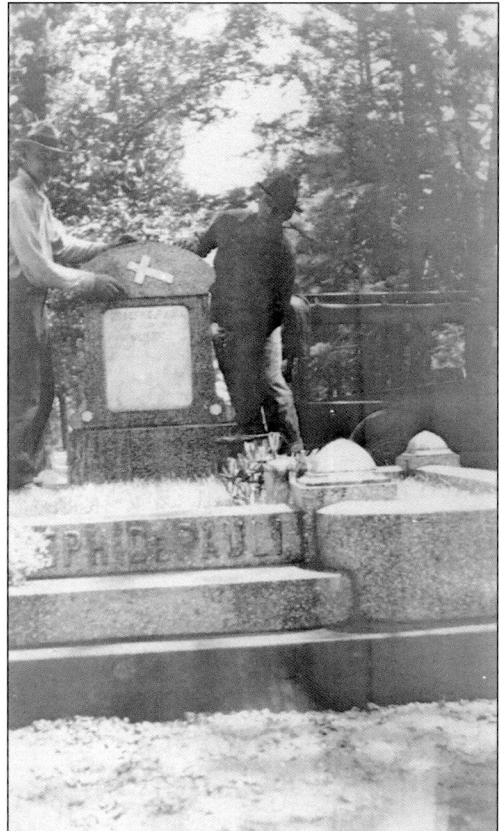

DEPAULI MONUMENT, STOCKTON. The monument of Joseph and Elizabeth DePauli (see page 17) was repaired in 1938 by cement contractor (and son of the deceased) David DePauli and his brothers William, Fred, and Joseph. The monument in the San Joaquin Cemetery remains in excellent condition and provides a connection to the past for this pioneer Italian family. (Courtesy of the DePauli family collection.)

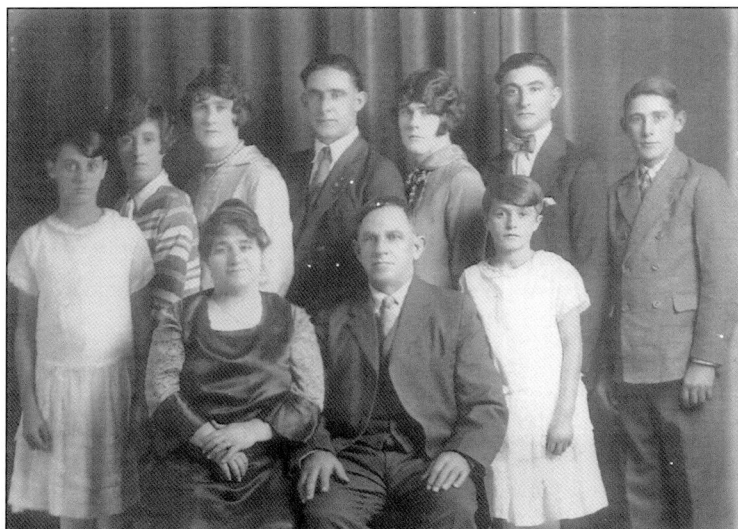

SALVETTI FAMILY, c. 1923. Zita and Annibale Salvetti (seated in center) had a large family after coming to the United States. All eight children were born in Stockton; they are, from left to right, Rose (Praschak), Vita (Morello), Marie (Minucciani), Dino, Eunice (Simoni), Jenny (Panelli), Louis, and Charles. (Courtesy of Dianne Gini.)

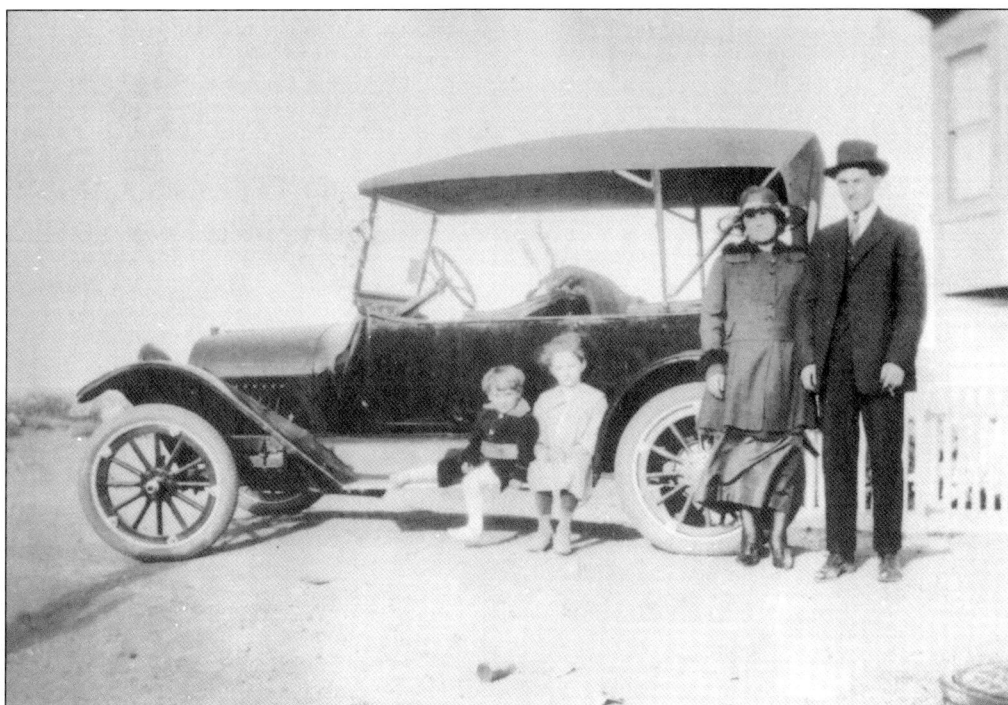

ANDREOTTI FAMILY CAR. Elizabeth and Guido Andreotti and their children, Leslie (left) and Ruby, show off the family car (most likely a Model T) in this photograph taken in 1921. Ruby would grow up to marry Charles Salvetti and have children Richard and Dianne (the contributor of this photograph). (Courtesy of Dianne Gini.)

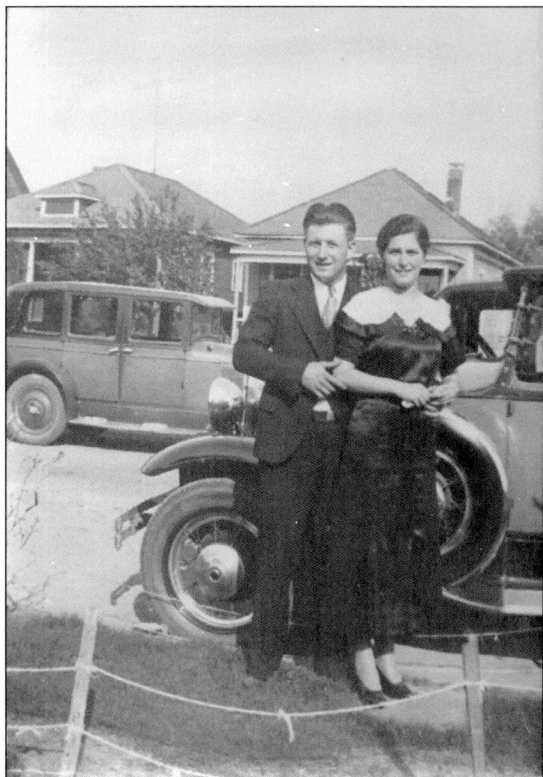

GINI FAMILY OF STOCKTON. Lido and Mary Gini took this photograph (left) in front of their residence in the 1100 block of East Clay Street in Stockton sometime in 1950. Sadly, Lido was tragically killed in a car crash while making arrangements for his own father's funeral in 1952. Lido often spent quality time with his son Gene (pictured below around 1949 or 1950) in the backyard of their home. Gene would grow up to eventually become the president/chief executive officer of Collin's Electrical Company, marry Dianne Salvetti, and have three sons and a daughter of his own. (Both, courtesy of Dianne Gini.)

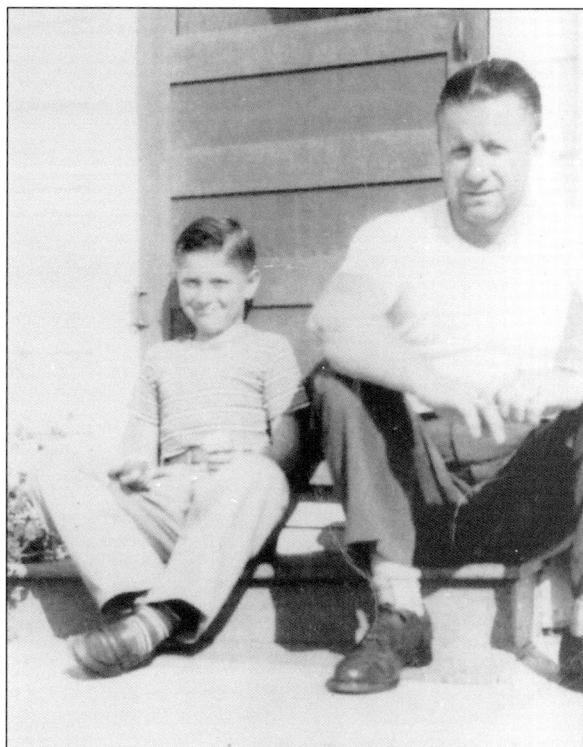

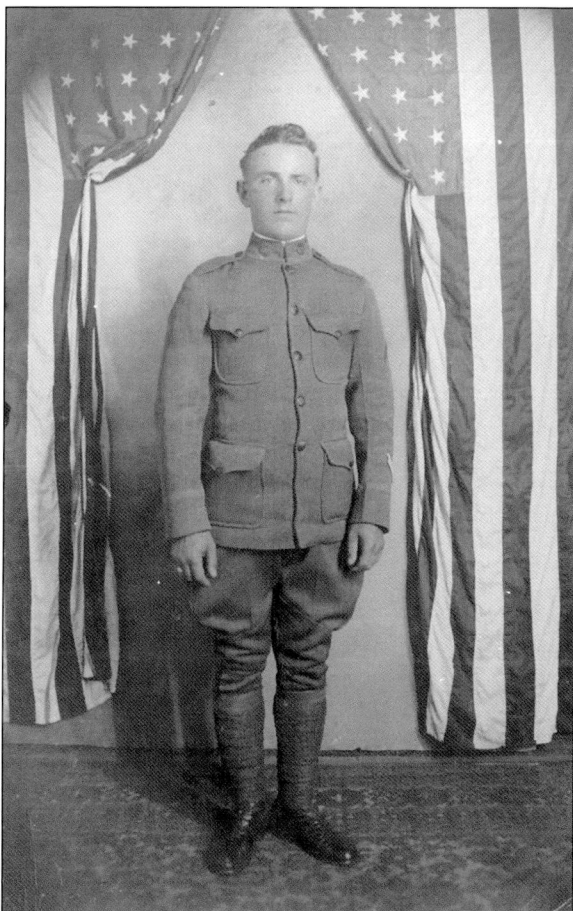

PROUD ITALIAN AMERICAN SOLDIER. Costanzo Michael Ciccone (right) was born in Compobasso in Southern Italy. He came to America when his brother Liberato Michael Ciccone (who immigrated in 1877) sent for him in 1917. His twin sister, Annalita, had died in Italy after falling down a hill while picking fruit when they were 10 years old. While coming through Ellis Island, he earned the nickname "Gus" after an immigration officer could not pronounce his name. In 1918, he was drafted into the Army, even though he could not speak English. He eventually learned English by reading an Army handbook and the *Stockton Record*. He distinguished himself among his fellow soldiers (shown below at Camp Kearny in California) with his cooking skills, and he often prepared meals for the officers returning late from their duties. (Both, courtesy of Gloria J. Ciccone.)

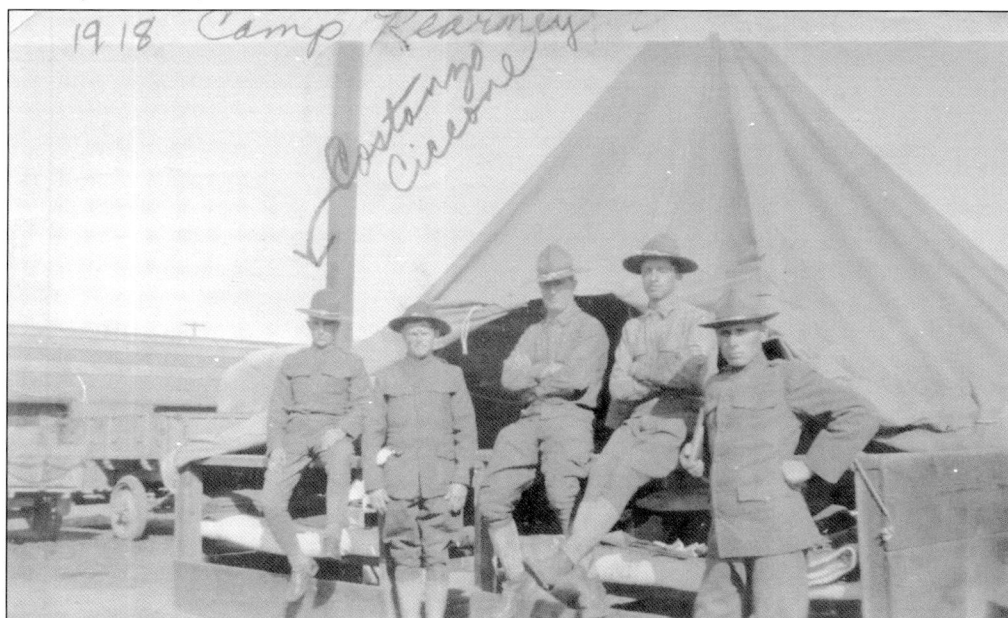

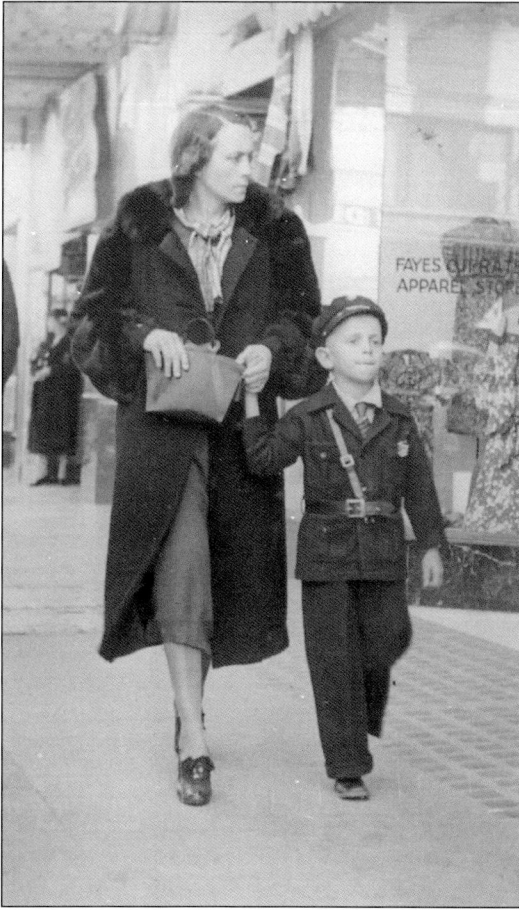

STROLLING ON MAIN STREET, STOCKTON, 1937. Emma Ciccone is escorted through downtown Stockton by her son Costanzo Michael Ciccone Jr. Emma Elizabeth Johnson met Gus Ciccone on a farm in Minnesota after he was discharged from the Army. They married and eventually made their way to California in a 1928 Ford that blew its radiator on an Indian reservation in Arizona. (Courtesy of Gloria J. Ciccone.)

PADULA'S SUBWAY INN, 1942. One could have a boisterous time at Padula's place at 1612 East Scotts Avenue in Stockton. Mrs. Padula, seated between an unidentified boy and Tony Richichi (on right), was a gracious woman who looked after the Italian community. Gus Ciccone (standing) sings happily and was a regular at the lively Saturday-night card games. (Courtesy of Gloria J. Ciccone.)

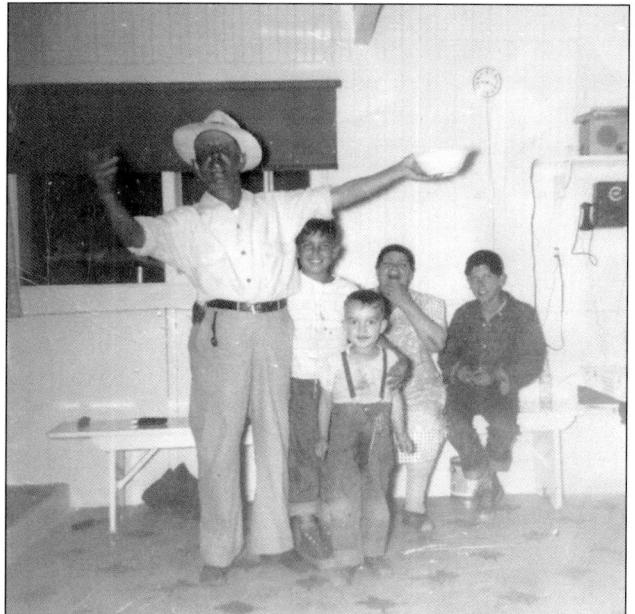

PRISONERS OF WAR. During World War II, several POW camps were located in California, including one in Lathrop (pictured) that housed captured Italian soldiers. In September 1943, the Badoglio government in Italy signed an armistice that turned Italy from an enemy to an ally. Prisoners like Luigi Maccini (left) and Mario Speroni chose to pledge allegiance to help the war effort, which allowed them limited freedom. (Courtesy of Diana M. Lowery.)

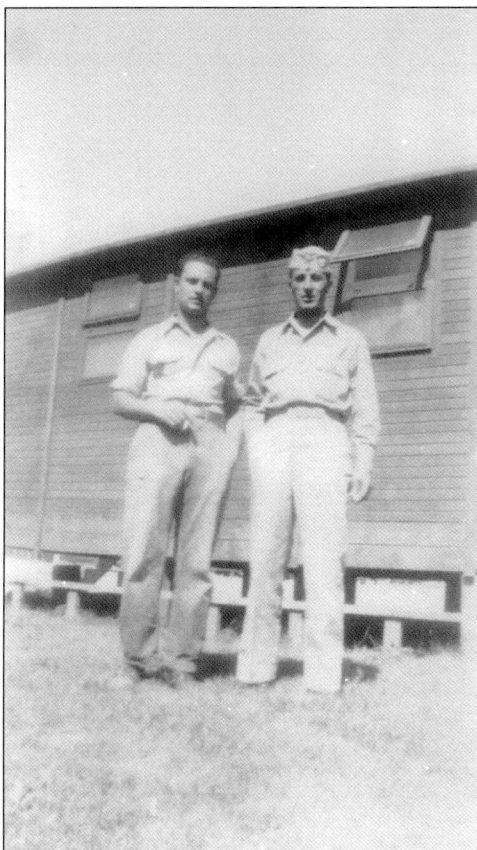

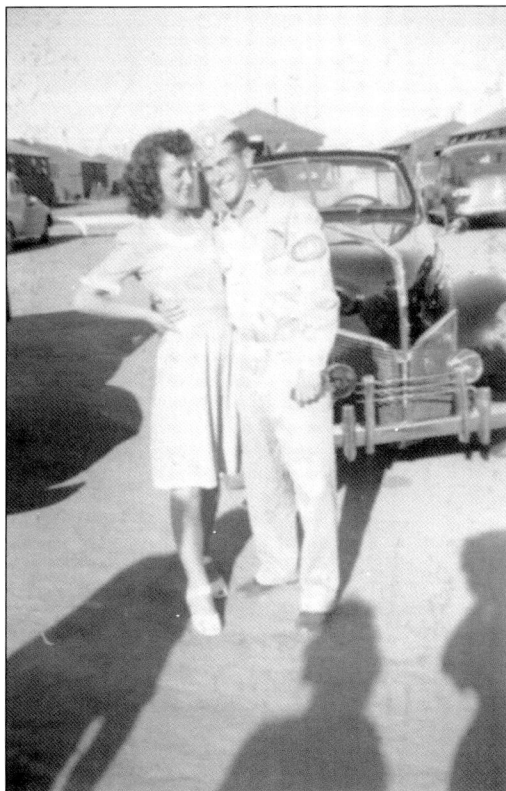

GENEROUS COMMUNITY. Many local Italian families extended their hospitality to the prisoners during their stay. The soldiers brought news of Italy and the possibility of knowing mutual acquaintances from "back home," so invitations to dinner were often extended. As the locals became comfortable with the POWs, picnics and even dances were held. Seen here are Elsie Prato and an unidentified prisoner of war. (Courtesy of the Sanguinetti/Prato family.)

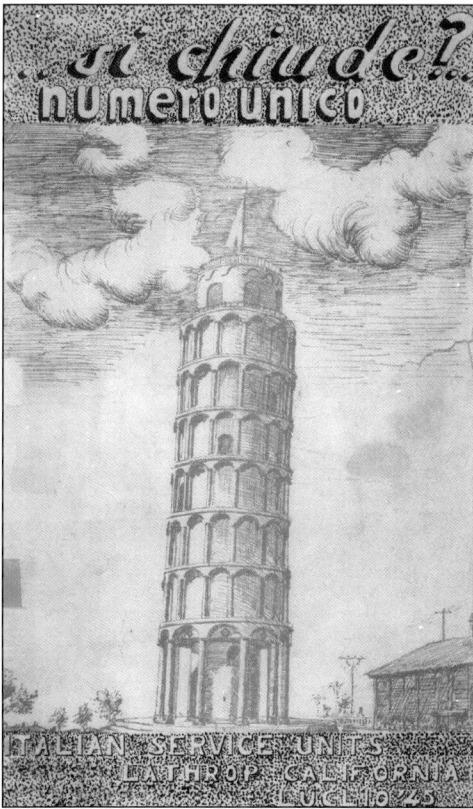

...si chiude?...
nUmero Unico

ITALIAN SERVICE UNITS
LATHROP CALIFORNIA
LUGLIO 45

LIFE IN THE BARRACKS. The Italian prisoners of war wrote and illustrated their own newspaper, *Si Chiude* ("Comes to a Close"), the first issue cover of which can be seen at left featuring a drawing of the famous Tower of Pisa. Topics included instructions on ordering ice cream in English and other items to help with life in San Joaquin County. After taking an oath of allegiance, many of the prisoners were placed with the 100th and 102nd Italian Engineering Company and worked for the Allied war effort. The unidentified soldier here stands next to a model of the Tower of Pisa (complete with lean), also built by the talented prisoners. (Left, courtesy of Diana M. Lowery; below, courtesy of the Sanguinetti/Prato family.)

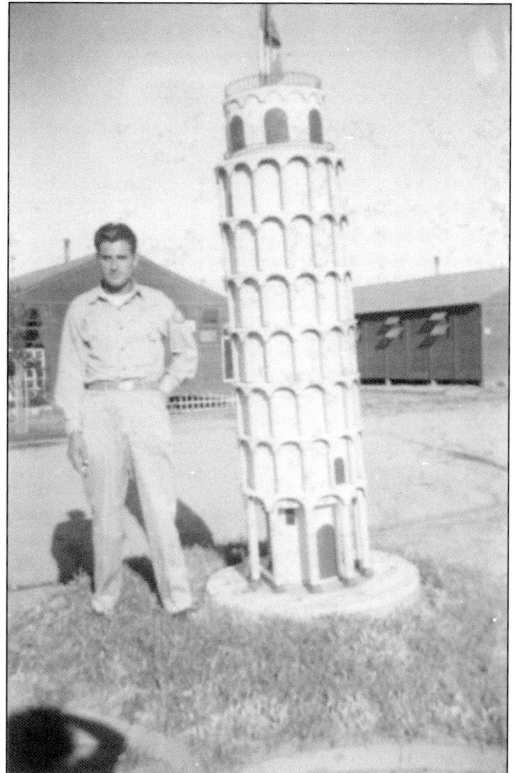

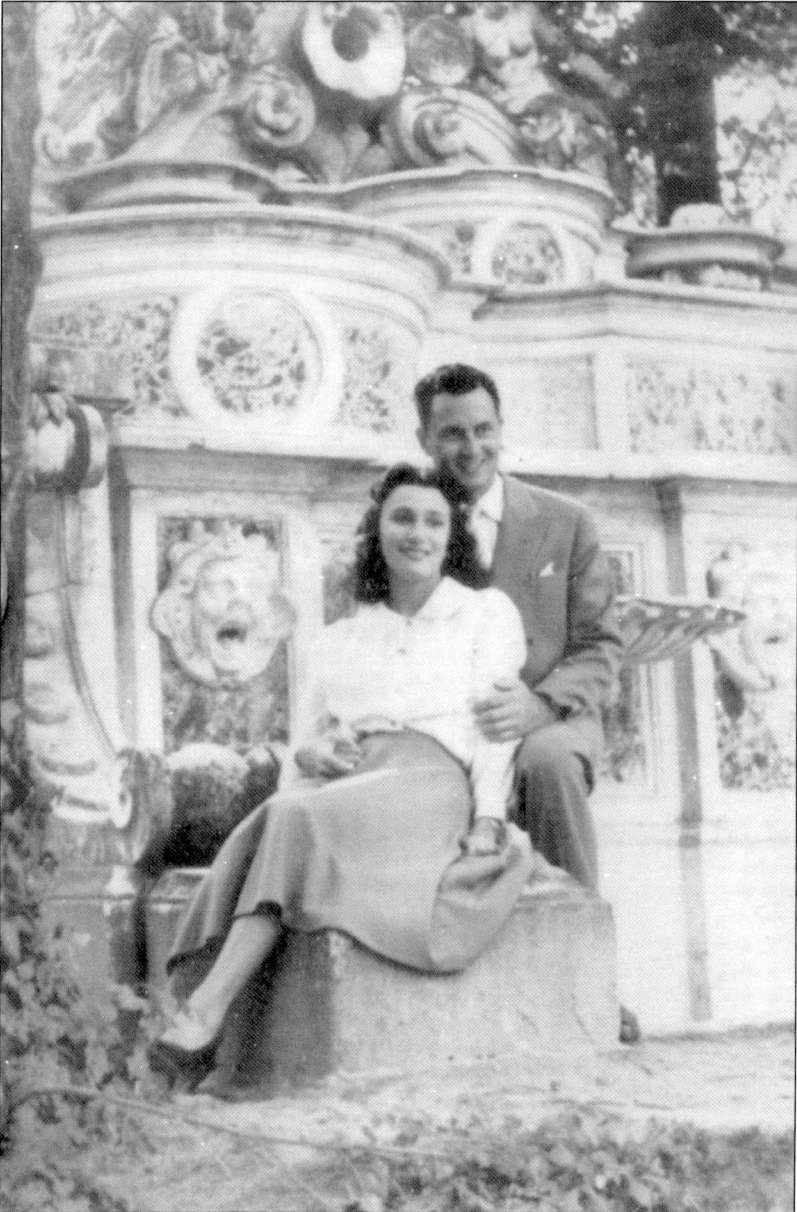

TRUE ROMANCE. Luigi "Louis" Maccini, a member of Mussolini's elite Bersaglieri (riflemen), was captured at El Alamein in Egypt during World War II. Once captured, he ended up a prisoner at a camp at Sharpe Army Depot in Lathrop. A friend of Tony Bacigalupi invited Louis and Mario Speroni to lunch one day, and they became regular guests at the Bacigalupi home for Sunday dinner. It was there that Louis first met Tony's daughter Alma, playing jacks with a friend on their front porch. He was 21 and she was 14. Louis became smitten with Alma, who wanted nothing to do with him at first, but the years went by, and he would later propose to her on that very same porch. It was decided that Alma should stay and finish school, and if after the war they still wanted to get married, they could. They wrote each other constantly, and in 1948, they were married in Parma, Italy. They returned to Stockton to make their home and raise a daughter. They were married for nearly 50 years. (Courtesy of Alma Maccini.)

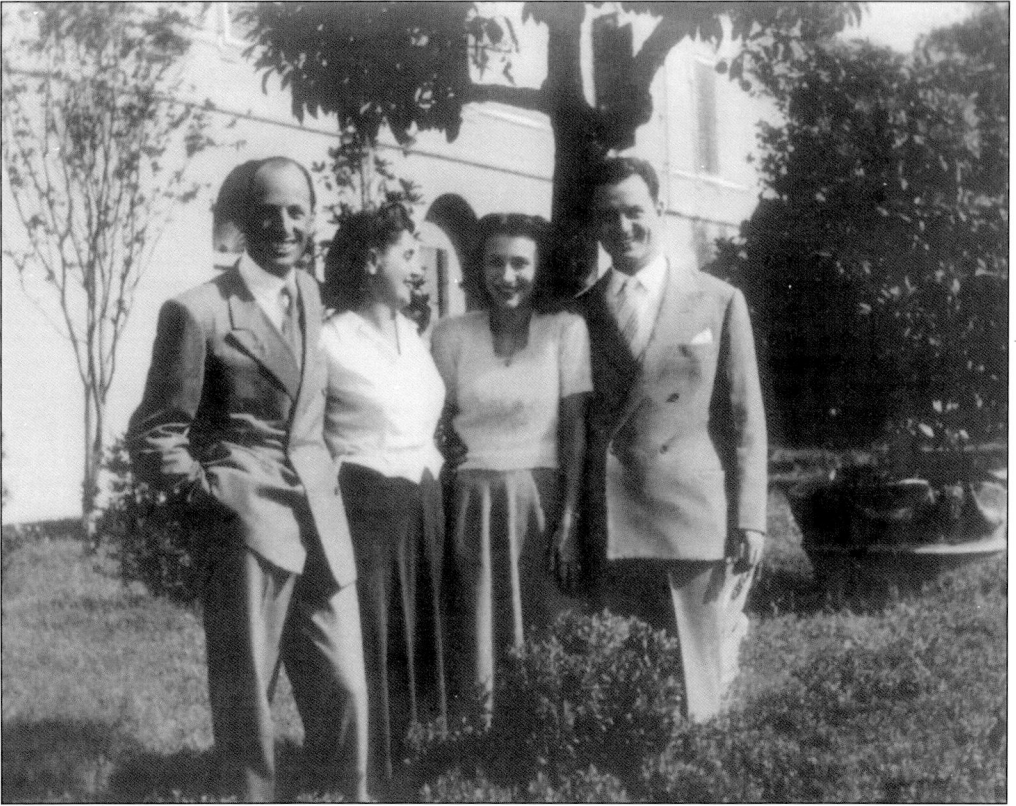

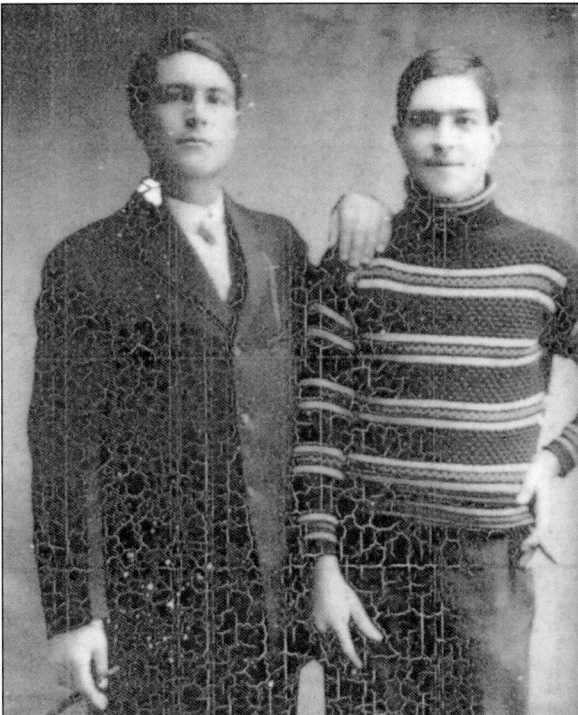

FAMILY FRIENDS. Standing from left to right, Marco and Bruna Speroni and Alma and Luigi Maccini enjoy time together in Parma, Italy. The Speronis and Maccinis enjoyed a long and deep friendship since their time as prisoners of war in San Joaquin County. Their children would help Stockton and Parma become sister cities in 1998. (Courtesy of Alma Maccini.)

BROTHERS LODUCA. This photograph, taken shortly after their arrival in the United States in 1917, shows brothers Giuseppe (left) and Francesco Loduca. The brothers immigrated from Custonaci, a village on the northwest coast of the island of Sicily. Francesco would eventually make his way to San Joaquin County and establish a large and productive family. (Courtesy of the Loduca family album.)

LODUCA FAMILY, C. 1923. In 1909, Francesco Paolo Loduca (seated) boarded a ship from Custonaci, Sicily, bound for New York. He met Giuseppa Columbo (standing), who had left Cinisi, Sicily, in 1916, and they married in Wyandotte, Michigan, in 1917. In 1926, they moved with their four young children—from left to right, Christina, Samuel, and Leonardo, as well as Rose (not pictured)—to California. (Courtesy of the Loduca family album.)

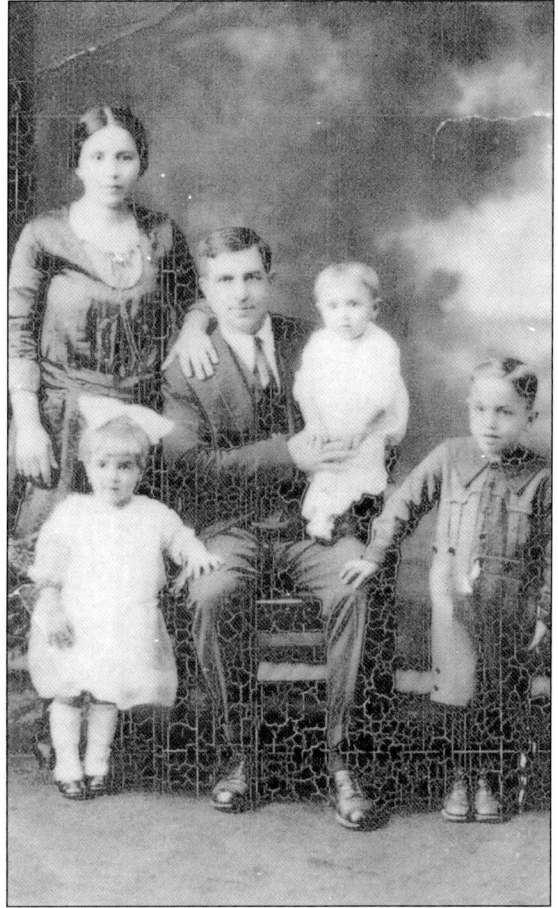

LODUCA'S HARVEST. After they settled in California, agriculture became the mainstay for the Loduca family. They would have 10 children (pictured here in the family orchard during the harvest of 1937). From left to right are (first row) Vincent "Phil," Frank Jr., and Angelo "Joe"; (second row) Mary, Rose, and Christina "Tena"; (third row) Sam, Frank Sr., Giuseppa, Leonora "Tootsie," and Pauline. Not pictured is Leonardo Loduca, who was serving in the military. (Courtesy of the Loduca family album.)

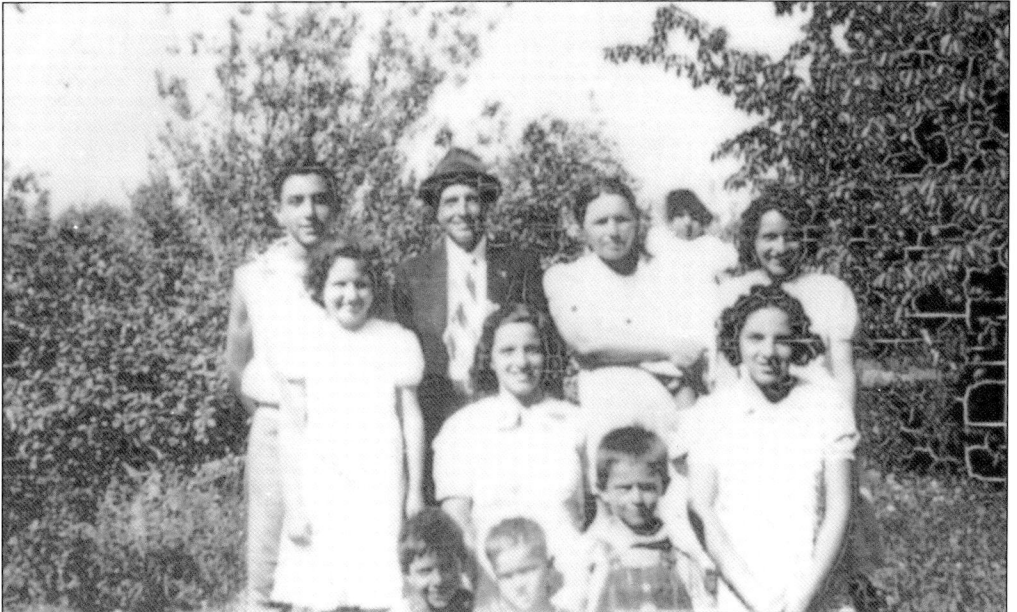

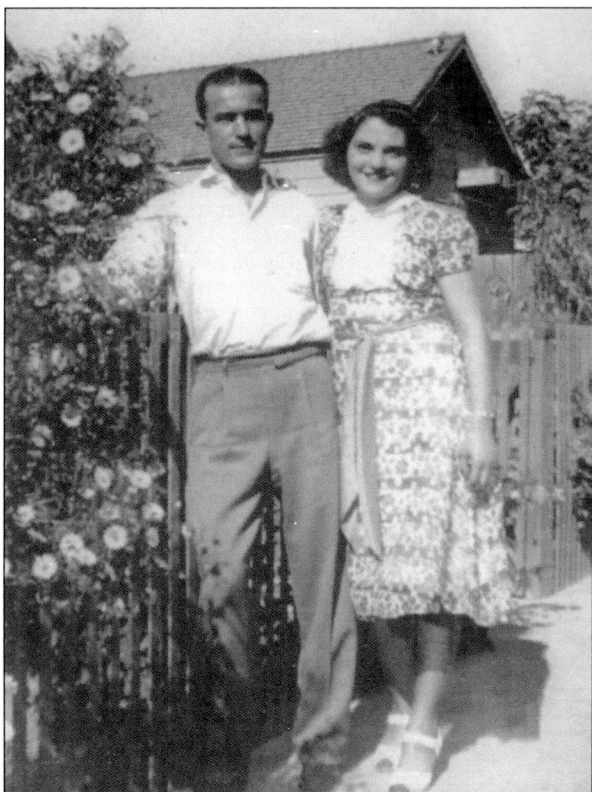

FRANK AND INA. Frank Lucchetti and Cristina "Ina" Ponsi were children of hardworking immigrants who had settled in San Joaquin County to make better lives for themselves and their children. Frank had three siblings—Dora, Esther, and Melvin—while Ina had three sisters—Alide, Gemma, and an older sibling who died young in Italy. Frank and Ina met by chance when her father, Ermenegildo Ponsi, was asked by his neighbor where he got his wine corks. Frank and his father, Giovanni, were also with the neighbor, as they were all avid winemakers. Ermenegildo was unable to leave, so he had his daughter Ina go with Frank to buy the corks. This encounter started their friendship. Frank was smitten and often drove past the Ponsi house repeatedly. They married in old St. Mary's Catholic Church in 1939. (Both, courtesy of the Lucchetti family.)

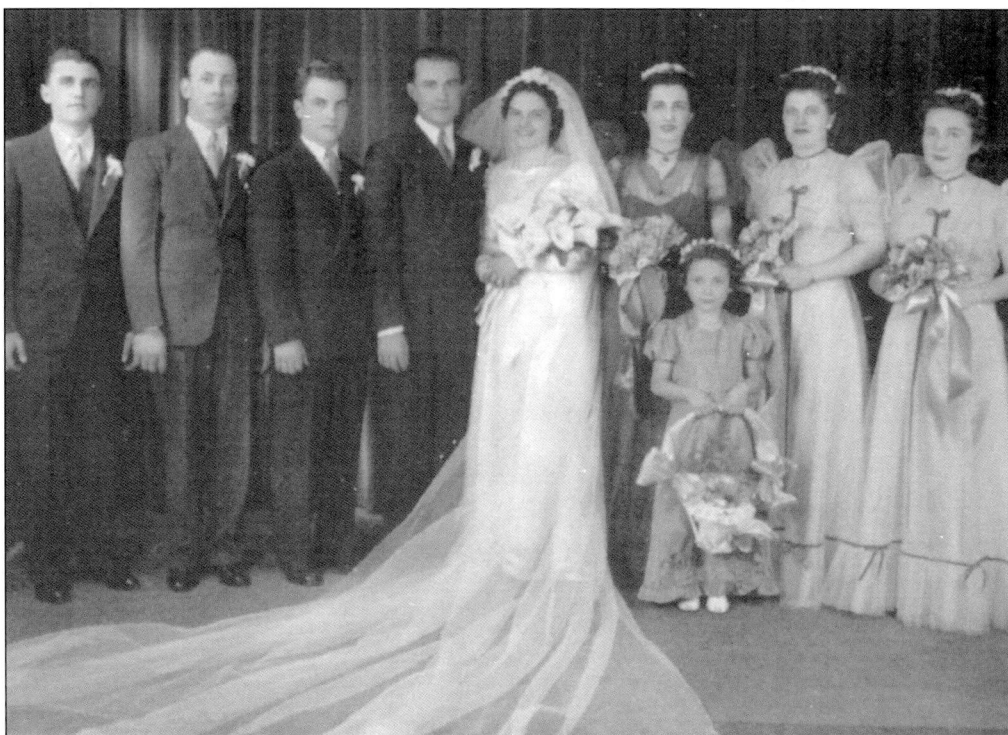

Three

BUSINESS, MERCHANTS, AND COMMERCE

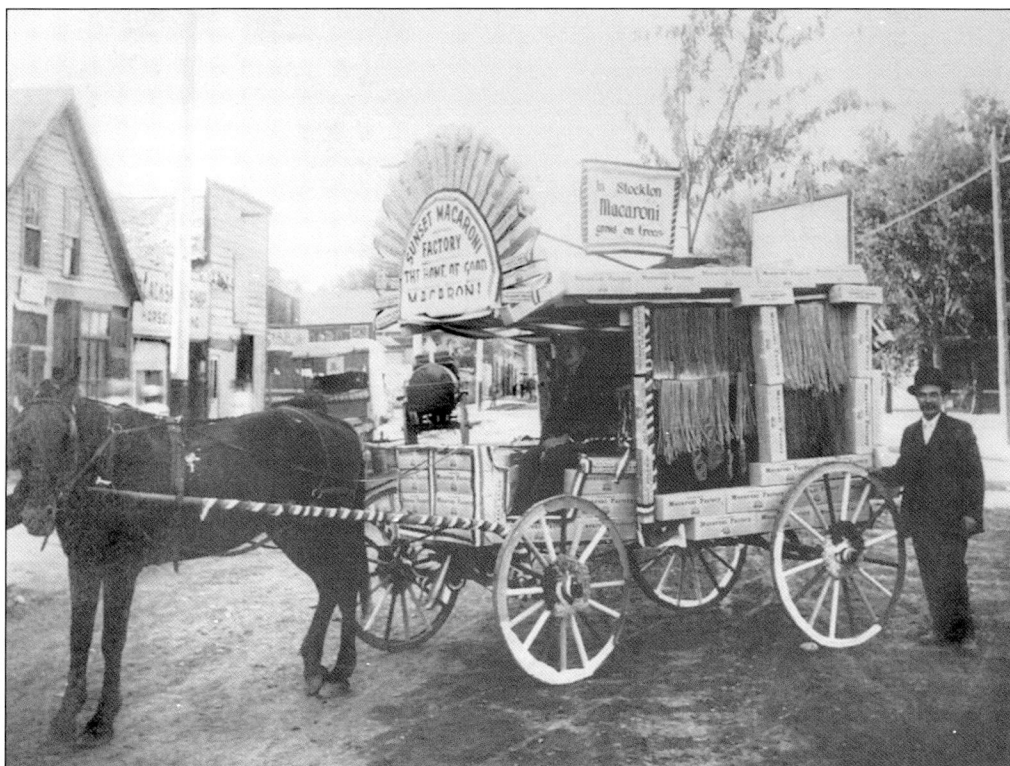

MACARONI WAGON. This colorful wagon is decorated and covered in labels of the Sunset Macaroni Factory, whose mottos were "Home of the Good Macaroni" and "In Stockton Macaroni Grows on Trees." This business was started by two immigrant brothers from Genova in 1905. (Courtesy of the Bank of Stockton Historical Photograph Collection.)

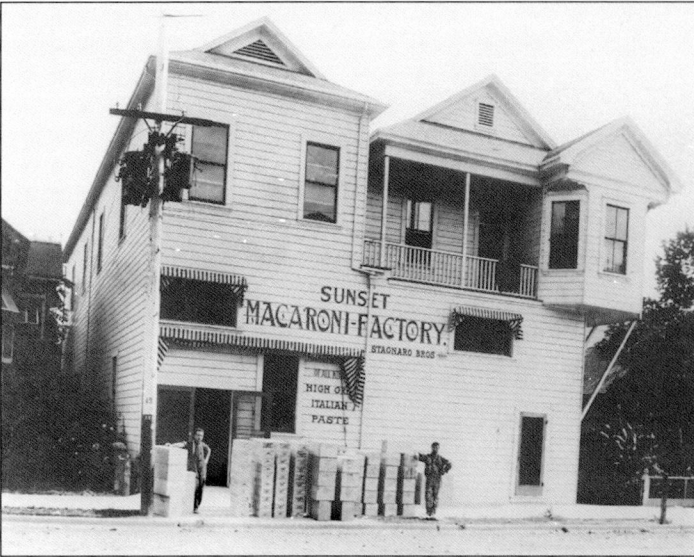

SUNSET MACARONI FACTORY, C. 1915. Brothers Frank and David Stagnaro were the proprietors of the Sunset Macaroni Factory located at 430 South American Avenue. Their factory was equipped with the latest machinery, and they produced 34 varieties of Italian pasta (their macaroni was a Stockton favorite). The factory remained in operation until the 1980s. (Courtesy of the Bank of Stockton Historical Photograph Collection.)

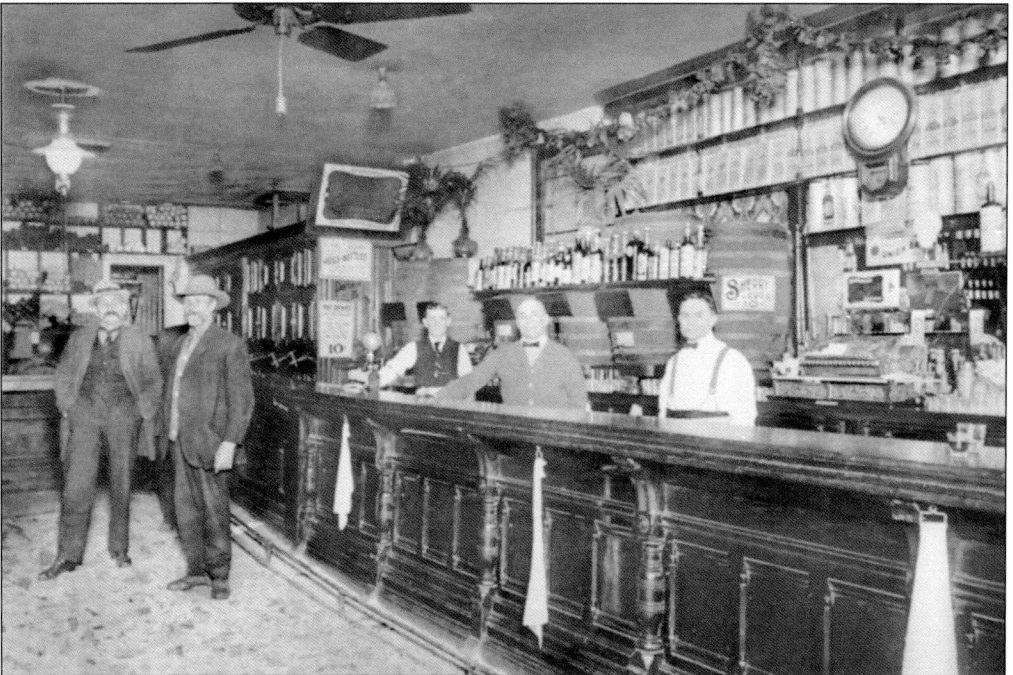

THE '49 SALOON. In 1905, August Genecco and Paul Trucco opened their establishment on East Weber Avenue near the channel, but they eventually moved to 47 North El Dorado Street. This photograph, taken around December 1910, shows unidentified customers and bartenders enjoying the saloon, which is decorated for the holidays. Bar towels hang for customers to wipe suds out of their mustaches. (Courtesy of the Bank of Stockton Historical Photograph Collection.)

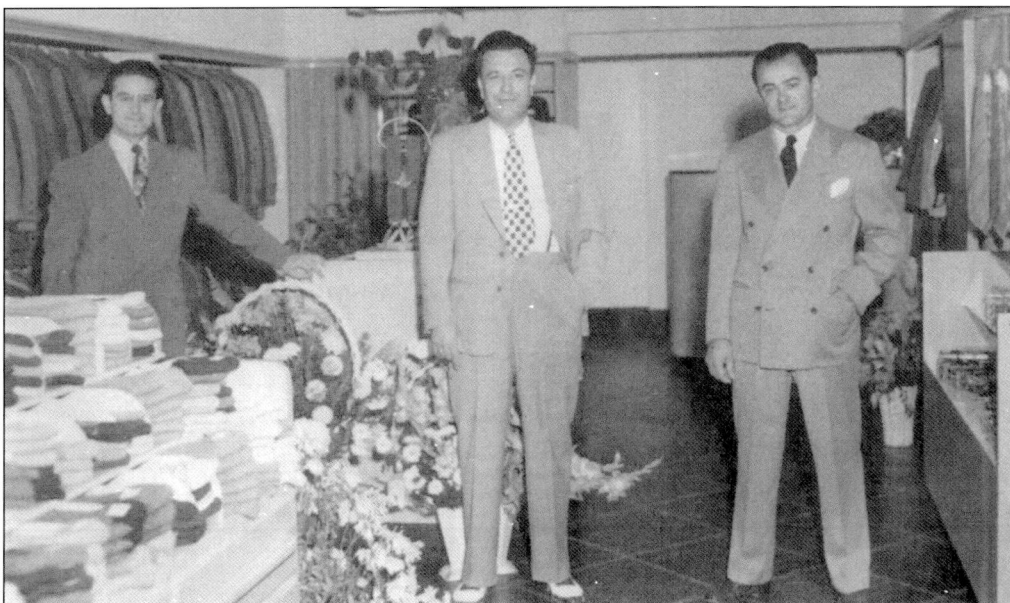

SQUIRES CLOTHIERS, 1947. This popular Lodi menswear shop opened on the School and Pine Streets block in August 1947. The three original proprietors are, from left to right, Bob Leonardini, Tony Borelli, and Sil Leonardini, seen here on the day of their grand opening. Sil bought out his partners in the mid-1950s and eventually sold the business to two employees. (Courtesy of the Leonardini Collection.)

PEIRANO'S MARKET. This very popular market was located at 119 East Pine Street in Lodi and served the area's significant Italian (and non-Italian) residents for many years. The founder was a Mr. G. Peirano, and the business went through several successive owners who eventually added a deli and restaurant. (Courtesy of the Lucchetti family.)

47

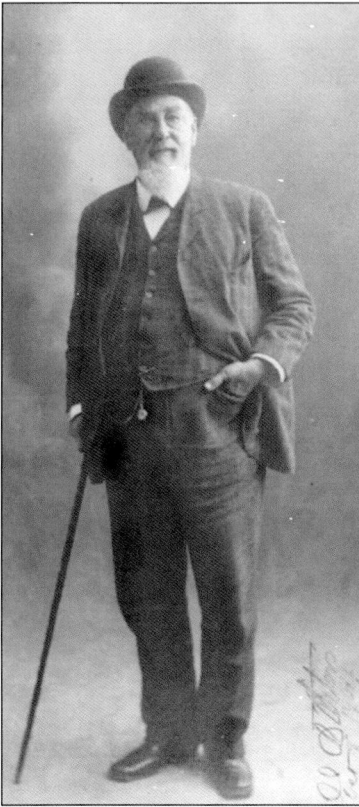

J.D. PETERS (GIUSEPPE DI PIETRI). Seen here in an 1890s portrait, di Pietri was born in Genova and went to sea at 11 years old. He came to America in 1838, anglicized his name to J.D. Peters, and joined the US Navy. In 1849, he came to California for the Gold Rush and worked as a miner and teamster. He settled in Stockton in 1853 and started a transportation business, buying grain and milling it to flour for the miners. He served as grand marshal for the centennial celebration of 1876—depicted below in this Ralph Yardley drawing—the largest and grandest event Stockton had ever seen. His ventures brought him enormous wealth, and Peters became one of the most respected and powerful men in the state. (Both, courtesy of the Bank of Stockton Historical Photograph Collection.)

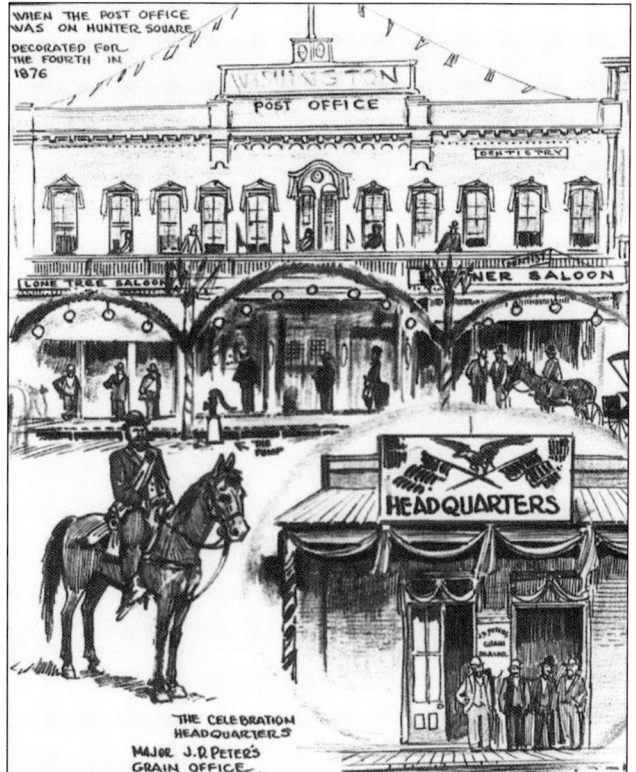

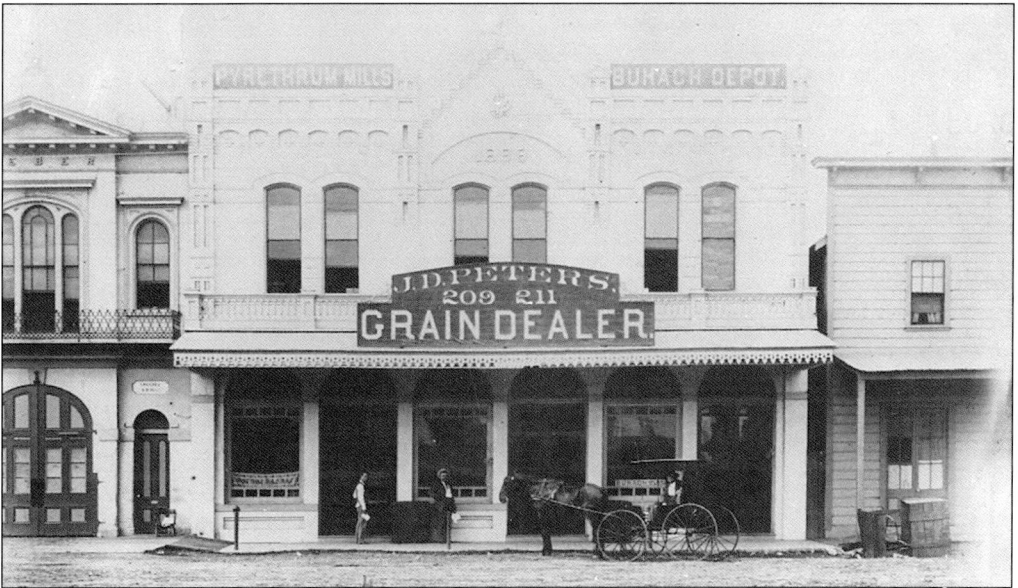

GRAIN AND BUHACH, 1888. At his headquarters at 209 and 211 East Channel Street (above), J.D. Peters ran his vast business empire. He founded and operated the San Joaquin Improvement Company, an early steamship company, which gave him control of river traffic throughout the region. He was the first to ship California wheat to Europe. In addition to his grain deals, Peters also produced a good called Buhach, an insecticide developed from a daisy-like flower in his pyrethrum mill (seen in the street view below). Peters also served as director of the Stockton Savings & Loan Society (the future Bank of Stockton), financed the Yosemite business block and St. Joseph's Hospital, owned part of the Copporopolis & Stockon Railroad, and published *Buzz Magazine*, dedicated to agriculture. (Above, courtesy of the Bank of Stockton Historical Photograph Collection; below, courtesy of the Haggin Museum.)

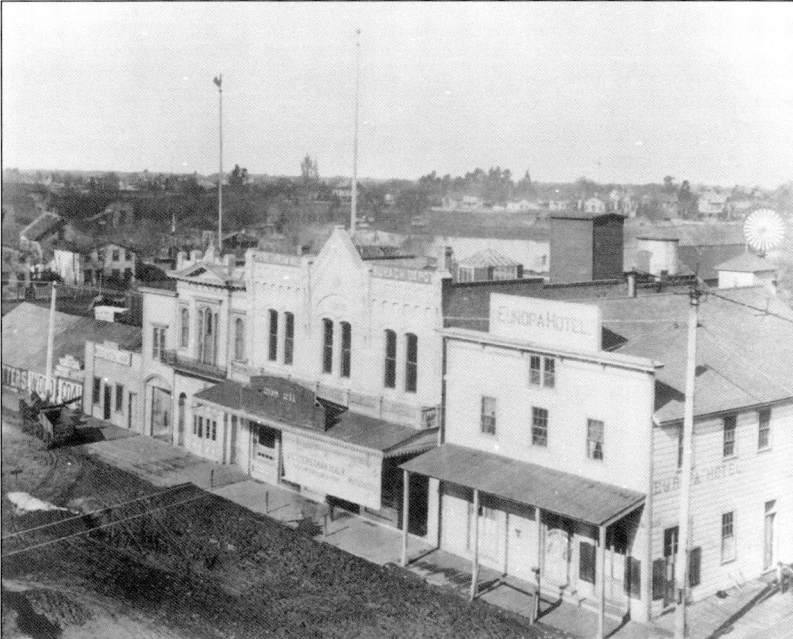

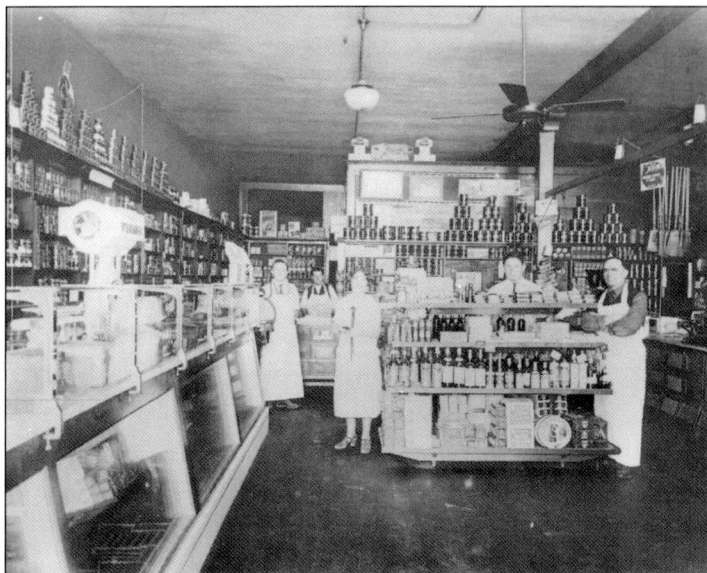

ORIGINAL GROCERY. This photograph shows, from left to right, Caesar Gaia, Berto Canepa, Elizabeth Cadematori, Louis Chipale, and Albert Puccini inside the original Gaia-Delucchi grocery around 1925. Gaia, a native of Torino, Italy, and Louis Delucchi partnered to open the grocery in 1917. They purchased E. Fontana's Ravioli Factory at 320 East Market Street in Stockton and became great successes. (Courtesy of the Haggin Museum.)

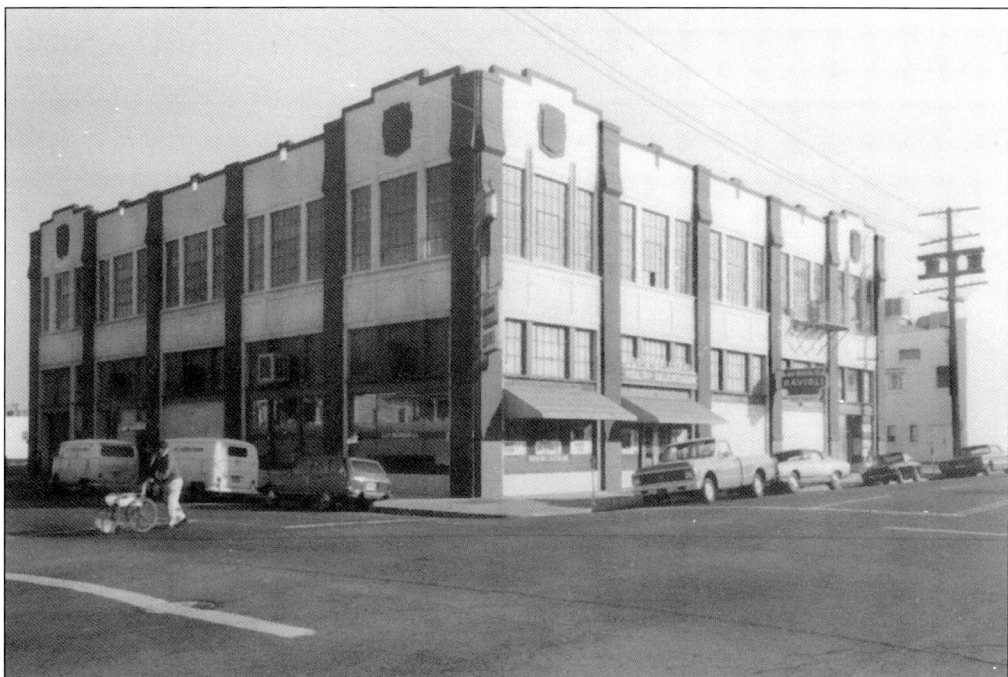

GAIA-DELUCCHI COMPANY. The success of the partnership facilitated a move to a new, grand location at 140 North American Street sometime in the late 1940s. The building housed a grocery and delicatessen in addition to the ravioli factory. Gaia-Delucchi was sold in 1974 and ceased all operations in 1982. This beautiful Art Deco structure was demolished in 2002. (Courtesy of the Bank of Stockton Historical Photograph Collection.)

QUALITY CATERING.
Another important part of
the company was its catering
business, and many Italian
American events would
not be complete without
food from Gaia-Delucchi.
The Italian Gardeners
picnic used its catering
service every year until the
company closed in 1974.
The partners pictured
here are, from left to right,
Anthony "Tony" Gotelli,
Al Bava, Tony Prato, and
Primo Valterza. (Courtesy of
historian Bennie Filippini,
Italian Gardeners Society.)

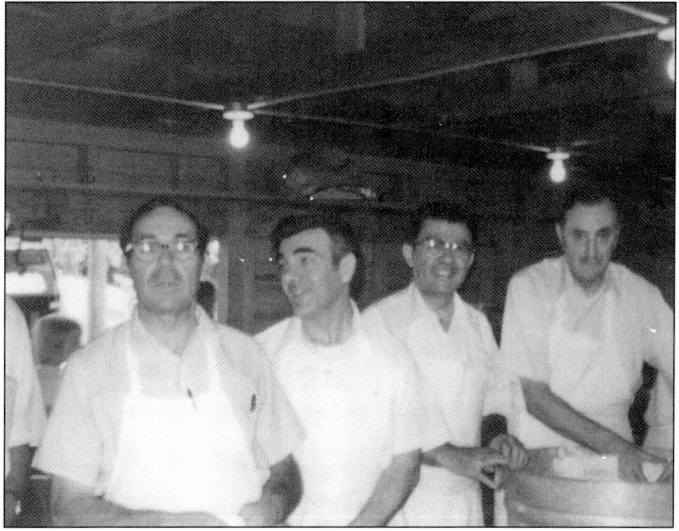

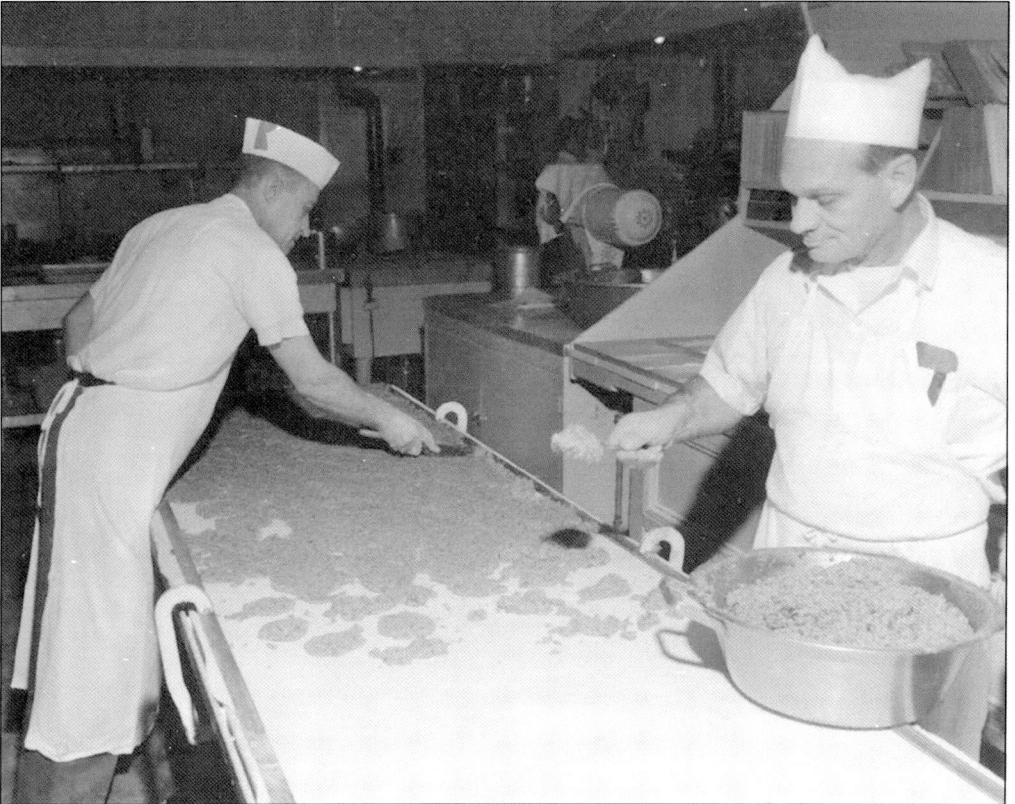

FAMOUS RAVIOLI. Employees at the Gaia-Delucchi Company make their famous ravioli in this photograph from the 1960s. Gaia-Delucchi became renowned for its ravioli, tagliarini, and Italian salami. Another specialty was its mushroom sauce, which was favored by Northern Italians. Delivery trucks brought the company's products to Lodi, Modesto, and the Sierra towns. (Courtesy of the Bank of Stockton Historical Photograph Collection.)

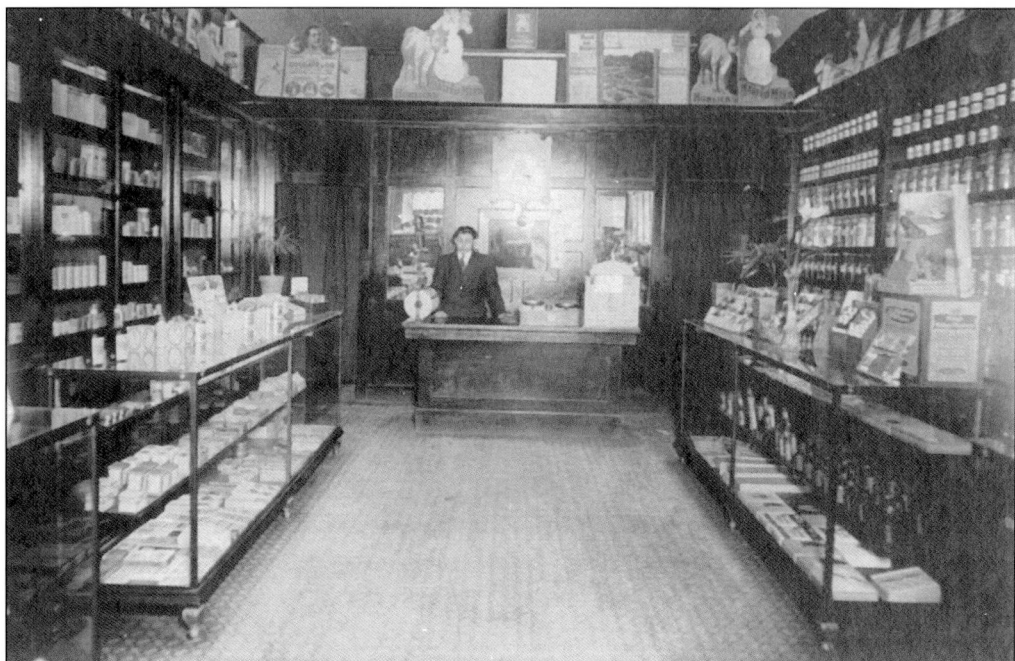

GENOVA PHARMACY. This pharmacy was operated by brothers Manlio and Tullio Silva and was originally located at 49 South Center Street in Stockton (seen in the c. 1915 image above, with Tullio behind the counter). The Silva brothers were from the region of Chiavari, Italy (near Genova), and immigrated in 1909. The pharmacy was a cornerstone of the Italian American community of Stockton. It eventually moved to a new location at 438 East Market Street (seen below around 1961) but has since been demolished. The pharmacy closed in 1964. (Both, courtesy of the Silva family.)

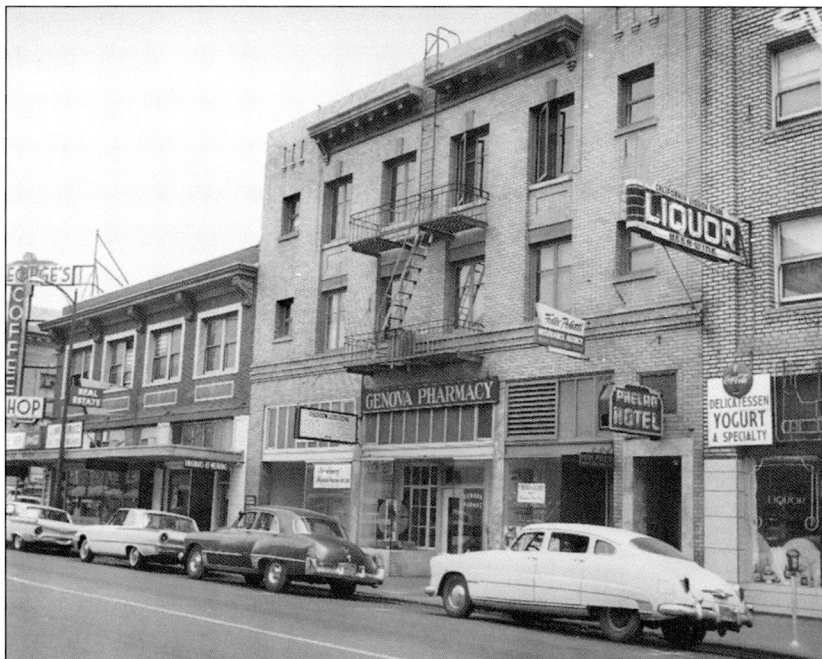

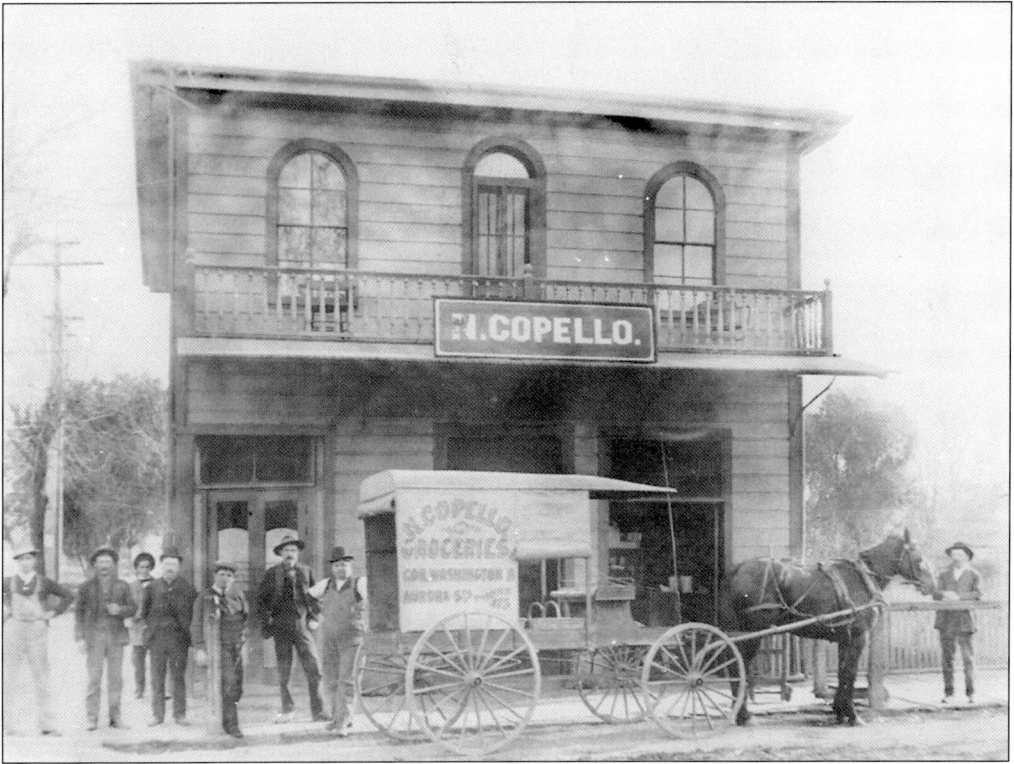

COPELLO GROCERY, C. 1900. Nick Copello was an immigrant's son and worked at a quartz mill as a boy. He helped his father run the Roma Hotel on Center Street in Stockton before buying a restaurant and this store on the corner of Aurora and Washington Streets. Free delivery, by horse and wagon, was a staple of early Italian groceries. (Courtesy of the Bank of Stockton Historical Photograph Collection.)

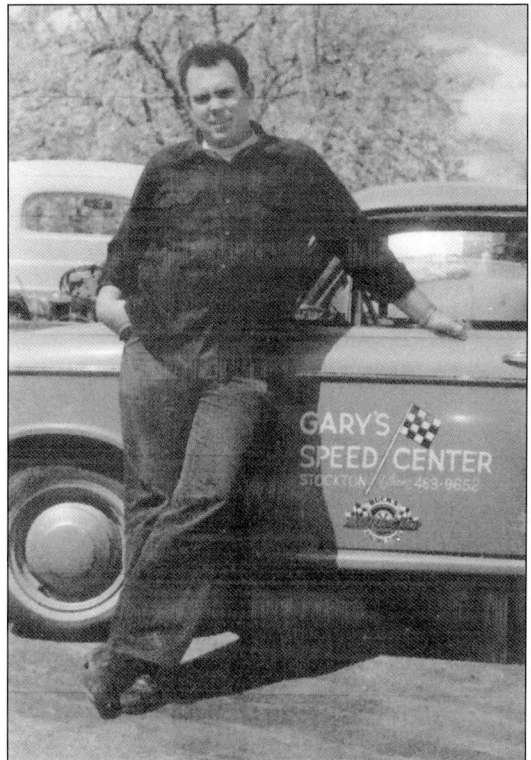

GARY'S SPEED CENTER. From age three, Gary DePauli (born October 31, 1940) loved cars. He once frightened everyone by disappearing and, after a search, was found inside his grandfather's Studebaker. Gary is pictured with his business car around 1965 at age 25. He sold auto parts and repair services from a welding unit towed behind his car at Stockton's 99 Speedway. Gary passed on August 29, 2012. (Courtesy of the DePauli family collection.)

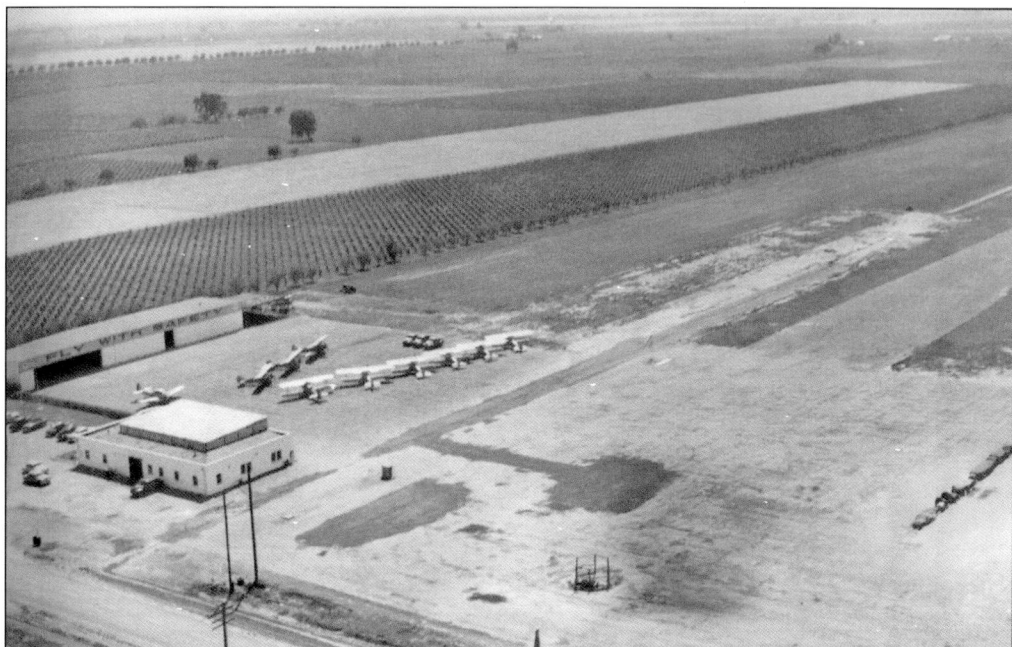

PRECISSI FLYING SERVICE. August, Joe, Louis, and Frank Precissi opened their flying service on 50 acres off of Lower Sacramento Road that they bought from Joseph Fillipi in 1945. This airfield became known as Lodi Air Park, seen above during the 1950s. The brothers learned to fly in the 1930s and served as instructors in the military during World War II. After the war, their business started with Civilian Pilot Training under the GI Bill but quickly moved to agricultural services and aerial application (or crop dusting). The new process of applying chemicals from the air became an important part in the farmers' war against pests. The photograph below shows Louis Precissi dusting grapes with sulfur in a signature Travelair Biplane around 1953. (Above, courtesy of the San Joaquin County Historical Society; below, courtesy of the Bank of Stockton Historical Photograph Collection.)

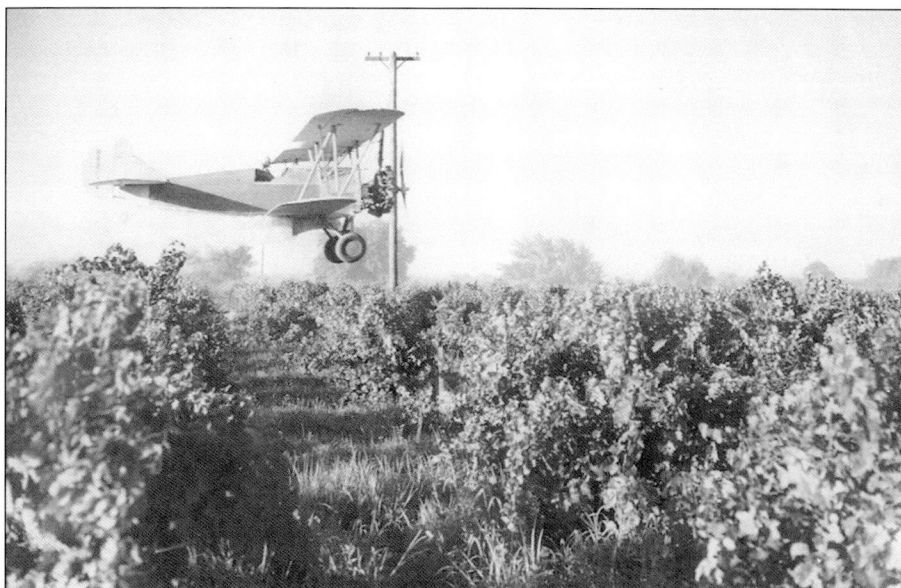

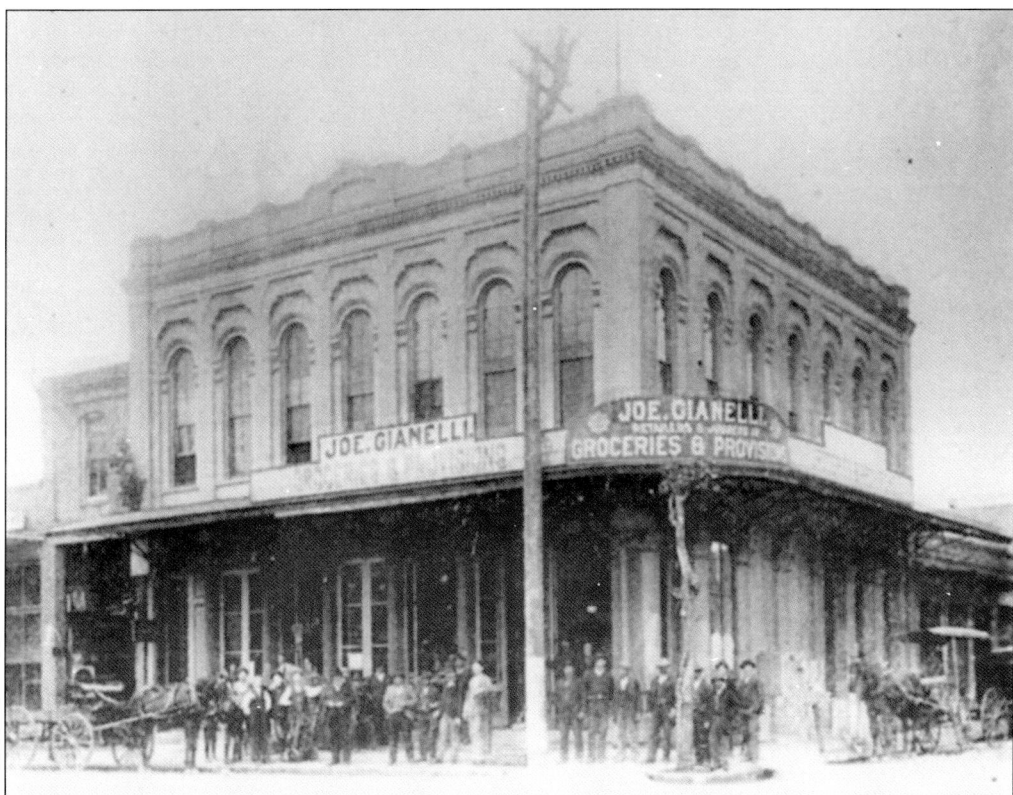

GIANELLI BROTHERS STORE. Giuseppi "Joseph" and Bernardo Gianelli were brothers, originally from Genova, Italy, who immigrated in 1873 and eventually made their way to Stockton. After working for other local Italian merchants, they opened their first grocery store together in November 1876 on California Street. In 1878, they moved to a new corner location at Fremont and California Streets. Older brother Joseph served as manager of this location, seen above, and Bernardo eventually managed a new Hunter Street location they opened in 1880. They did a brisk business delivering to residences and providing farms and ranches with their yearly supplies of provisions. Below, a rare look inside the store (taken around 1910) shows unidentified men shopping the quality goods that the Gianelli grocery stores were known for. (Both, courtesy of the Bank of Stockton Historical Photograph Collection.)

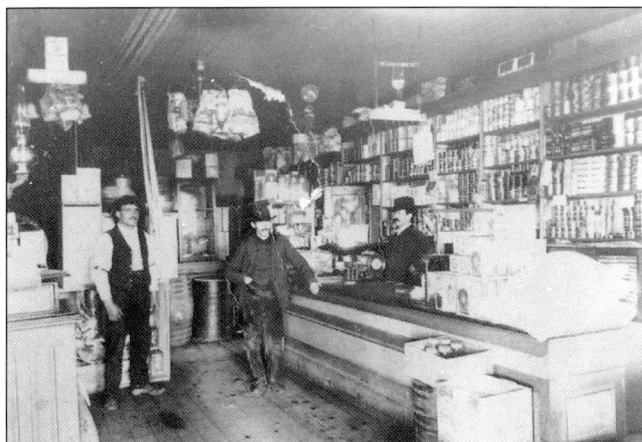

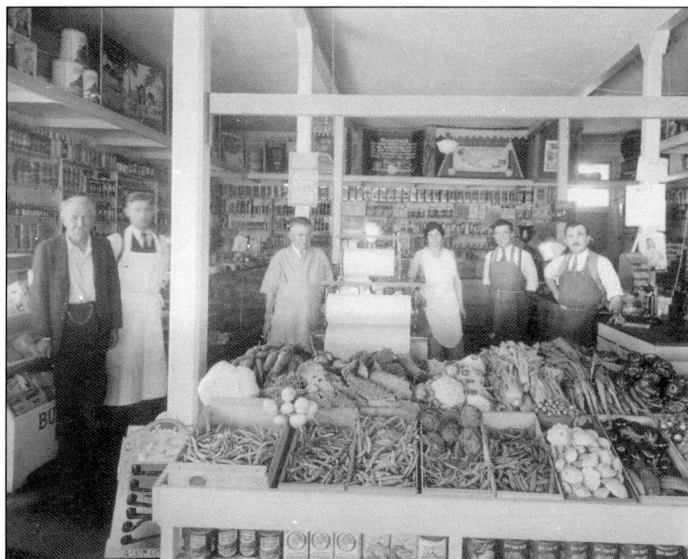

ZAPPETTINI MARKET. The market was managed by Giuseppe "Joe" Zappettini, known to friends and customers as "Zap." This c. 1930 photograph shows, from left to right, an unidentified man, an unidentified butcher, Zap, Adele (Lagorio) Zappettini, an unidentified employee, and Leo Dentoni (Zap's cousin). The market was located at 701 North Ophir Street (now Airport Way) in Stockton. (Courtesy of Lucia Olivieri-Grillo.)

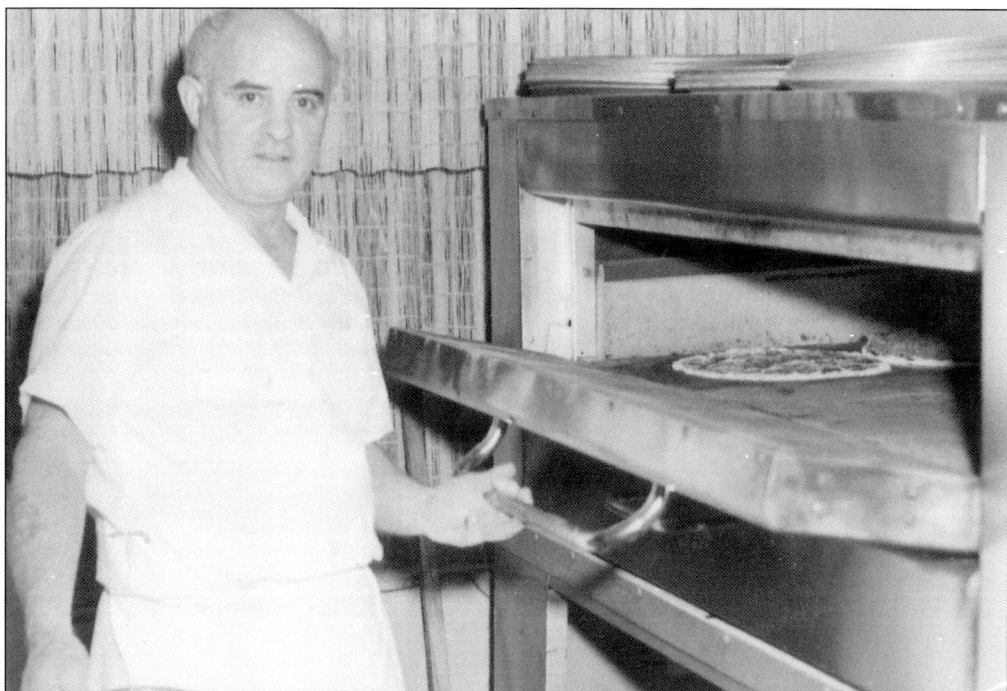

FRANK'S PIZZA PARLOR. Frank A. Sannella stands in front of his restaurant's pizza oven. Frank emigrated from the Naples region in Italy to Boston and eventually arrived in Stockton by 1949. He opened the first pizza parlor in Stockton at Harding and Wilson Ways and operated the popular establishment until 1978. Frank volunteered at St. Mary's Church and cooked for those in need downtown. (Courtesy of the Sannella family.)

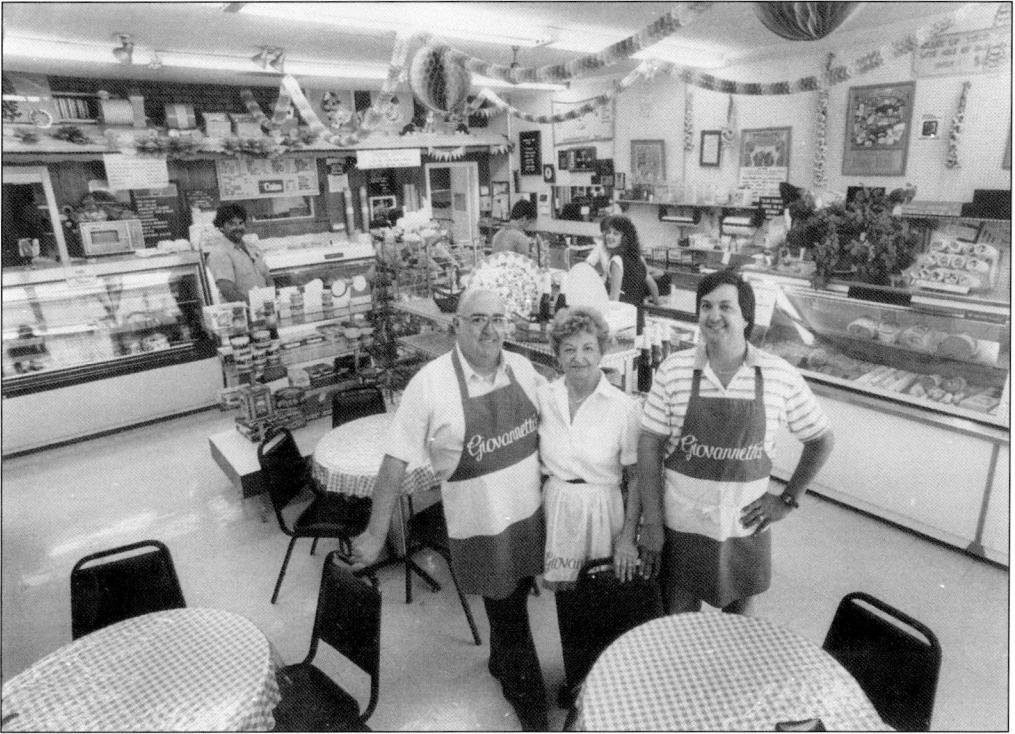

GIOVANNETTI'S ITALIAN DELICATESSEN & CATERING. Lino, Tillie, and Gary Giovanetti (pictured above) pose for a photograph inside their delicatessen in 1986 while customers shop. The Giovanetti family purchased longtime local business Webb's Bakery (opened in 1911) and started their deli and catering business alongside it in May 1980 on Pacific Avenue. It was the largest family-owned bakery and deli in Stockton, offering traditional Dutch pastries and Italian cuisine. The Giovanettis reverted to the traditional spelling of their name (with two *n*'s) for their business name (seen on the ravioli box to the right) after somehow losing one *n* during immigration, a common occurrence for Italian families with difficult-to-spell names. Unfortunately, the historic bakery and deli closed up shop in 1992. (Both, courtesy of the Giovanetti family.)

Giovannetti's

ITALIAN
DELICATESSEN & CATERING

RAVIOLI
"Fresh, like Grandma used to make."

Italian Cooked Foods
Imported & Domestic Foods
Catering For All Occasions
3228 N. Pacific Ave. at Alpine
Stockton, California 95204
209·464·4781

— DIRECTIONS FOR COOKING FINE PASTES —

TO COOK RAVIOLI USE HALF GALLON OF WATER ADDING ONE TEASPOONFUL OF SALT. WHEN THE WATER BOILS PUT IN THE RAVIOLI STIRRING LIGHTLY NOW AND THEN. COOK FOR THREE OR FOUR MINUTES. STRAIN WELL OF WATER AND PLACE IN VESSEL, ADDING GRATED CHEESE TO TASTE. NOW ADD MEAT AND MUSHROOM SAUCE WHICH HAS PREVIOUSLY BEEN SLOWLY WARMED IN ANOTHER DISH. MIX THOROUGHLY AND THE RAVIOLI ARE READY TO SERVE. INGREDIENTS: FLOUR, FILLING (BREAD CRUMBS), SWISS CHARD, SPINACH, BEEF, EGGS, CHEESE, SALT, SEASONING. PERISHABLE — KEEP REFRIGERATED.

Try Giovannetti's Meat & Mushroom Sauce

54 count   *   15 ozs. net weight

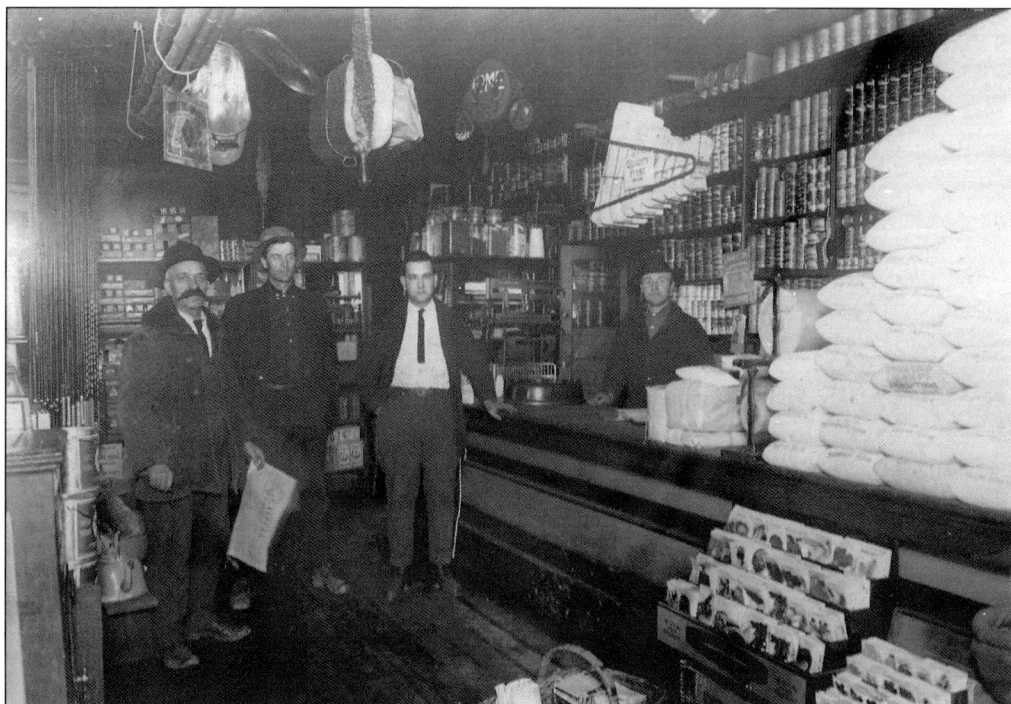

GENOVA STORE AND BAKERY. This business was opened in 1918 by brothers Giovanni and Angelo Rolleri along with their brother-in-law Domenico Gianelli. Giovanni stands behind the counter in this early photograph of the building's interior, taken in November 1918 (the same year they opened). The man in the white shirt is identified as Anthony Gianelli; the other men are unidentified. (Courtesy of the John A. Rolleri Archives.)

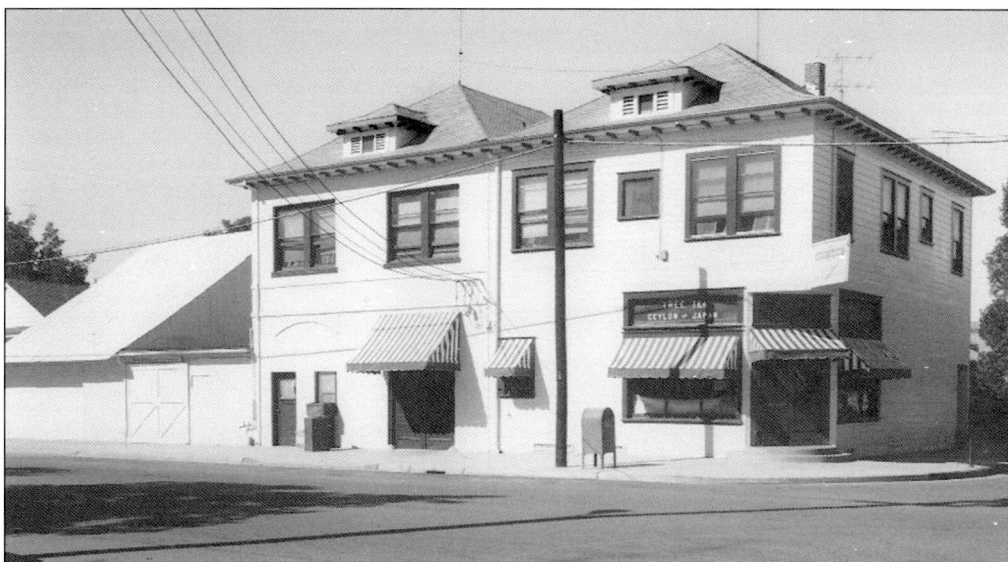

HISTORIC BUILDING. A historical institution, the bakery's location at 749 on the corner of Flora and North Sierra Nevada Streets, seen here in 1971, has changed very little since it first opened for business. The building was named a historic landmark by the City of Stockton in 1985. (Courtesy of the Bank of Stockton Historical Photograph Collection.)

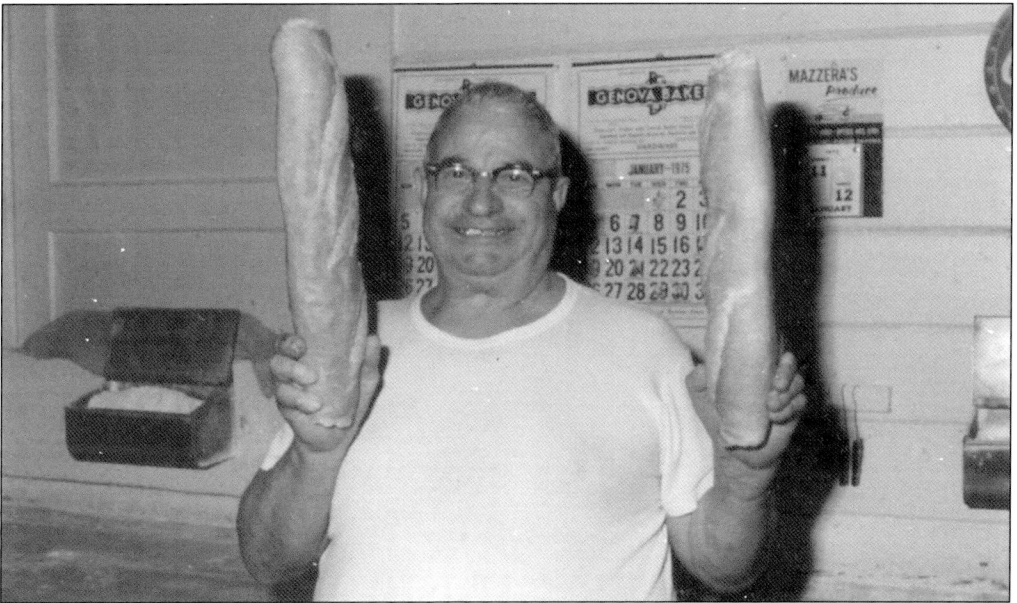

ANGELO ROLLERI. Angelo arrived in the United States in November 1914 at only 15 years old. He worked several jobs before helping his brother start the bakery. After Giovanni retired, he passed his share of the business to his sons John A. and Donald Rolleri. Angelo eventually bought out his nephews and became the sole owner, although both his nephews continued working there. (Courtesy of the Lucchetti family.)

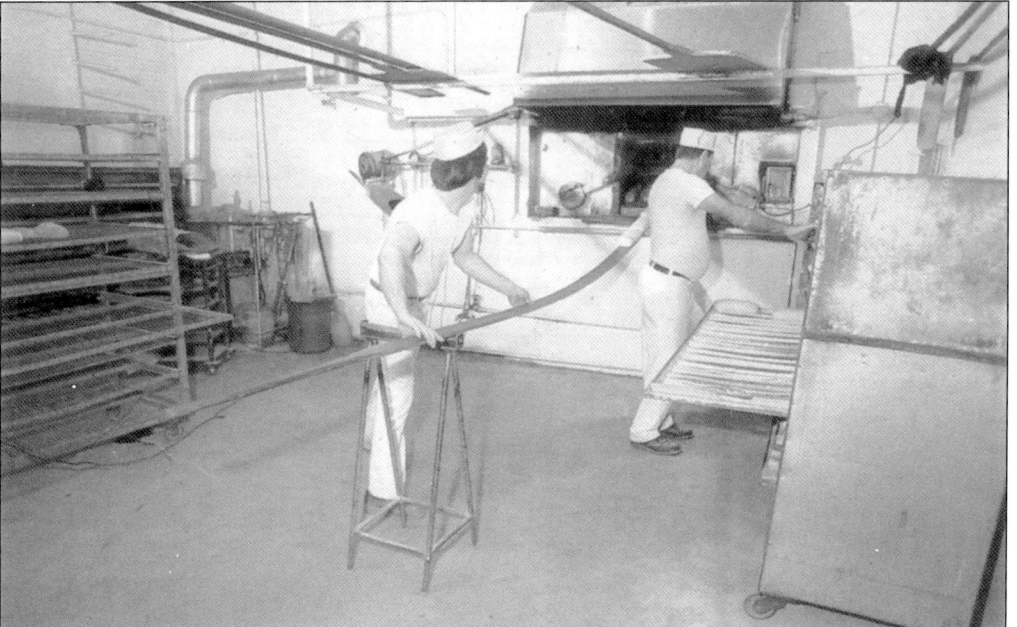

BAKING THE BREAD. In this photograph, Mike Amodeo (left) and Riccardo "Enrico" Rolleri (nephew from Italy) slide loaves into the brick oven with the help of a long paddle. The unique brick oven, built by German immigrants in 1921, would be heated to 500 degrees and then turned off to allow the bricks to cook the dough. Two shifts baked daily to meet the demand. (Courtesy of the Haggin Museum.)

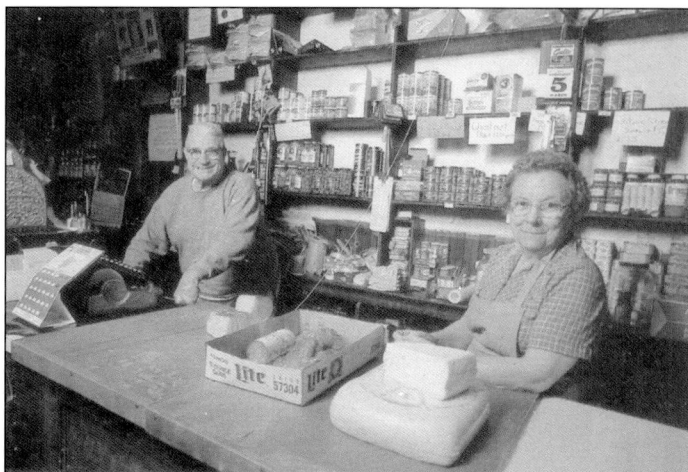

MINDING THE COUNTER.
Angelo Rolleri and his
niece-in-law Edna Rolleri
tend the counter at the
grocery store adjacent to
the bakery. Edna was the
wife of Donald Rolleri,
who delivered the bread
until his untimely death
in the 1950s. The process
of baking the loaves has
been repeated countless
times over the 96 years
of the Genova Bakery's
history. (Courtesy of the
Haggin Museum.)

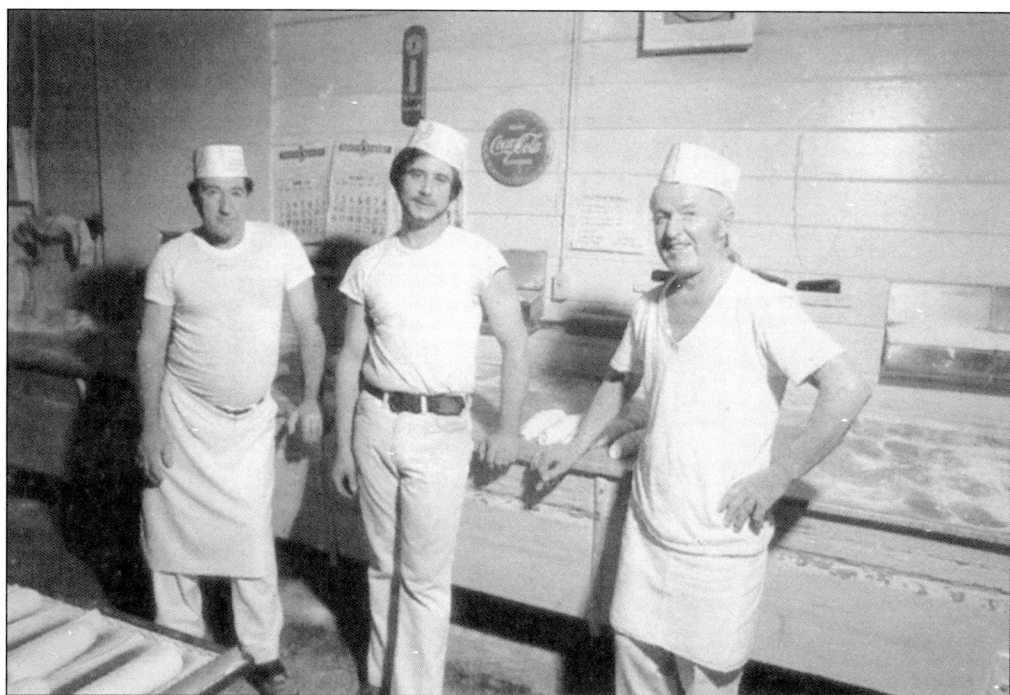

PASSING THE TORCH. The crew includes, from left to right, Enrico Rolleri , Mike Amodeo, and
John A. Rolleri, Giovanni's son who worked at the bakery for over 52 years. Angelo sold the
business to his nephew and two other employees, John G. Rolleri (a cousin) and Bart Bona, in
1980. Tim Canevari, also an employee, took over in 2004 and continues the tradition. (Courtesy
of the Haggin Museum.)

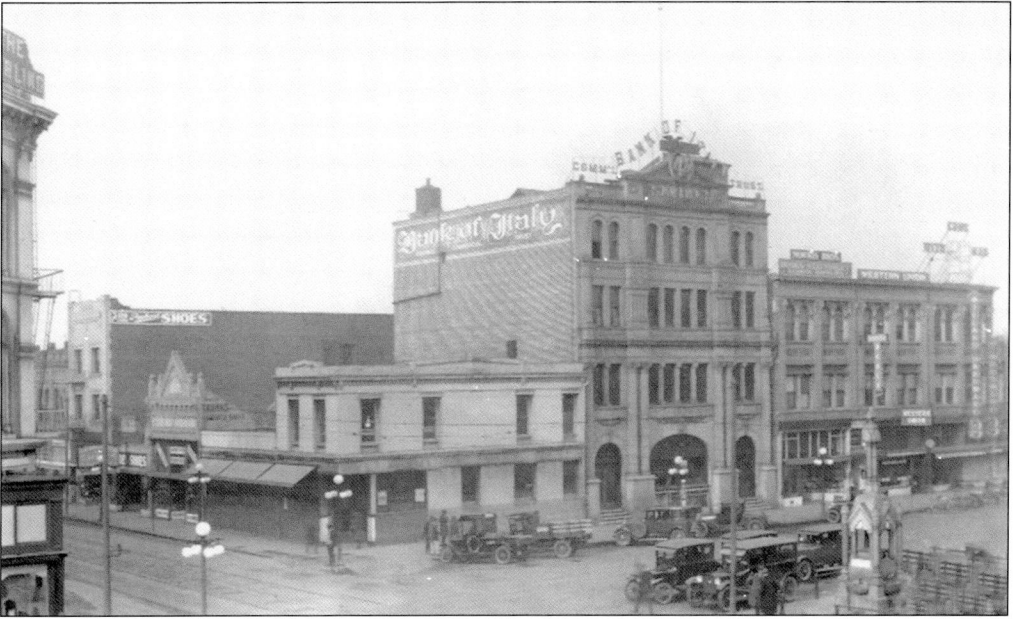

BANK OF ITALY, 1920. The Bank of Italy was founded in 1904 in San Francisco by Amadeo Pietro Giannini, a son of a Genovese immigrant forty-niner. After surviving the Great 1906 Earthquake, it merged with other banks, becoming the Bank of America in 1930. The Stockton branch (seen here) faced Hunter Plaza on the northwest corner of Main and Hunter Streets. (Courtesy of the Bank of Stockton Historical Photograph Collection.)

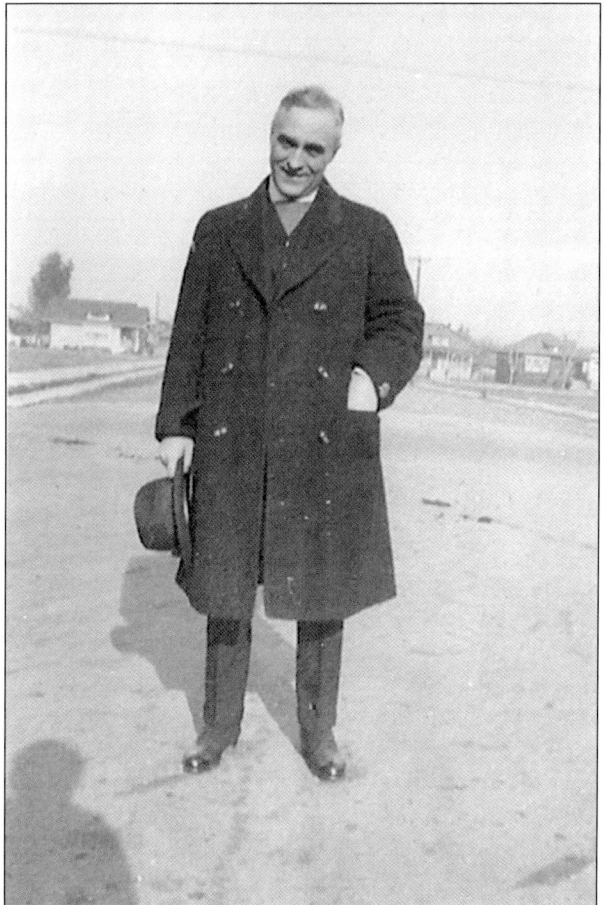

DR. JOHN CRAVIOTTO. Dr. Craviotto came to San Francisco from Genova with his parents at the age of five and would eventually graduate from the University of California in 1899 and receive his medical degree from Cooper Medical College in 1904. In 1905, he moved to Stockton to establish his medical practice. He quickly became a leader in the Italian community of San Joaquin County. (Courtesy of the Bank of Stockton Historical Photograph Collection.)

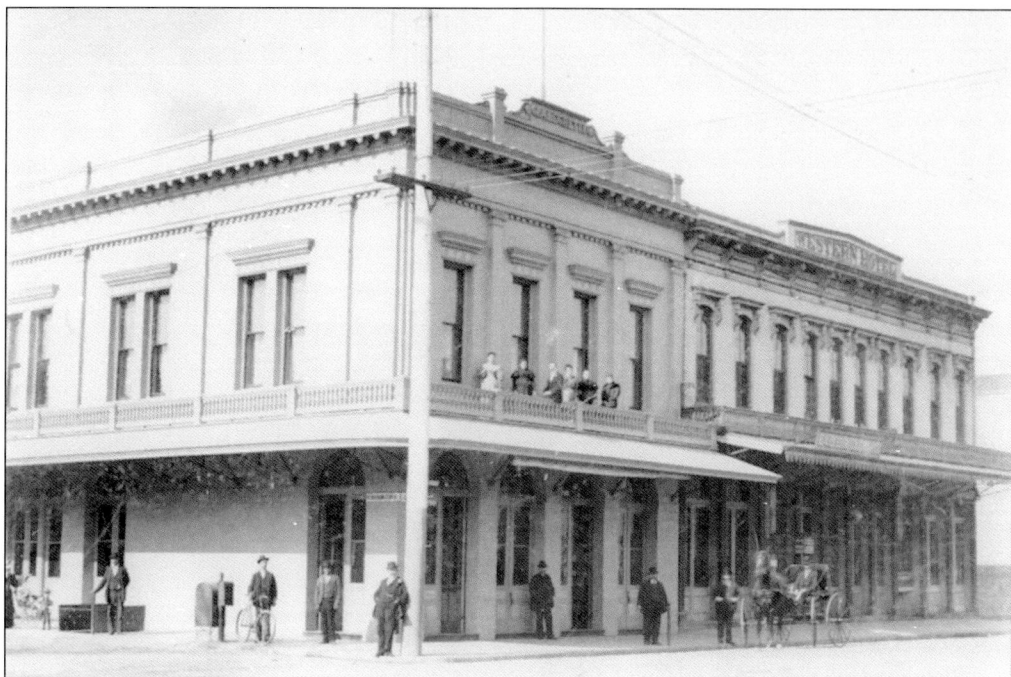

GAETANO ALEGRETTI. Popular early Italian businessman Gaetano Alegretti was born in Chiavari, Italy, and came to America in 1864 to make his fortune. He worked for his uncle in San Francisco before making his way to Stockton. He worked hard and eventually bought his uncle's business interests in San Joaquin County. Alegretti invested in real estate and became quite wealthy. He built the Alegretti Building at 403 Center Street (pictured above around 1890) in 1869, which housed his grocery store and saloon (pictured below around 1900). Alegretti was a pillar of the community, often helping his countrymen and offering advice on how to deal and thrive in their new homeland. (Above, courtesy of the Bank of Stockton Historical Photograph Collection; below, courtesy of the San Joaquin County Historical Society.)

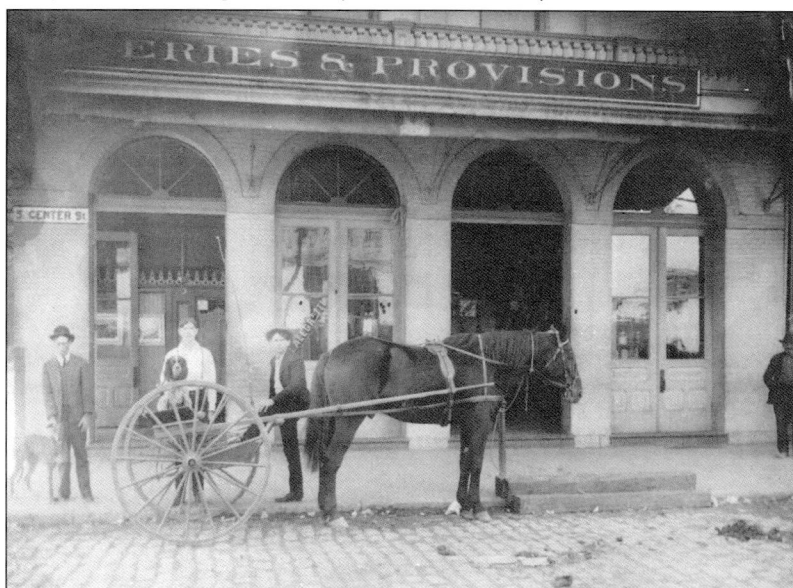

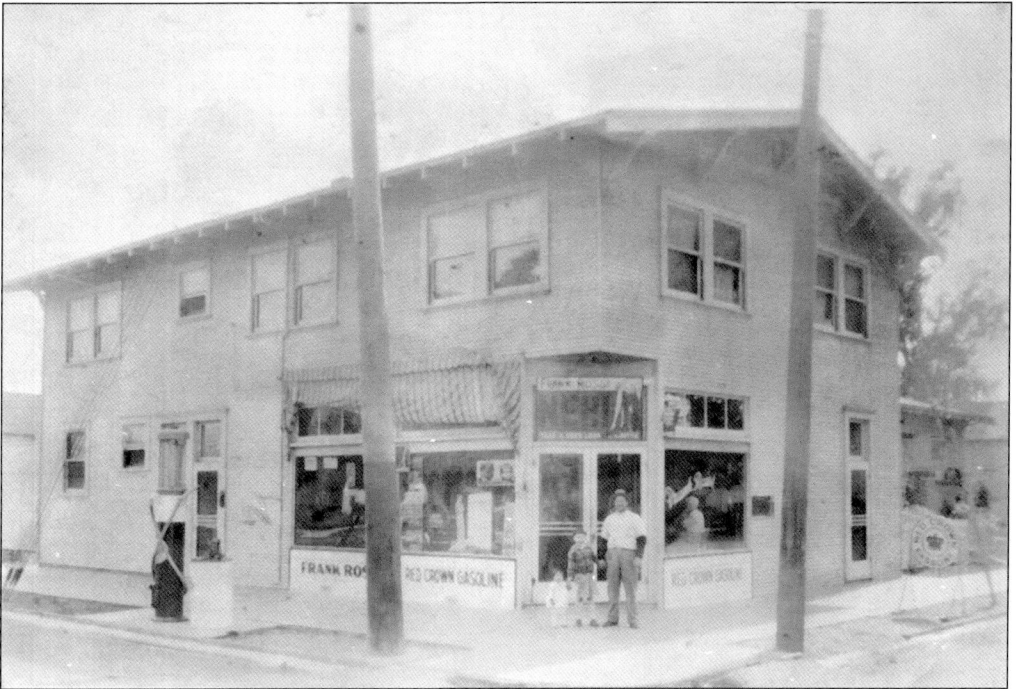

ROSSI STORE, 1930. The Rossi Store was located on the southwest corner of South El Dorado and Anderson Streets in Stockton. The Ponsi family lived above the store in 1928 and in a flat on the first floor for several years. Standing in front of the store are Frank Rossi and his young sons Carlo (right) and Aldo. (Courtesy of the Lucchetti family.)

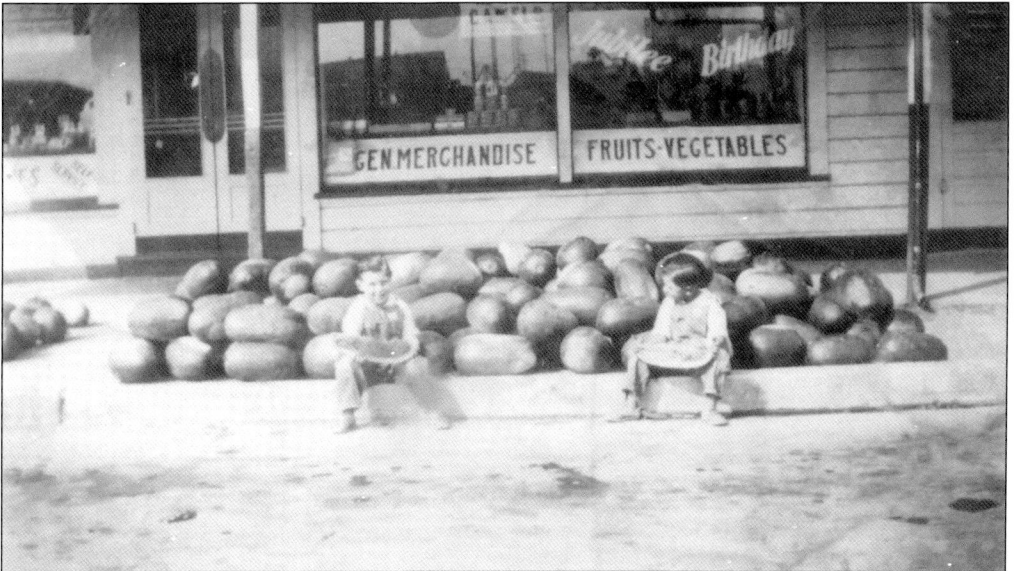

GERLOMES GROCERY STORE, 1934. Brothers George (left) and Ray "Babe" Gerlomes enjoy slices of watermelon on a hot afternoon in August in front of their parents' grocery store. The family-owned store was located on South Lincoln Street in Stockton and was in business until the early 1970s. The family's name was originally Girolami but was changed at some point to Gerlomes. (Courtesy of Angie Gerlomes Nunes.)

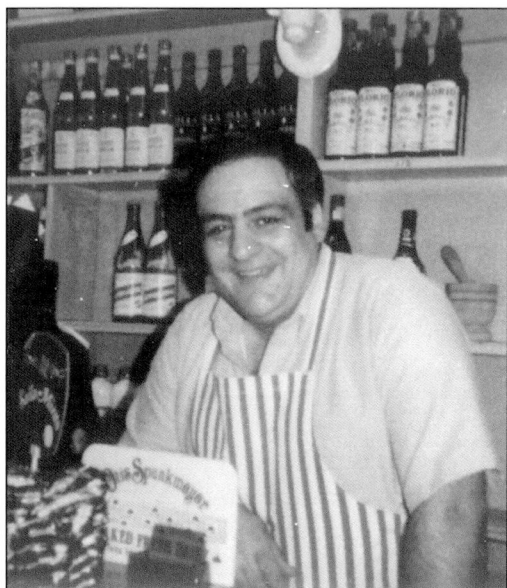

GIAN'S DELI. Dario Angelini and Lorenzo Ferrari opened their delicatessen at 19 San Joaquin Street in Stockton in 1924. It soon became a favorite among the Italians of the area. At the age of 16, Giavanni "Gian" Bolognini, Lorenzo's wife's nephew, came from Corfino, Italy, to Stockton and worked in the delicatessen for many years (at right, behind the original counter). In 1972, the original partners sold the business to Gian, who built it into a Stockton institution (seen below at the original location). Gian used recipes from Angelini and Ferrari along with his own recipes that were passed down in his family. Since its opening, several generations of families have patronized the deli. Sadly, Gian passed away of cancer in 2008, but his second son, Jeffery, now owns and runs the daily operations of the business. (Both, courtesy of Gian's Deli.)

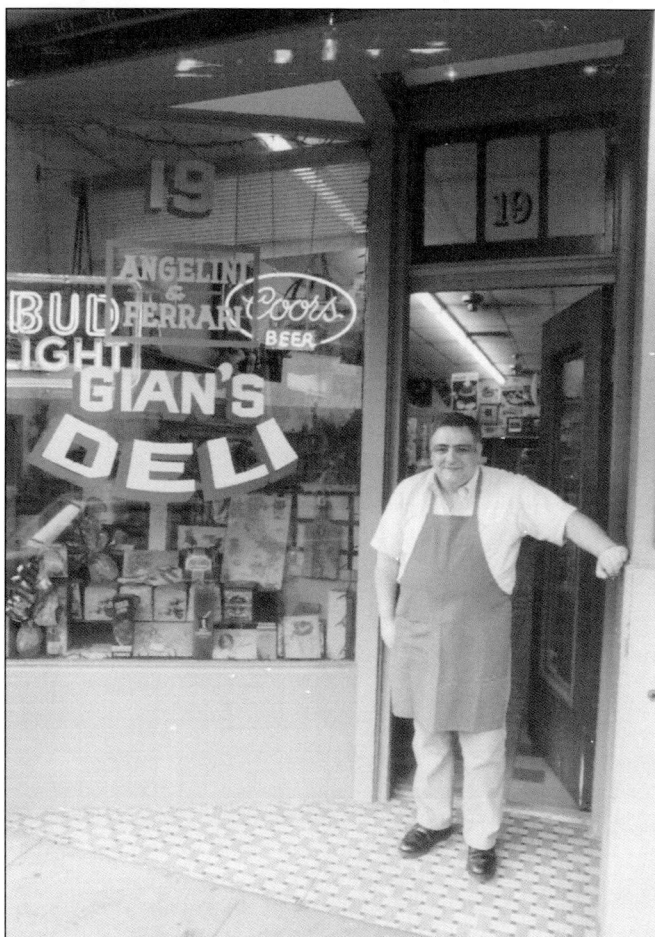

New Deli Location. After its many moves to different locations over the years, Gian; Gian's mother, Maria; and his son Jeffery Bolognini stand in front of the current location of Gian's Deli at 2112 Pacific Avenue off of Stockton's Miracle Mile. For over 89 years, the delicatessen has remained a family business serving the community. (Courtesy of Gian's Deli.)

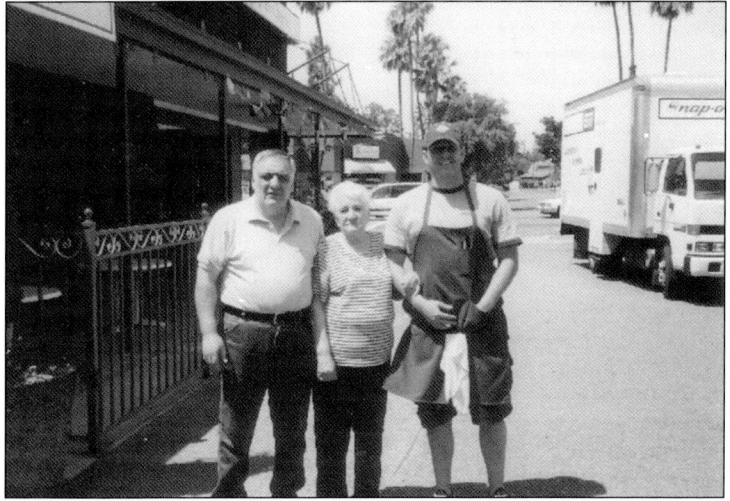

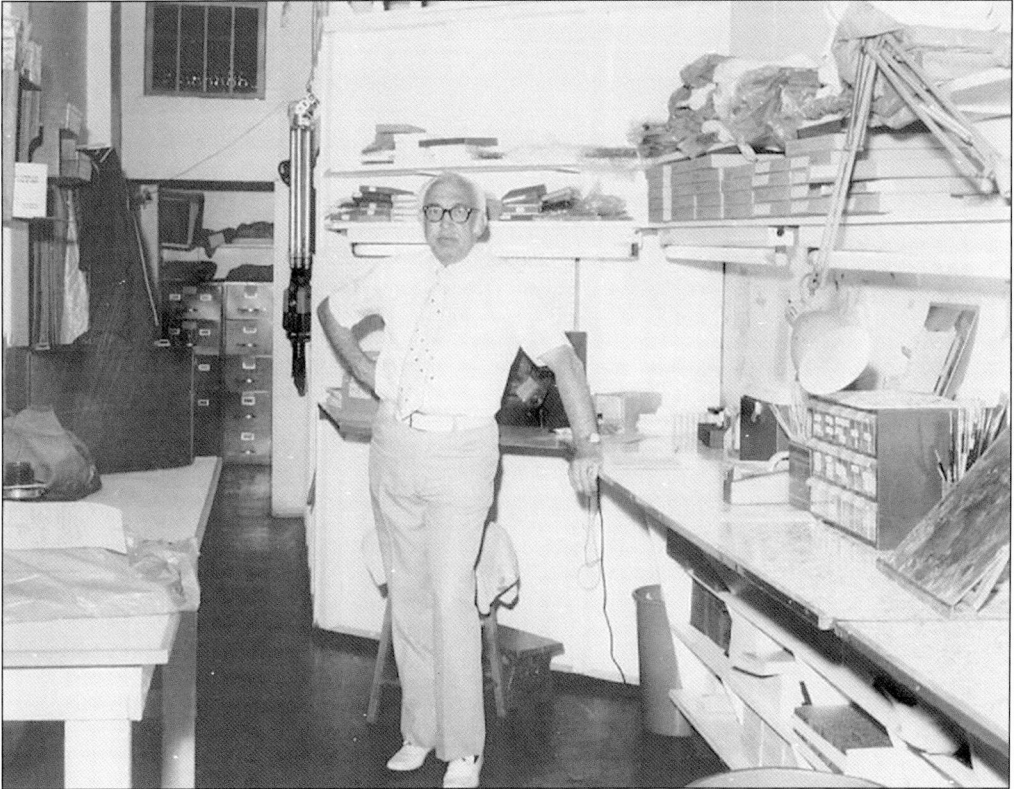

History's Photographer. Noted photographer and historian Leonard Covello, an Italian immigrant, traded a career in music (see page 86) for one in professional photography. Covello began collecting thousands of historical images (now part of the Bank of Stockton Archives) and cowrote three books on local history. He is seen here in his studio at 2007 Pacific Avenue on the Miracle Mile around the 1970s. (Courtesy of the Bank of Stockton Historical Photograph Collection.)

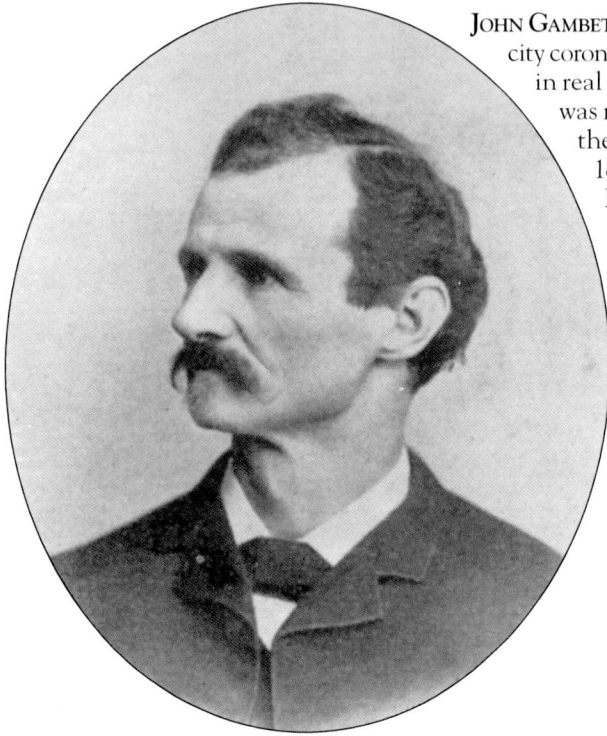

JOHN GAMBETTA. Gambetta was a skilled businessman, city coroner, and public administrator who invested in real estate in the early days of Stockton and was responsible for the first land addition to the city. His family came from Genova in 1855 and was one of the first complete Italian families in the area. (Courtesy of the Haggin Museum.)

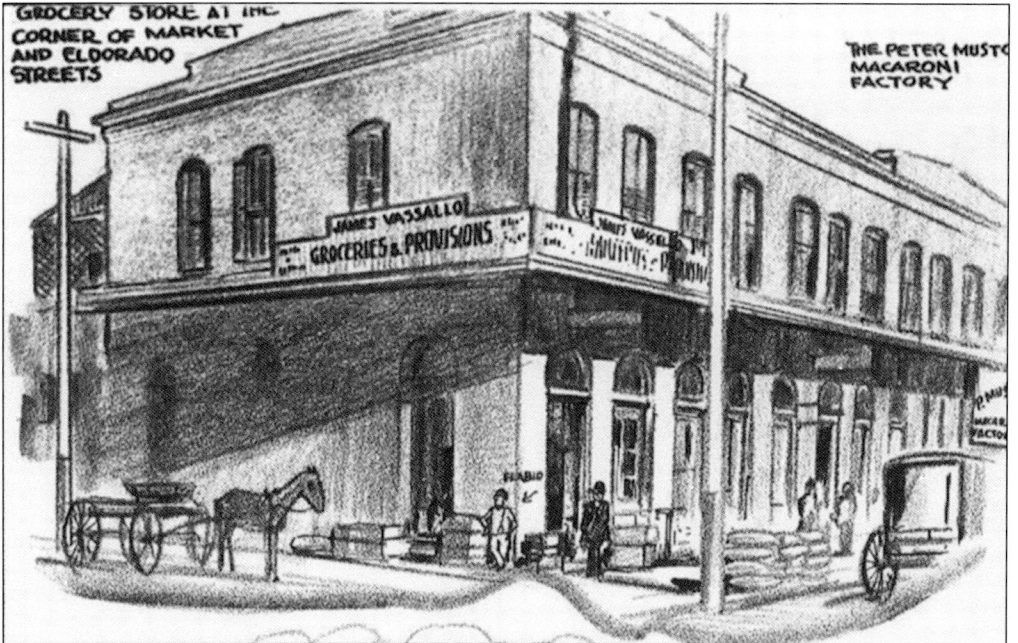

PETER MUSTO. Musto was an early entrepreneur and businessman who immigrated to San Joaquin County around 1872. He started and operated a grocery store and the Stockton Macaroni Factory (seen in this Ralph Yardley sketch), a successful Italian food producer at the turn of the century. Unfortunately, the business closed its doors in 1917, eight years after Musto's death. (Courtesy of the Bank of Stockton Historical Photograph Collection.)

Four

Traditions, Customs, and Entertainment

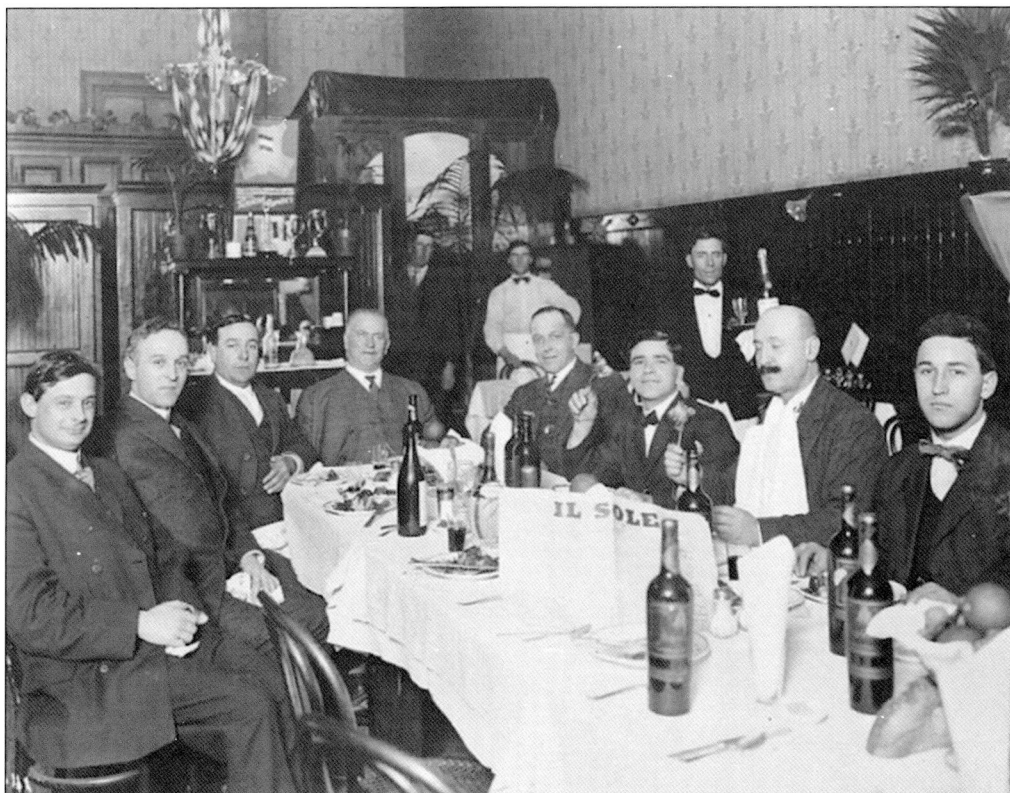

CIBO E VINO (FOOD AND WINE). Although many community members achieved a level of success that was unobtainable in Italy, they kept their beliefs, customs, and traditions, such as a love of food, wine, and good company, as evidenced here around 1910 at a restaurant in Stockton. The only man identified is Dr. John Craviotto (second from left). *Il Sole*, an Italian-language newspaper, is featured prominently. (Courtesy of the Bank of Stockton Historical Photograph Collection.)

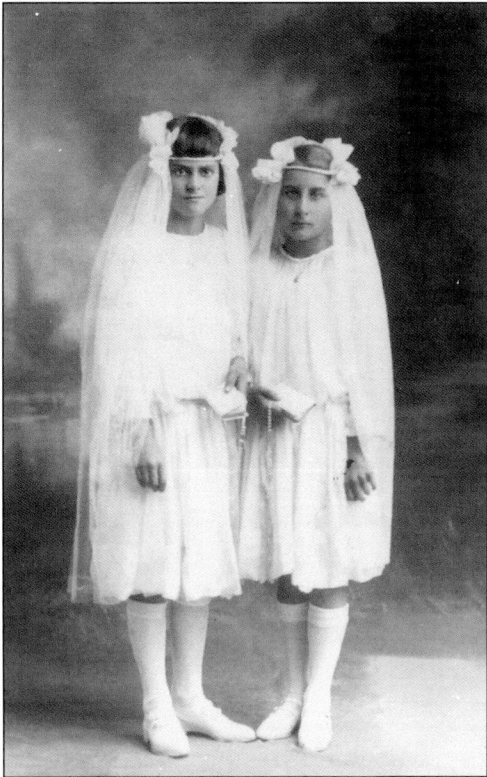

FIRST COMMUNION DRESSES. Many important milestones in Italian culture are linked to the practices of the Roman Catholic Church. Here, Elsie Corradi (later Boggiano), on the left, and sister Lucy Corradi (later Pitto) pose in their Communion dresses sometime between 1915 and 1920. The beautiful dresses and veils were handmade by their mother, Catherina (Guerrini) Corradi. (Courtesy of the Macfarlane/Boggiano/Corradi family.)

FIRST COMMUNION. First Communion is an important rite of passage in the Roman Catholic Church. Here, Giavanni "Gian" Bolognini (first row, third from left) and his parents Maria and Antonio (directly behind him, in the second row) are ready to receive the sacrament in Corfino, Italy. (Courtesy of Gian's Deli.)

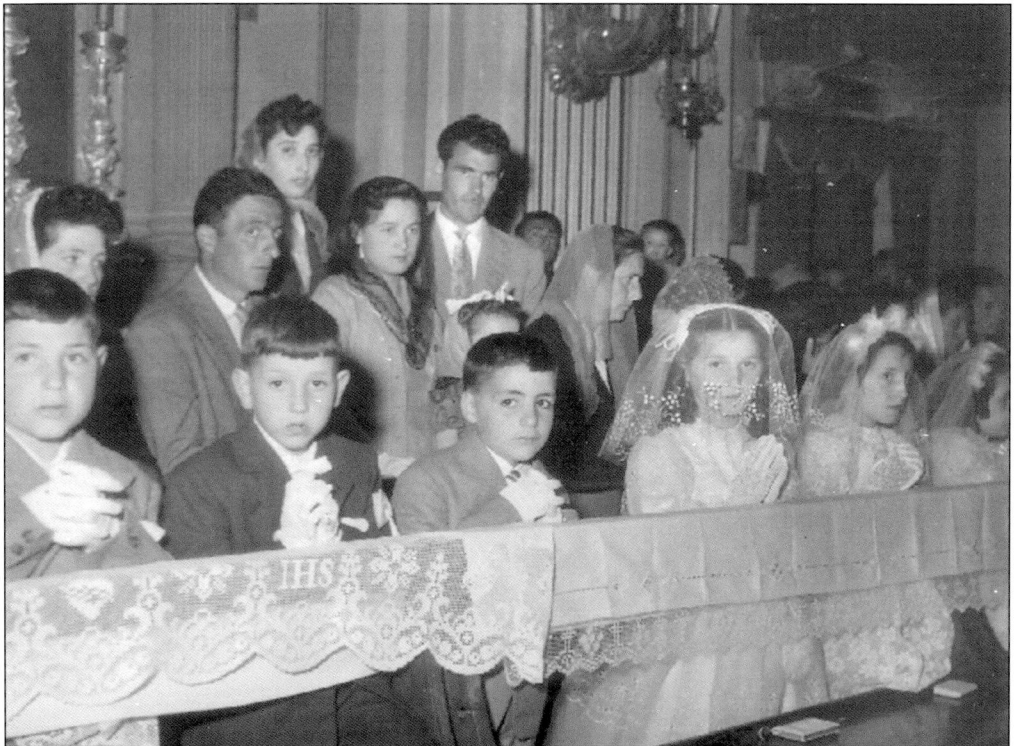

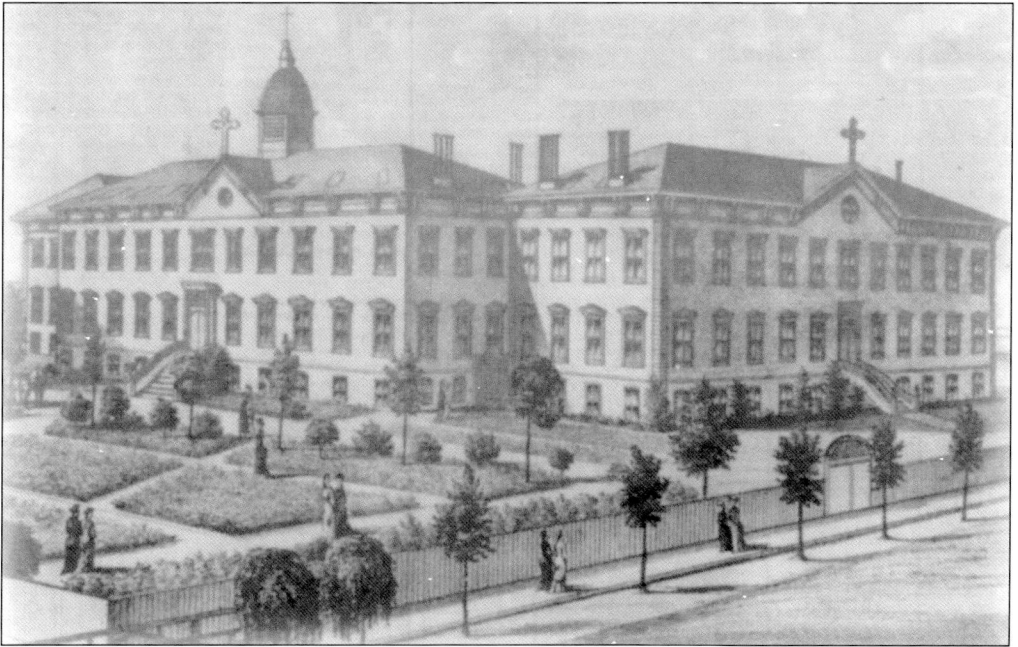

ST. AGNES ACADEMY. On March 17, 1876, Archbishop Joseph Alemany of San Francisco dedicated St. Agnes Academy, located between San Joaquin and California Streets in Stockton. It cost $22,000, which was raised by the Catholic community with the help of Fr. William Bernard O'Connor and the Dominican Sisters who traveled through the county raising subscriptions from area Catholics. (Courtesy of St. Mary's High School.)

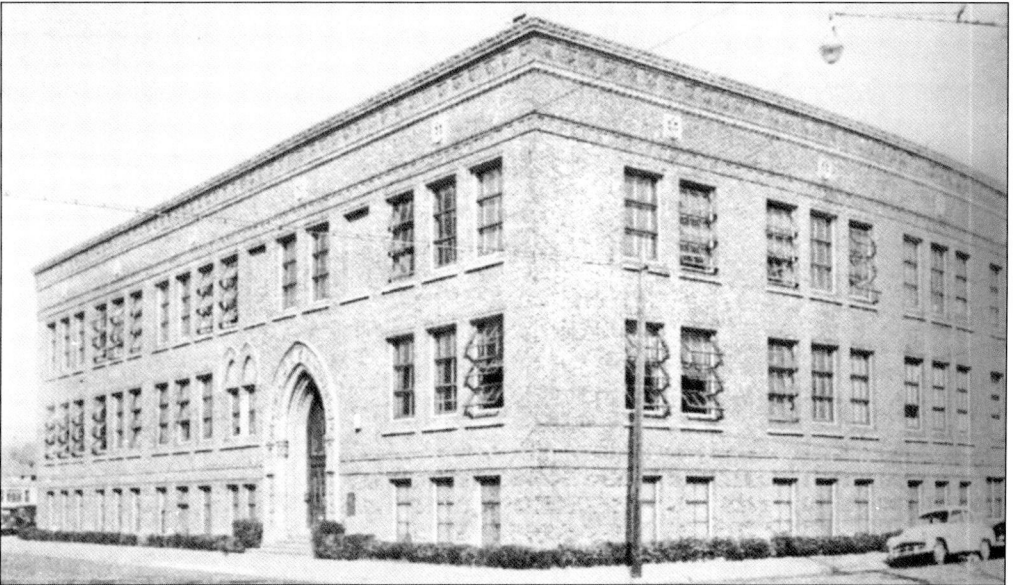

ST. MARY'S HIGH SCHOOL. After several incarnations and locations (the building seen here was used from 1927 to 1956), a new school facility was needed to meet the enrollment demand. Money was raised by the community, and in 1956, a new campus opened on El Dorado Street. It continues to provide high-quality education to this day. Italian families were instrumental in establishing Catholic education in the area. (Courtesy of St. Mary's High School.)

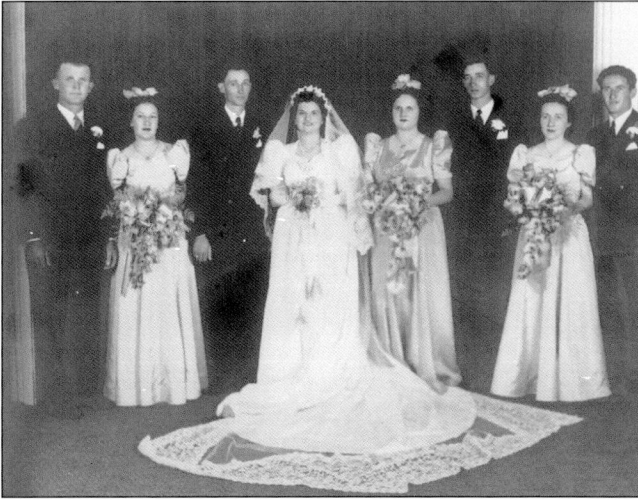

ITALIAN AMERICAN WEDDING, STOCKTON. Weddings were extremely important to the Italian community and could be large affairs. Pictured here is the Ceresola/Ghiglieri wedding on September 15, 1940. In the wedding party are, from left to right, Simon Van Steenberge, Rose Forenti Derivi, Eddie Ghiglieri (groom), Mary Ceresola (bride), Margaret Giannocchio Avansino, Leslie Ghiglieri, Esther Lucchetti, and Fred DeBenedetti. (Courtesy of the estate of Rose Forenti Derivi.)

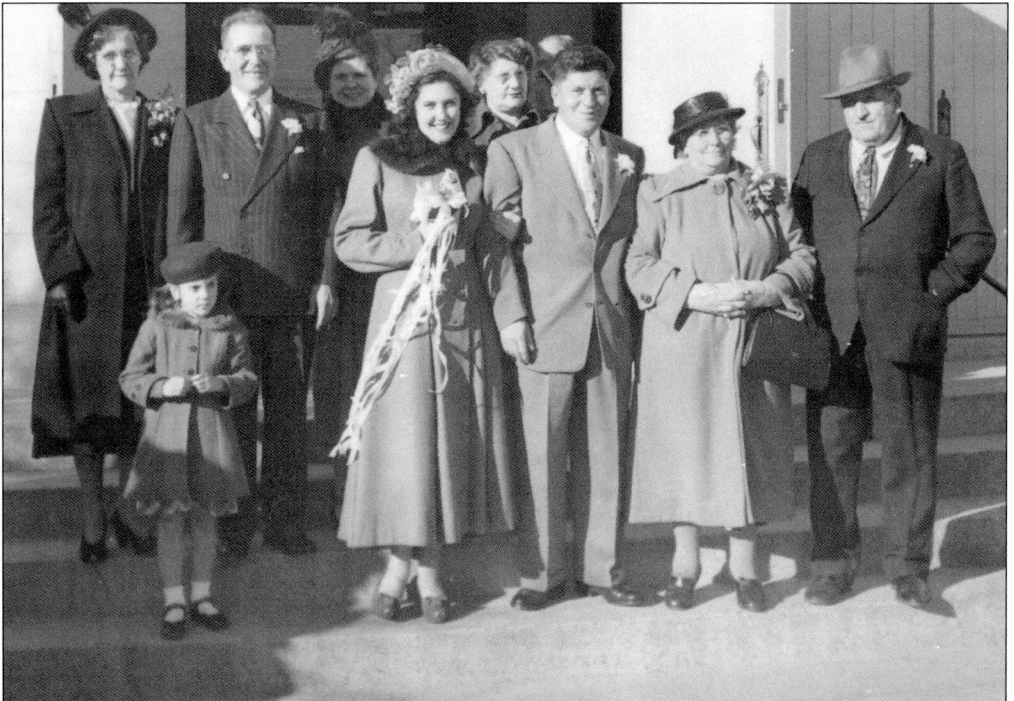

PRECISSI/ZAPPETTINI WEDDING. Adriana Zappettini emigrated in 1948 from Genova, where several of her family had already settled. There, she met Frank Precissi of Precissi Flying Service, and they married in January 1950 at St. Gertrude's in Stockton. From left to right are Adele Zappettini, little Sandy Bertocelli, Zap Zappettini, Amelia Olivieri, Adriana Precissi (bride), Josephine Bertocelli, Frank Precissi (groom), and Angela and Pietro Precissi (Courtesy of Lucia Olivieri-Grillo.)

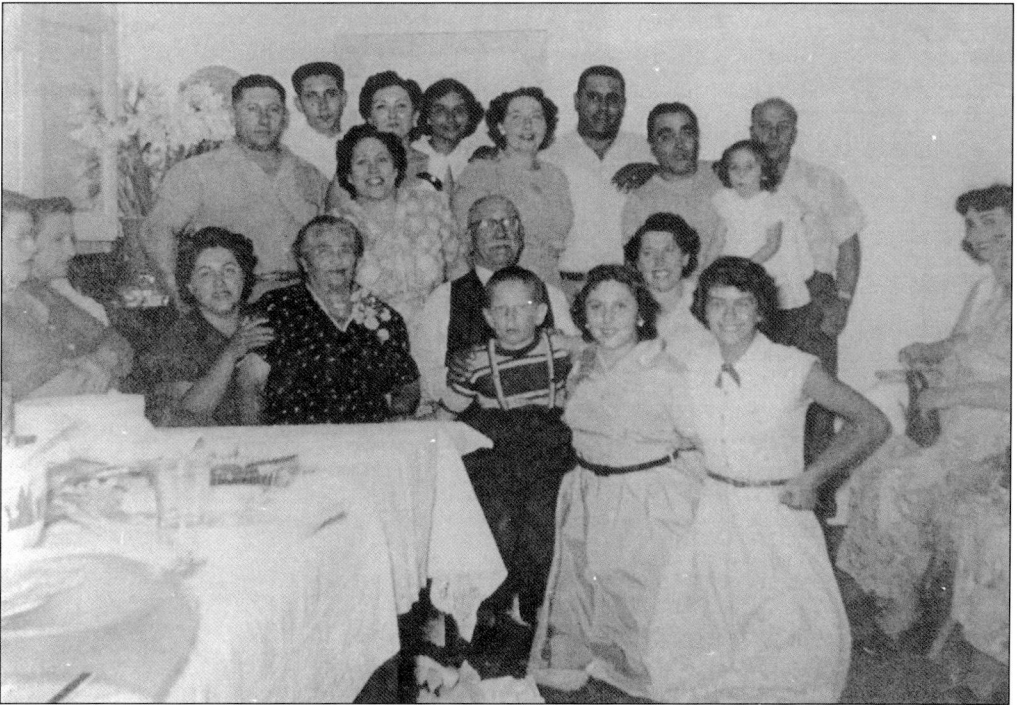

MAZZILLI FAMILY TABLE. An important part of gatherings and a source of tremendous pride is the family table, like the one seen here during the 50th wedding anniversary of Antonio and Maria Mazzilli. Gathered around the table in the image above are, from left to right, (first row) Merle Pulas, Eileen Garrett, Josephine Honkenon, Maria Mazzilli, Carmel Mazzilli, Antonio Mazzilli, Paul A. Mazzilli, Donna Francisco, Roxine Francisco, and Toni Mazzilli; (second row) Vincent James Mazzilli, Donald Anthony Mazzilli, Delores Mazzilli, Diane Mazzilli, Dorothy Mazzilli, John Anthony Mazzilli, Peter Francisco, Ero Honkenon, Doreen Francisco, Millie Caparusso, and Catherine Caparusso. The table graced the basement of their familial home at 326 South Union Street in Stockton, and it serves the family to this day. Generations sharing a meal around the table, as seen below during the 1980s, is an important tradition for many Italian American families. (Both, courtesy of the Mazzilli family.)

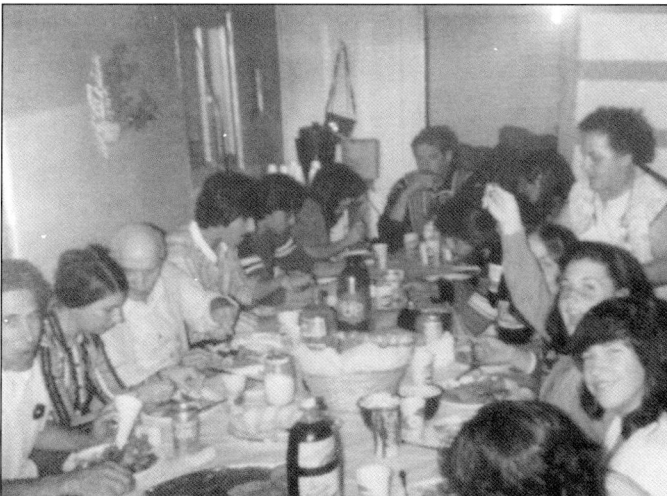

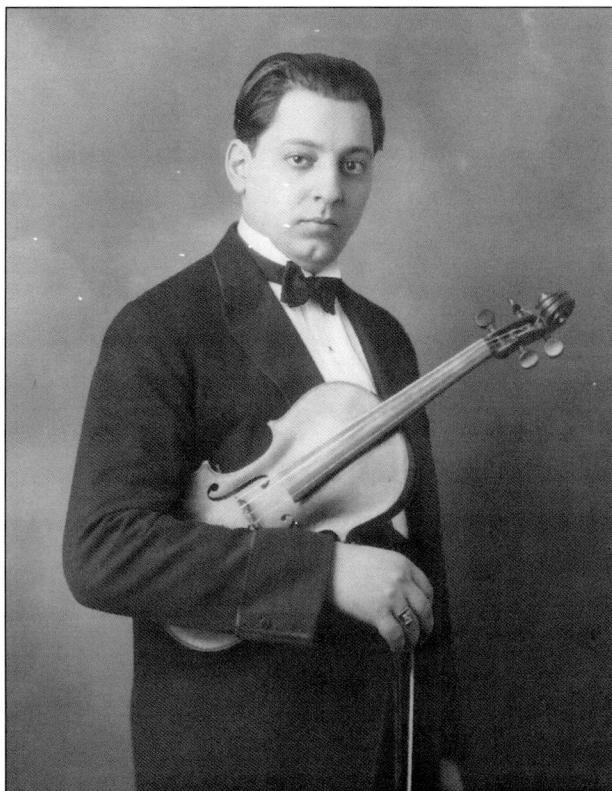

MAESTRO MANLIO SILVA. Manlio was born in Chiavari, near Genova, on November 4, 1893. His family (along with brother Tullio) came to the United States in 1909. Trained as a pharmacist, Manlio operated the Genova Pharmacy with Tullio, but his true passion was music. He studied at the Ginnasio and at the Liceo Musicale di Chiavari under Prof. Giulio Gamberini, who was a notable violinist. Manlio married Margaret Gianelli, and they had a daughter named Carmen. He conducted both the State and Orpheum Theater Orchestras and was instrumental in the establishment of the Stockton Symphony Orchestra, which he conducted for 31 years until his death on October 27, 1958. An elementary school in Stockton is named in his honor. (Left, courtesy of San Joaquin County Historical Society; below, courtesy of the Silva family.)

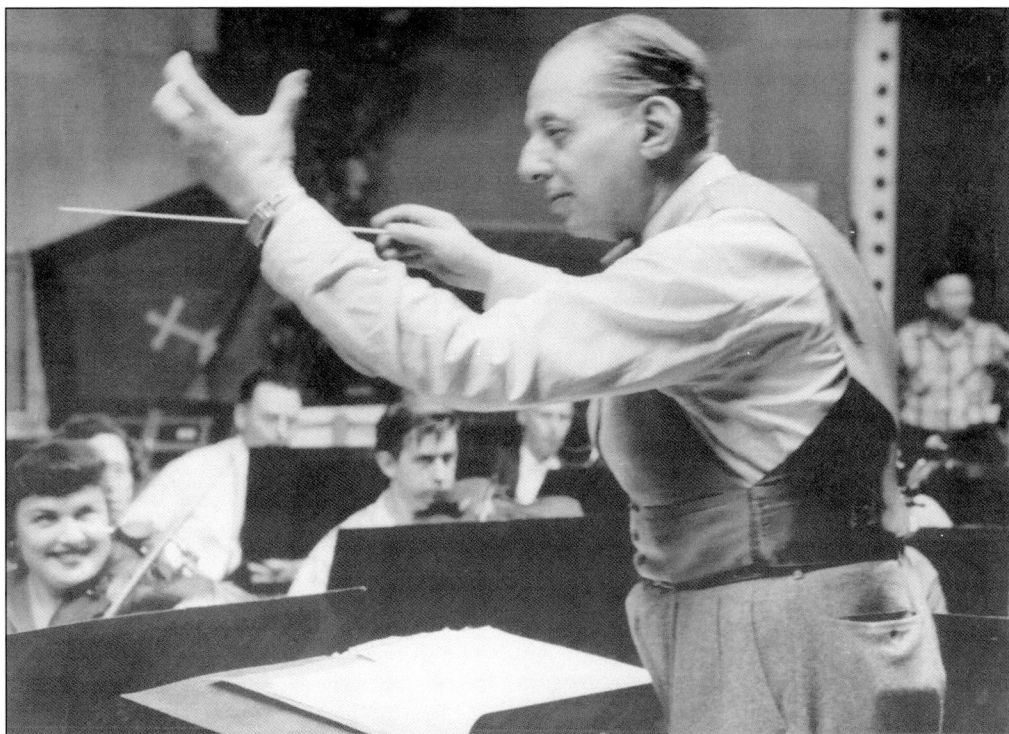

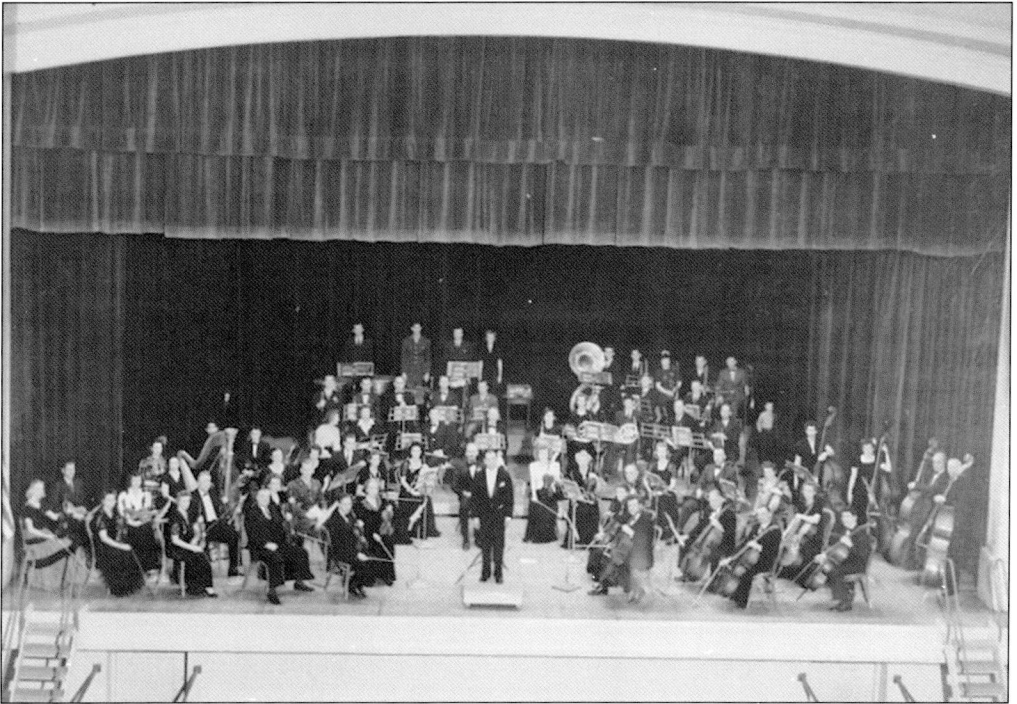

STOCKTON SYMPHONY. In the spring of 1926, an ensemble of 20 musicians gathered for a Stockton Music Club concert. The group called itself the Little Symphony Orchestra and would meet weekly after 1:00 p.m. after its founder, Manlio Silva, fulfilled his duties at a local theater. Silva served as business and musical director and conductor, and he paid expenses out of his own pocket the first few years of operation until the group became successful. The company grew and changed its name to the Stockton Symphony Orchestra. It made appearances throughout the area, including at the Stockton High School Auditorium in 1929 (above) and at the San Joaquin County Fairgrounds in 1958 (below), which was one of the last performances by Maestro Silva before his death. (Both, courtesy of the Bank of Stockton Historical Photograph Collection.)

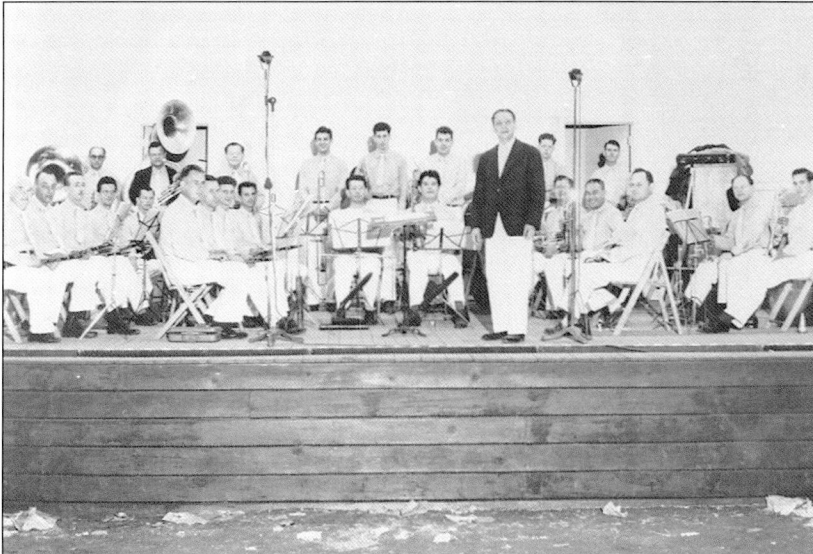

73

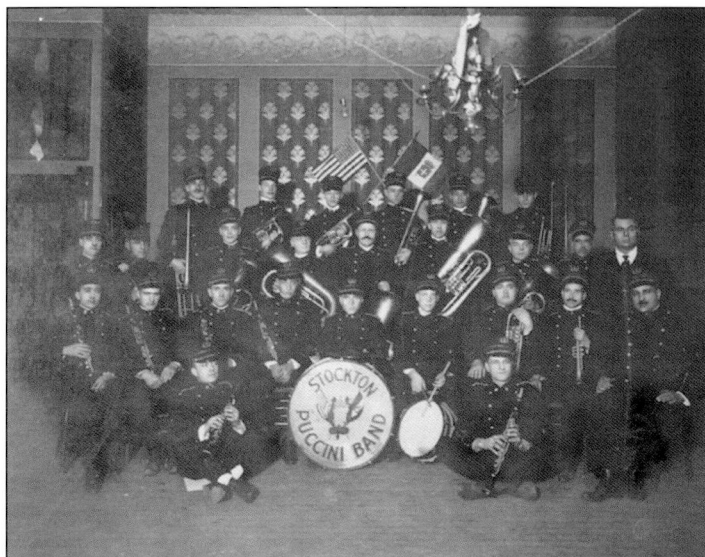

STOCKTON PUCCINI BAND. Music has always been an important part of the Italian culture, a tradition maintained by the local Italian community. One of the earliest bands organized by immigrants was the Puccini Band, seen here around 1900. The group specialized in the works of Puccini, a native of Lucca, Tuscany, and one of the world's greatest composers. (Courtesy of the Bank of Stockton Historical Photograph Collection.)

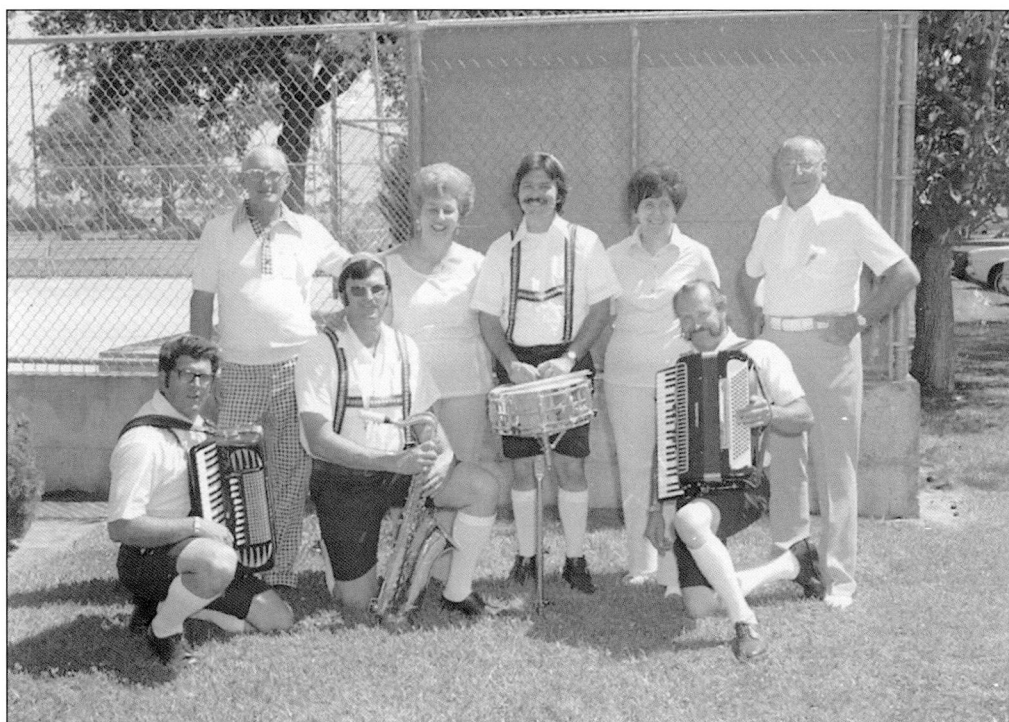

STEVE TRUCCO BAND. Steve Trucco (far left, with accordion) and his band of strolling *paesani* (countrymen) delighted audiences for years at the Italian Gardener Society's annual picnics. This photograph was taken at the 1974 picnic at Micke Grove. (Courtesy of the Bank of Stockton Historical Photograph Collection.)

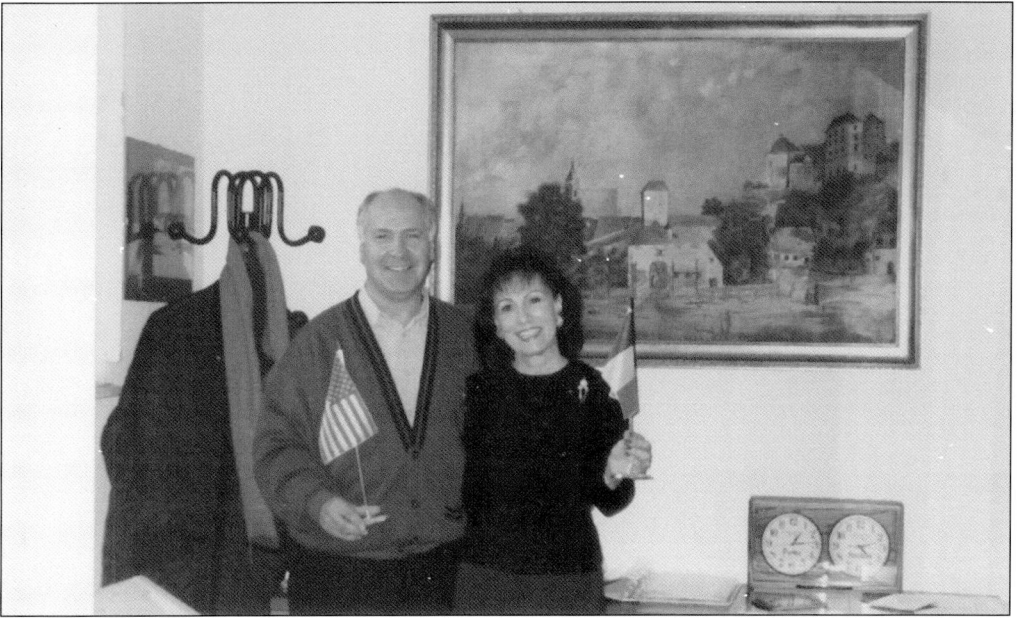

ITALIAN SISTER CITY. Michele Speroni (left), an official with the Province of Parma, and future Stockton city councilwoman Diana Lowery were instrumental in making the city of Parma, Emilia-Romagna, the first European sister city of Stockton in 1998. As longtime family friends and the children of Italian POWs held in the county, they represent the deep connection between both nations. (Courtesy of Diana M. Lowery.)

ITALY'S SONS, 1962. The Order of the Sons of Italy in America, founded in 1905, was the largest Italian American fraternal organization in the country. The local Meucci lodge formed in 1924 and went inactive when the Stockton lodge took its place in 1947. Delegates hosting a convention are, from left to right, Larry Weaver, Al DeNevi, Dan D'Amico, Anthony Indelicato, and unidentified. (Courtesy of the Bank of Stockton Historical Photograph Collection.)

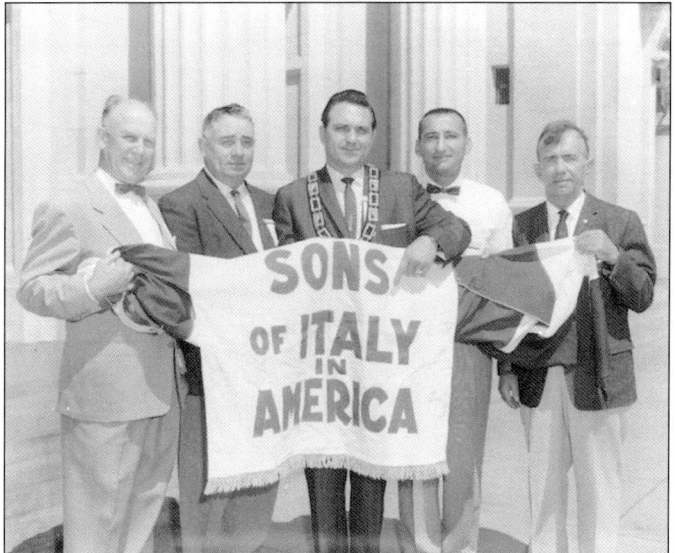

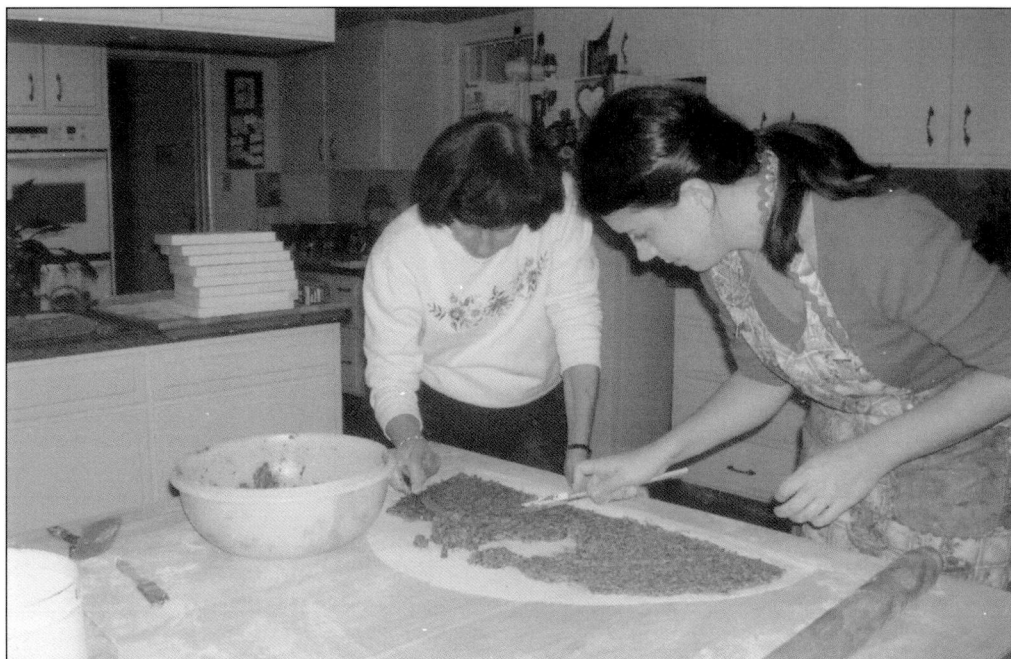

HOMEMADE RAVIOLI. Josephine Gerlomes (left) and her granddaughter Nicolle Harrity carry on the tradition of making ravioli together the old-fashioned way. Ravioli dough is rolled out in a circle and folded back halfway. The filling is spread on the lower half of the dough, and then the top half is rolled to cover the filling, as seen above. Below, Nicolle then firmly presses a ravioli rolling pin across the dough to seal in the filling at her grandmother's home. A crimped-edge ravioli cutter is then used to cut the individual ravioli. Making homemade raviolis for special occasions and holidays is an important tradition for Italian American families. (Both, courtesy of Tim and Lynnette Gerlomes Harrity.)

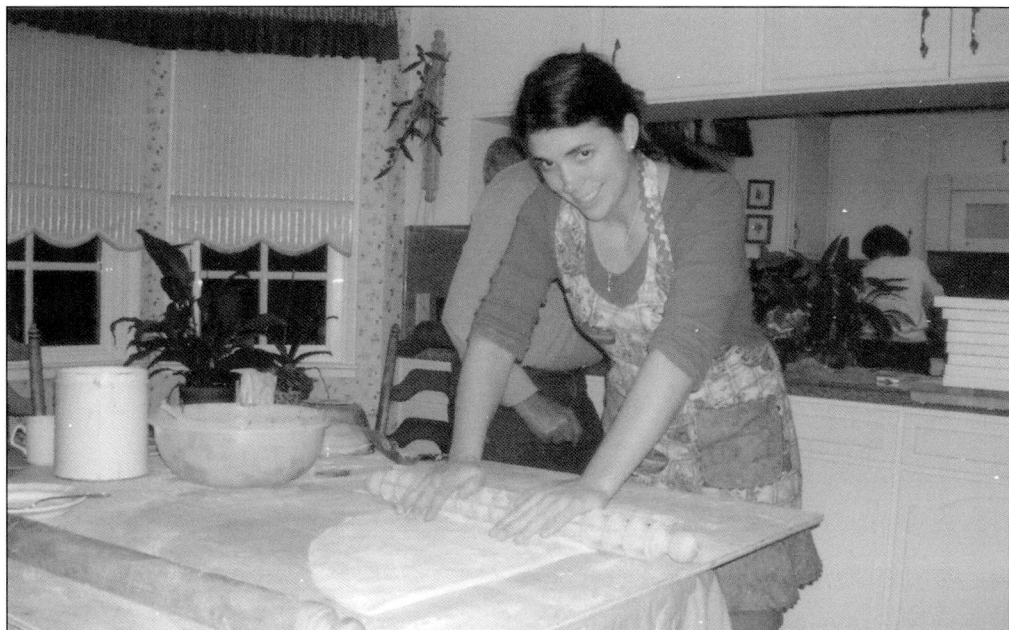

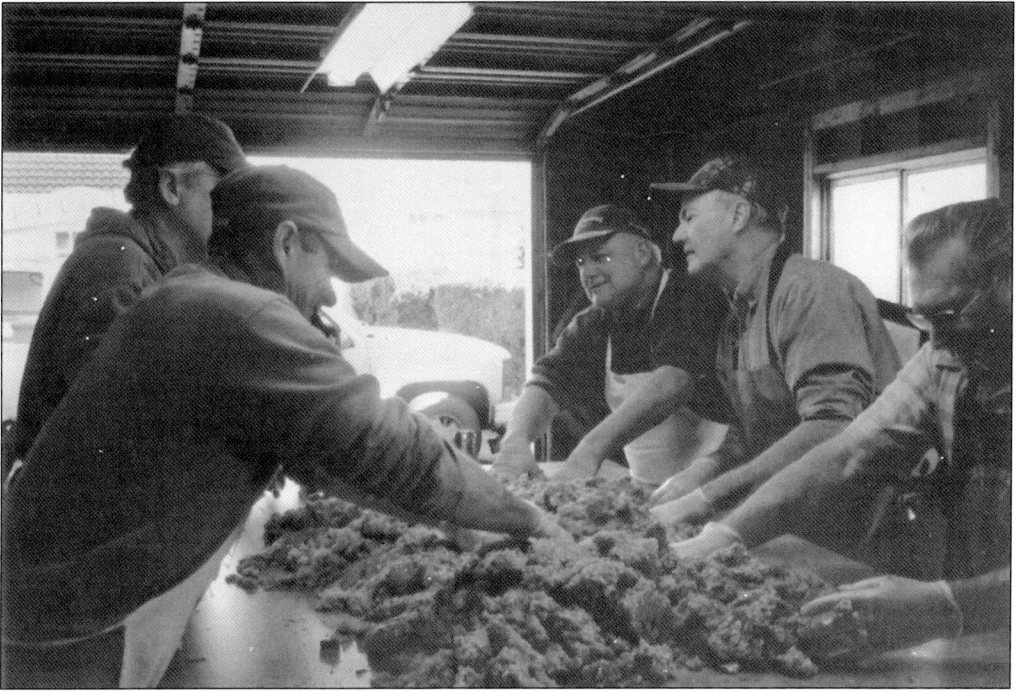

MAKING HOMEMADE SALAMI. Every January, the Gerlomes family and friends gather to make homemade salami, as seen above in 2012 at the home of Greg and Jeanette Gerlomes. The men hand mix ground pork and spices, which are then packed in casings and cured. The salami makers are, from left to right, Greg Gerlomes (front), Kevin Schneider, Tim Harrity, Phil Lawson, and George Gerlomes. After packing the casings, they tie twine around the stick of salami to prepare it to hang and cure, as demonstrated at right by George Gerlomes. Traditions such as these help to pass knowledge on to future generations and maintain cultural identity. (Both, courtesy of George and Josephine Gerlomes and family.)

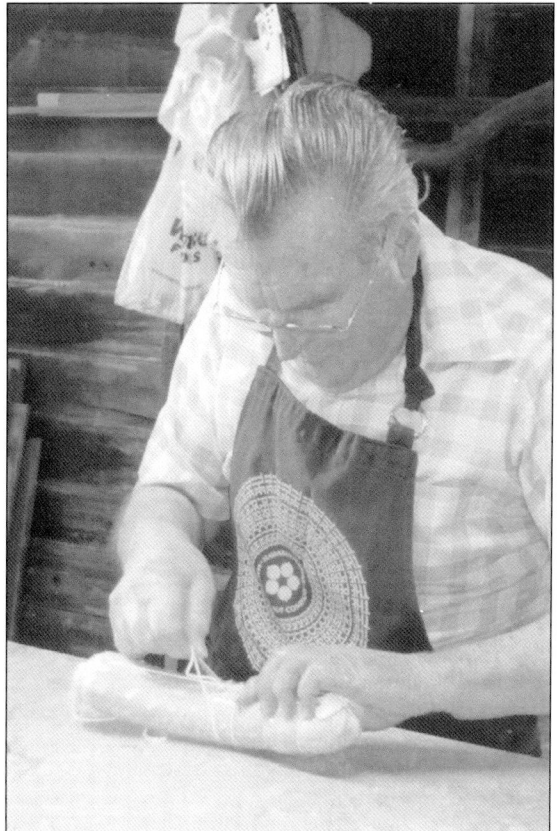

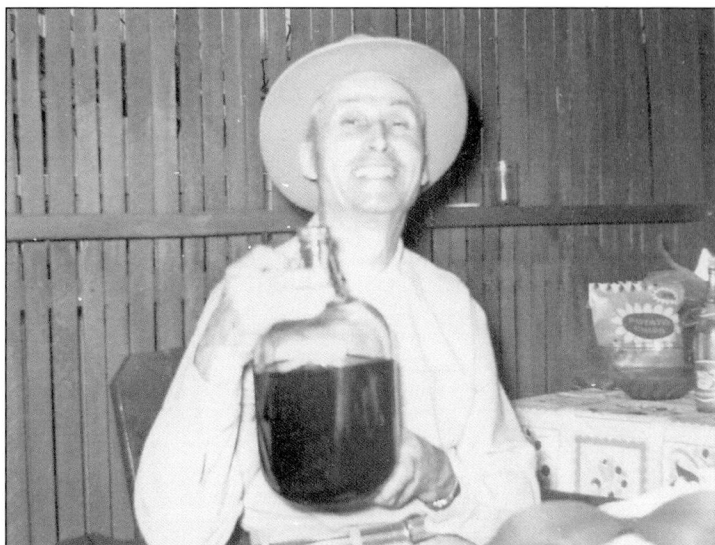

HOMEMADE VINO, 1956.
A beaming Tony Basalto
raises a jug of homemade
wine in a toast at his
son John's engagement
party in May 1956.
Following a strong
tradition in many Italian
families, Tony made his
own wine every year,
and his wife, Giulia,
made wine vinegar.
Amazingly, when it
was time to make more
wine, the previous year's
supply was all used
up. (Courtesy of the
Basalto family.)

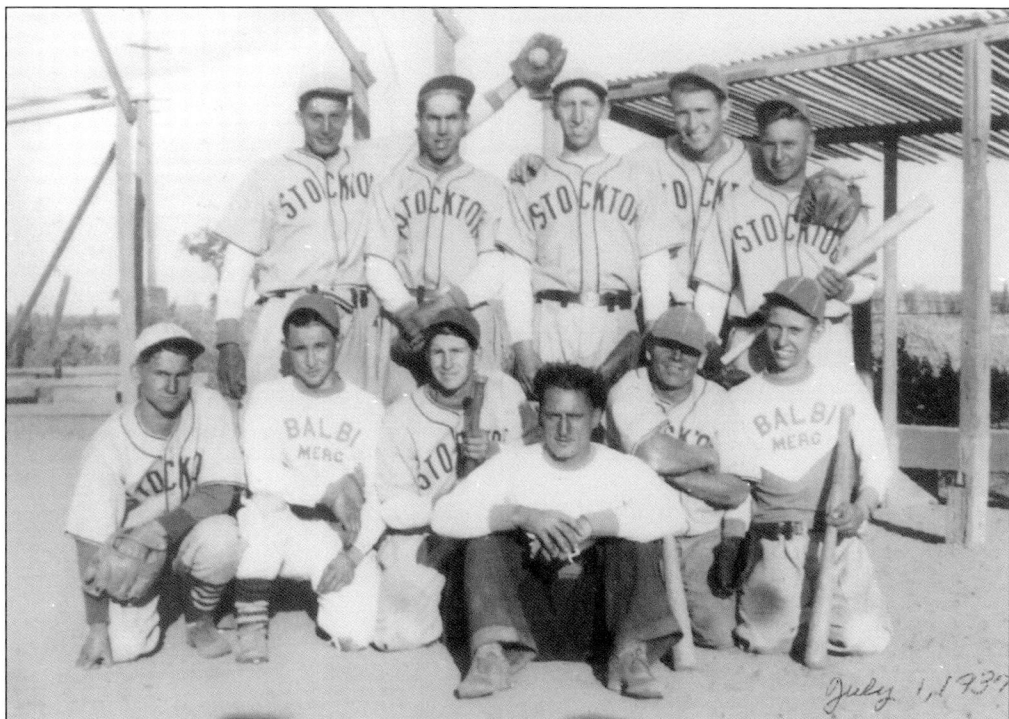

BALBI'S SANDLOT BASEBALL. The team played in a dirt field behind the store on the corner of
Linden and Alpine Roads (called Balbi's Corner). The team members seen here on July 1, 1937,
are, from left to right, (first row) Leroy Bava, Jack Solegue, John Armanino, Andrew Boggiano
(manager), unidentified, and George Rugani; (second row) Joe Mangili, Dante Canepa, Louis
Tassano, Ray Rugani, and Ray Luchetti. (Courtesy of the Macfarlane/Boggiano family.)

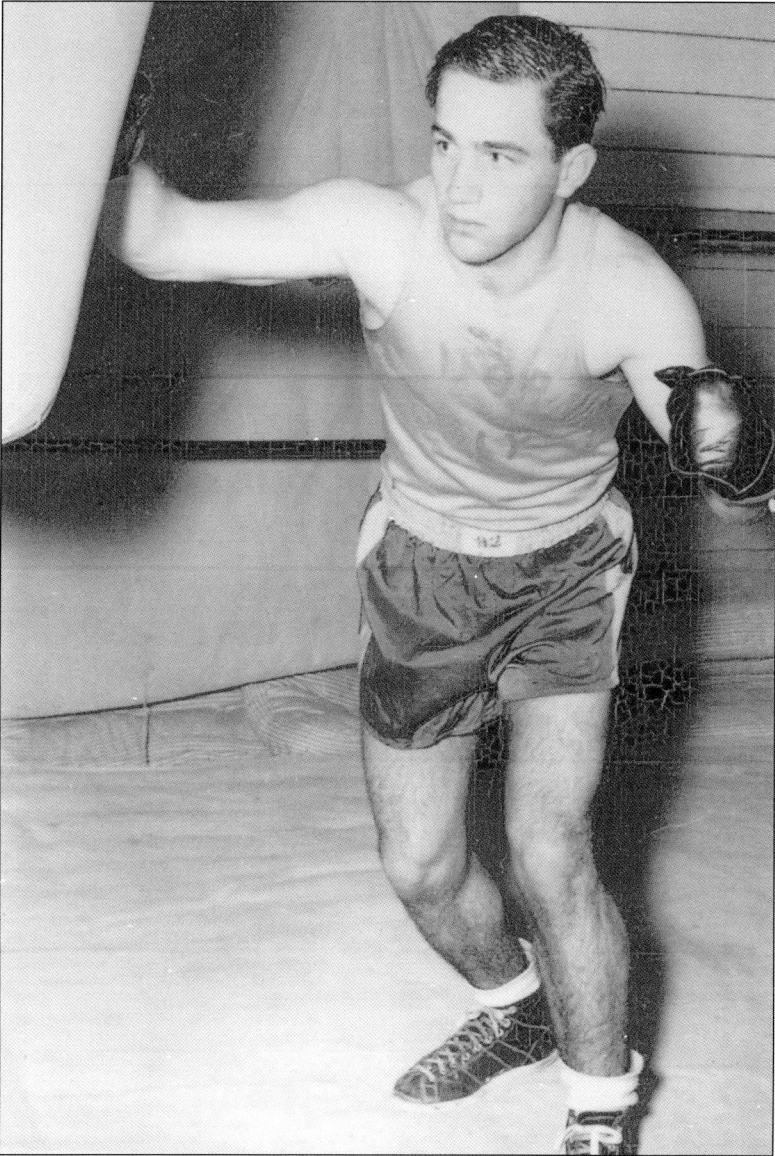

BOXING CHAMPION. A National Intercollegiate Boxing Coaches All-American boxer, Francesco "Frank" Paolo Loduca Jr. grew up in San Joaquin County, the son of Sicilian immigrants who came to America for new opportunities. Frank attended California Polytechnic University in San Luis Obispo to study agriculture and is considered one of the all-time greatest boxers in the school's history. He was a two-time NCAA finalist and a Pacific Coast Intercollegiate Conference Champion (welterweight, 1956), one of only two boxers from California to achieve this honor. He also achieved the Outstanding Boxer of the Year Award in 1956. He was inducted into the university's hall of fame in 1997. After graduating in 1957, he worked in the agriculture and food-processing industry. In 1982, he and his wife Maria established the LnL Transplant Company, which specializes in vegetable transplants. They have three children—Frank III, Gina, and James—and 5 grandchildren. Maria continued her career in education as the business became established. Frank III continues the agricultural legacy as the grower manager for the family company. (Courtesy of the Loduca family album.)

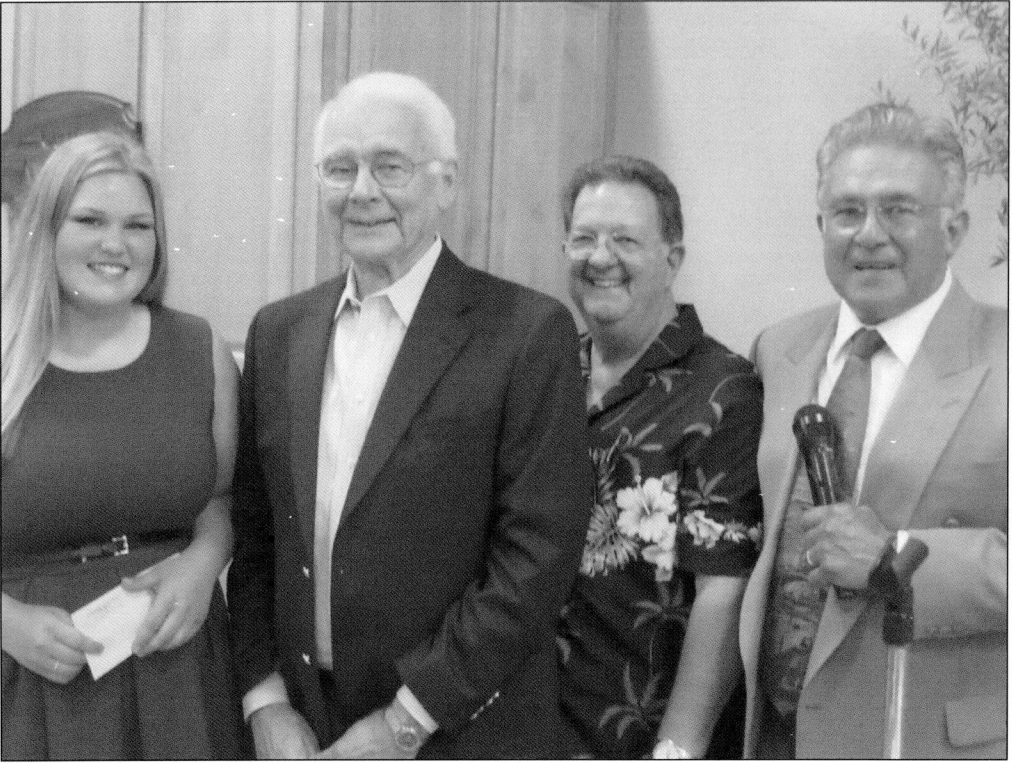

LIGURI NEL MONDO SCHOLARSHIP. This scholarship program, established in 1992, has awarded almost $100,000 to college students who are related to members. Funding for the scholarships comes from the annual Reverse Raffle Dinner and generous donations from the public. Pictured here, from left to right, are the 2014 Daniel J. Caminata Pacific Italian Alliance Scholarship recipient, Reanna Peters, and members Daniel J. Caminata, Gary S. Giovanetti, and George Piccardo Jr. (Courtesy of Liguri Nel Mondo.)

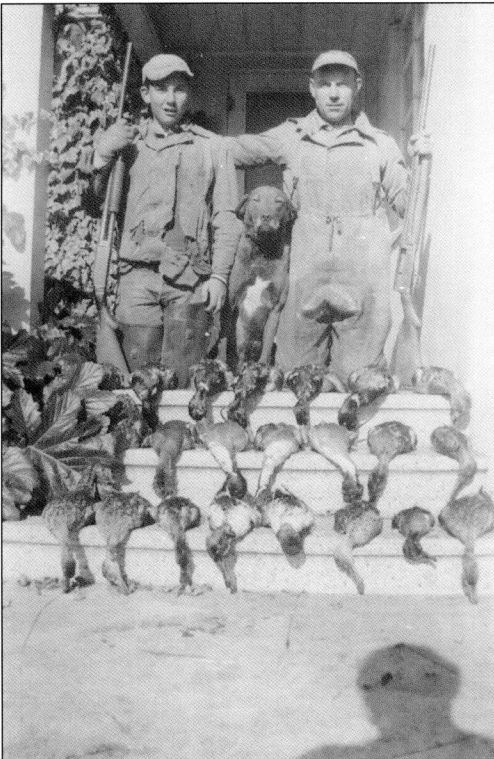

FAMILY HUNT, C. 1952. Dave Canclini (right) and his son David pose with their Chesapeake Bay retriever Skeet after a successful duck hunt in front of their home on the Weber Ranch on McAllen Road. Also on the hunt but not pictured was Dave Pizzorno (David's uncle) from San Francisco. (Courtesy of the Canclini family.)

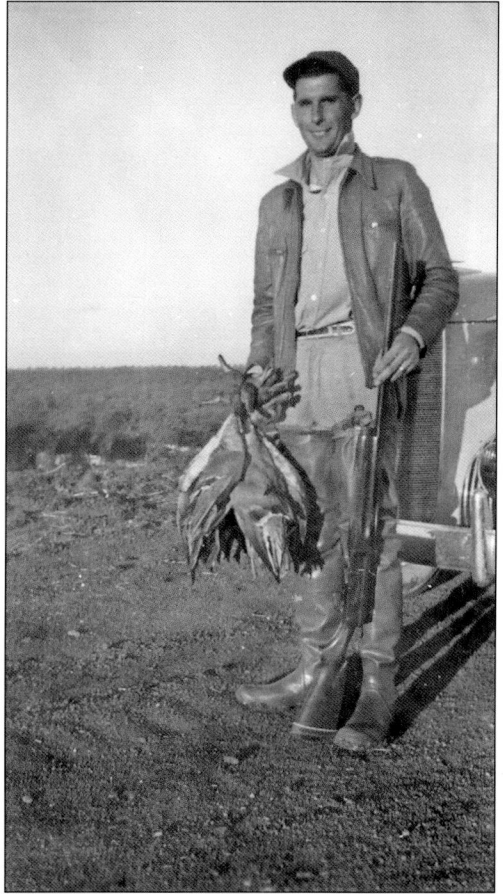

BALDOCCHI BROTHERS. These pictures show Baldocchi brothers Armando (right) and Guido (below) with the ducks they shot during a day of hunting. The photographs were taken sometime in 1939 or 1940. The 1939 Cadillac was owned by Guido. Hunting remains an important part of life in the delta region, and duck and pheasant were plentiful in the 1930s and 1940s as the region is part of the Pacific Flyway. Anything the hunters brought back home was always eaten by their families. Armando's wife, Nancy Marchini Baldocchi, often made spaghetti sauce with pheasant meat, and the family still talks about how great it tasted. (Both, courtesy of the Armando Baldocchi family.)

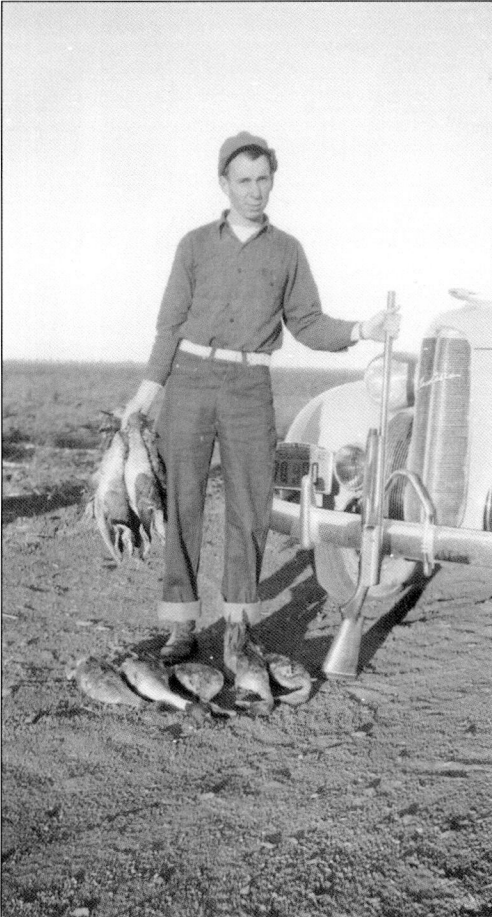

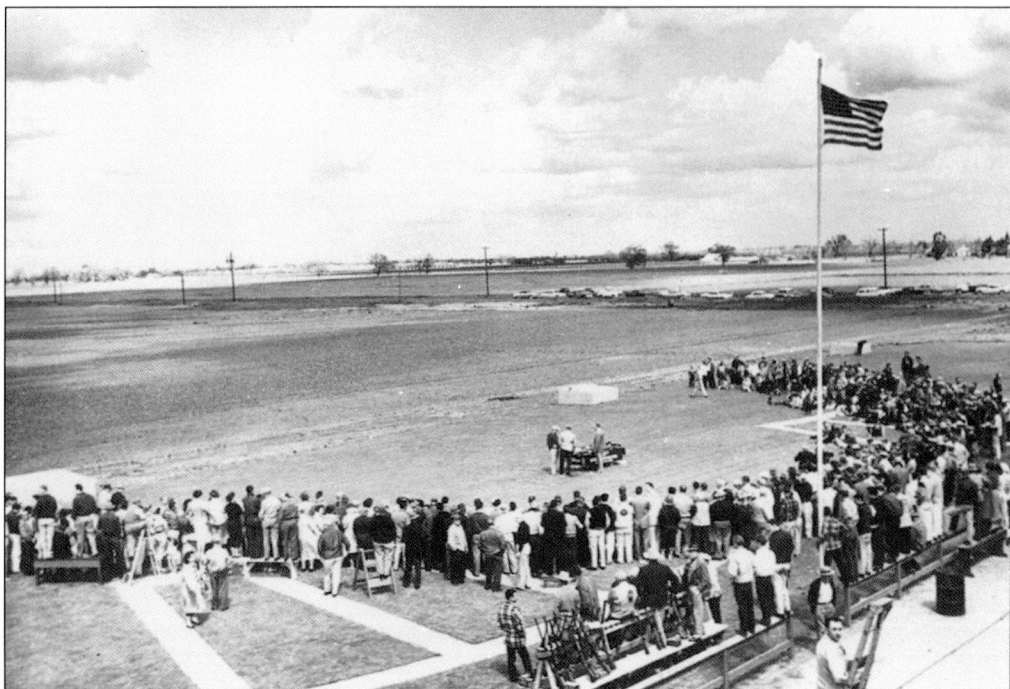

WATERLOO GUN & BOCCE CLUB. The club began with a group of shooters who met to shoot trap on the north end of Lucky Ranch, along Mosher Slough. In 1948, Louis Cadamartori and Roy DeVencenzi led the group to a new location on Jack Tone Road, and it became known as the Calaveras Blue Rock Gun Club. The group eventually relocated to 4343 Ashley Lane, renting two acres with an option to purchase the full 35-acre parcel (seen above in 1960 during a competition) from Fred Tozi and Emil Delucchi. A clubhouse was built and the group became the Waterloo Gun Club. Later, a group of bocce players approached the group, and the Stockton Waterloo Gun & Bocce Club was born and incorporated in 1953. (Above, courtesy of the Bank of Stockton; below, courtesy of the Haggin Museum.)

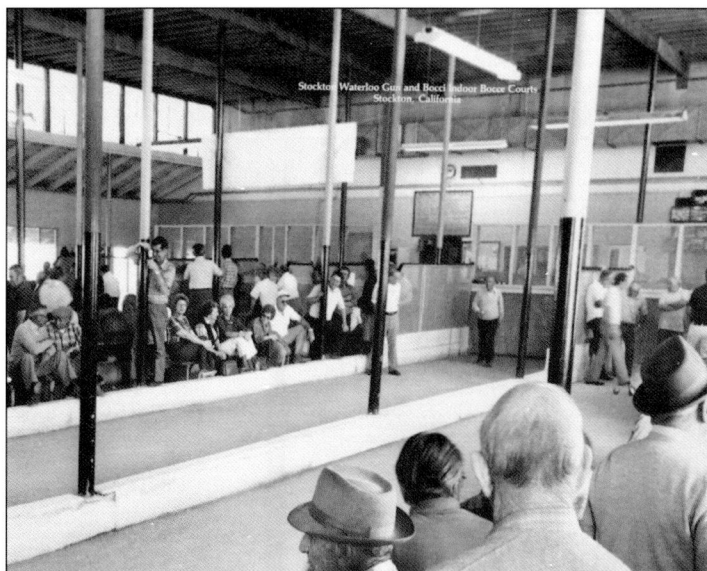

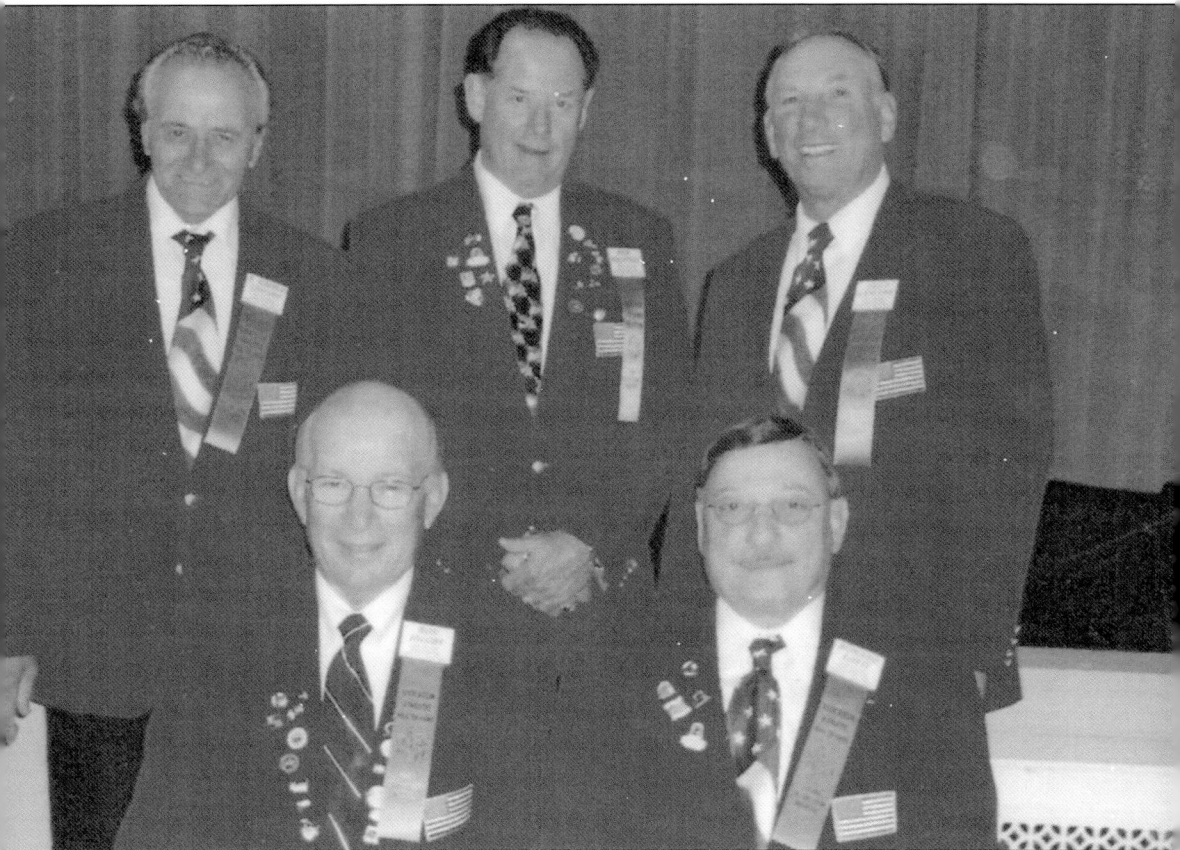

HALL OF FAME BOCCE TEAM. Bocce is an ancient and traditional Italian game in which players on two teams score points by rolling a bocce ball closer to a target ball than their opponents. Stockton hosted the United States National Bocce Tournament for the first time in 1985 at the Waterloo Gun & Bocce Club. In 2002, the Italian Athletic Club Bocce Team won all the team events at the national championships, which had never been done before. The successful team would go on to represent the United States at the World Bocce Championships in Passo Fundo, Brazil, and ultimately place ninth in the world. The team members are, from left to right, (first row) Ron Jacobs and Romano Lotti; (second row) Alberico Leonardi, Rick Wagstaff, and David Canclini. They were inducted into the Stockton Athletic Hall of Fame in November 2007. (Courtesy of the Canclini family.)

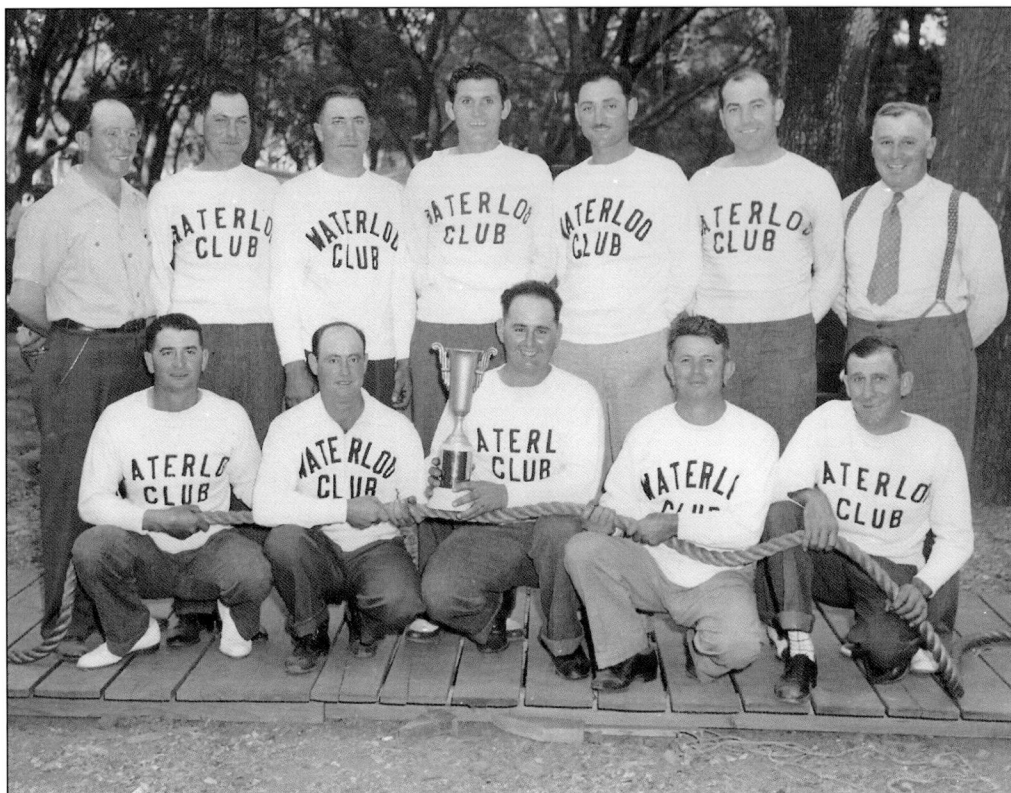

TUG-OF-WAR CHAMPIONS. This team took top honors from the Waterloo Gun & Bocce Club sometime in 1940. The team members are, from left to right, (first row) Amerigo Cortopassi, Ning Pezzi, John Avansino, John Garibaldi, and Dave Sanguinetti; (second row) Steve Sanguinetti, Louis Barosso, Marione Gogna, Joe Zolezzi, Fred Tozi, Louis Conti, and coach Lloyd Rizzi. (Courtesy of Joe Avansino.)

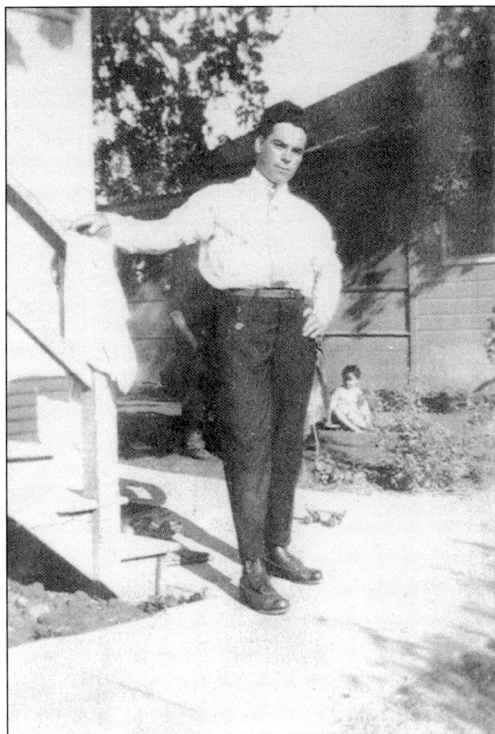

HORSESHOE CHAMPION. John Galli garnered front-page attention in the *Stockton Record* when he became horseshoe champion of Central California at Oak Park in 1929. An employee of Geiger Iron Works, he won 18 straight matches and was undefeated in the tournament. The *Record* states that Galli started out behind, but steady and consistent pitching put him over the top. (Courtesy of the DalPorto/Galli family.)

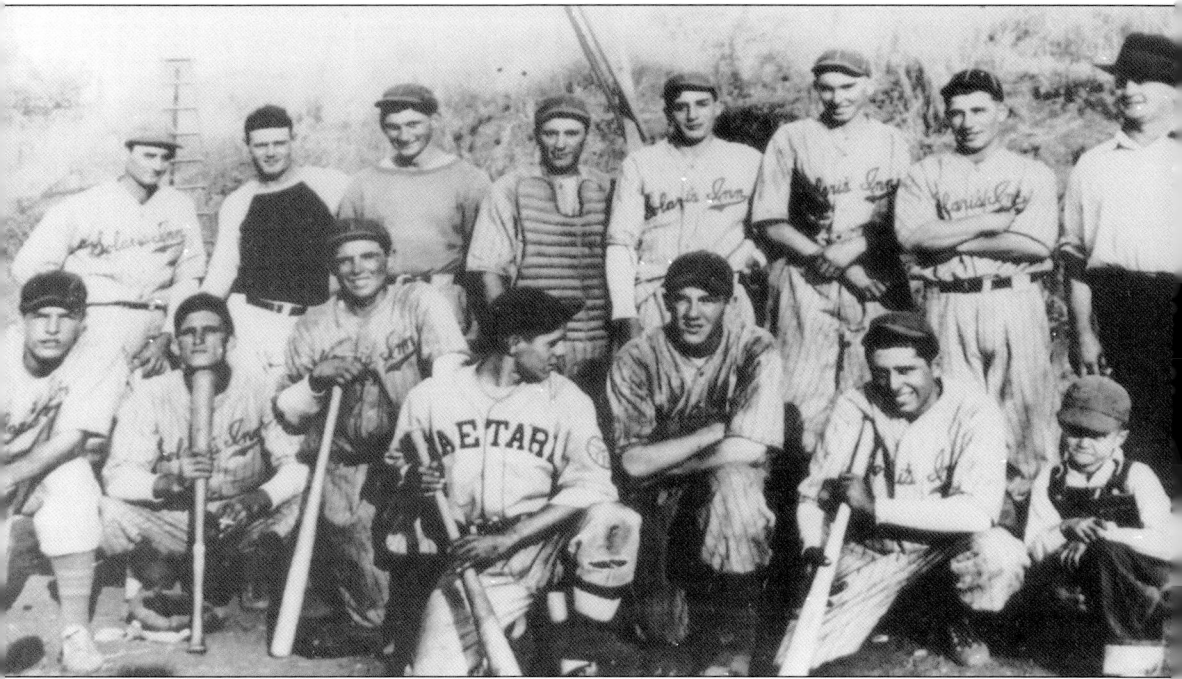

SOLARI'S INN BASEBALL TEAM, 1934. Baseball has always been an important part of life for Italian men in San Joaquin County. Every Sunday after church, games would be held between local and visiting teams. This team played on a field built by Vic Solari across the street from the family home in Linden. Teams would come from as far away as the Bay Area to play and then happily cross the street to feast on the renowned homemade raviolis, pasta, and bread prepared by Mary Solari, Vic's wife. Vic would also bring out his legendary homemade wine to soothe any hurt feelings or lopsided final scores. Pictured, from left to right, are players (first row) Frank Budiselich, Tillio Boggiano, Tommy Prato, two unidentified, Emil Sciuti, and Vic Solari Jr.; (second row) Henry Boggiano, Blain Simonich, Dick Mangili, Frank Boggiano, Enrico Mangili, Larry Sciuti, John Dondero, and team owner Vic Solari Sr. (Courtesy of the Macfarlane/Boggiano family.)

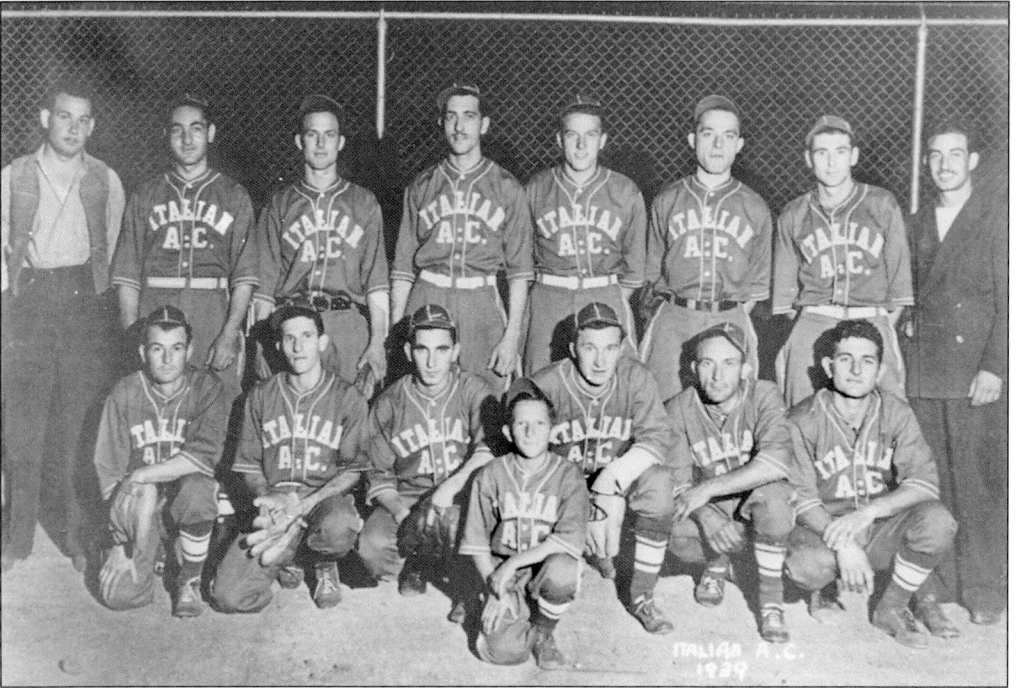

ITALIAN ATHLETIC CLUB. The club was founded in 1936 to help Italian Americans participate in sports. Over the years, it has raised money for equipment and uniforms and has sponsored numerous local teams, including this 1939 baseball team. The current office is located at 3451 Cherryland Avenue in Stockton. (Courtesy of historian Bennie Filippini, Italian Gardeners Society.)

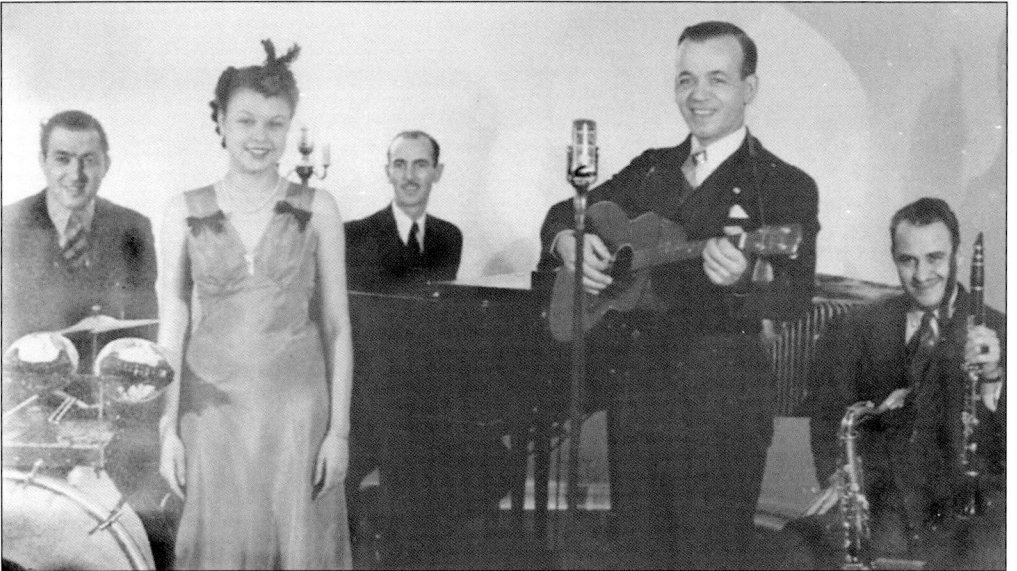

COVELLO BAND. Leonard Covello played many venues with his band pictured here. This photograph was taken at a performance at the El Capitan Club in Redding in 1939. Pictured, from left to right, are Covello (drums), Dorothy "Dot" Eulie (vocalist), Claude Gribble (piano), an unidentified guitar player, and Duke Chappell (saxophone). (Courtesy of the Bank of Stockton Historical Photograph Collection.)

Five

AGRICULTURE

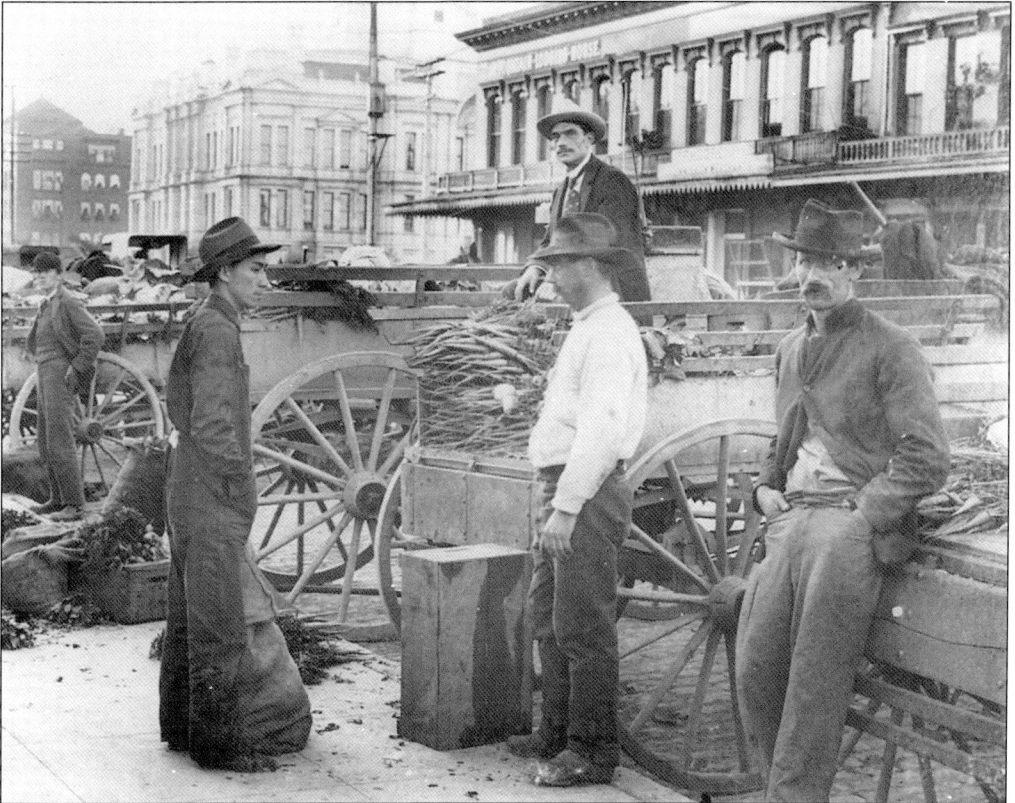

TRUCK GARDENERS. Italian farmers would bring produce from their gardens in wagons and, later, in trucks, to sell along Stockton's city streets, as seen in this 1905 image of Weber Avenue. In 1922, the city outlawed the truck gardening, which prompted the construction of the Growers Hall in 1923 by members of the Italian Gardeners Society. (Courtesy of the Bank of Stockton Historical Photograph Collection.)

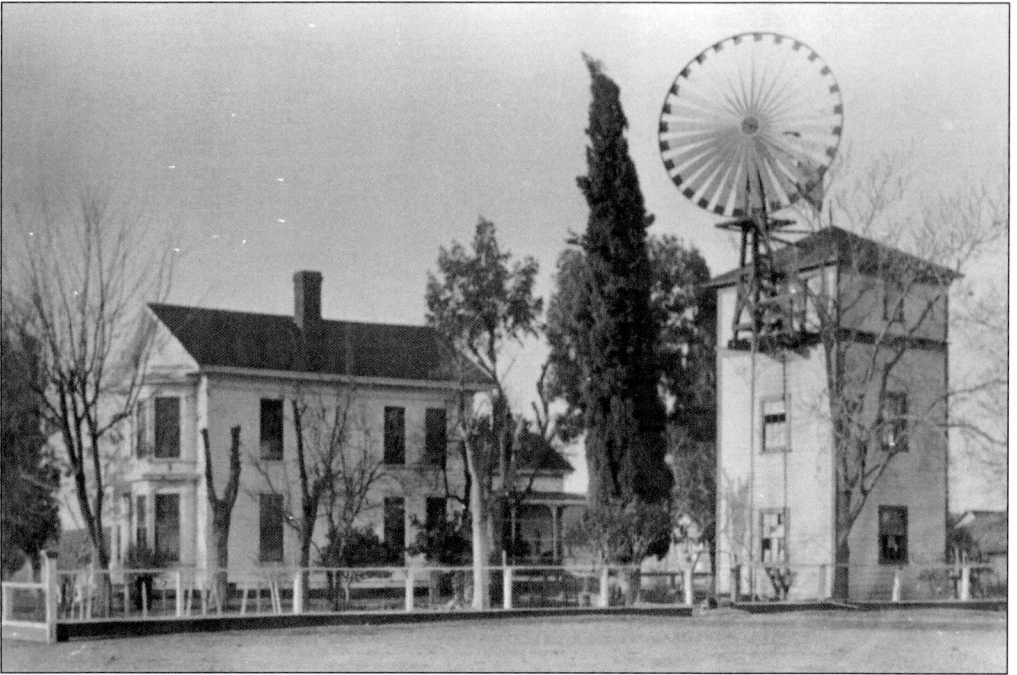

ITALIAN WINDMILLS. This windmill was originally built by the Davis Regulating Windmill Company of Stockton and officially called the Improved Davis Windmill. Large structures like this one quickly became known locally as Italian windmills because so many Italian truck farmers purchased and used them to irrigate the variety of crops grown in their gardens. (Courtesy of the San Joaquin County Historical Society.)

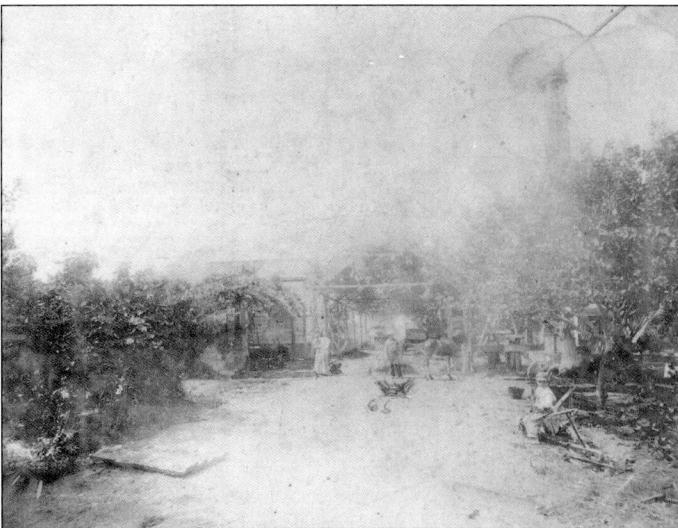

SCHENONE FARM. This faded and extremely old photograph (taken around 1897) shows the Italian garden of Giovanni Schenone on Beyer Lane. Schenone (standing center, near horse) was the first president of the Italian Gardeners Society and had six children. Note the different variety of trees, the large grape arbor, and the Italian windmill, all typical of early Italian homesteads. (Courtesy of historian Bennie Filippini, Italian Gardeners Society.)

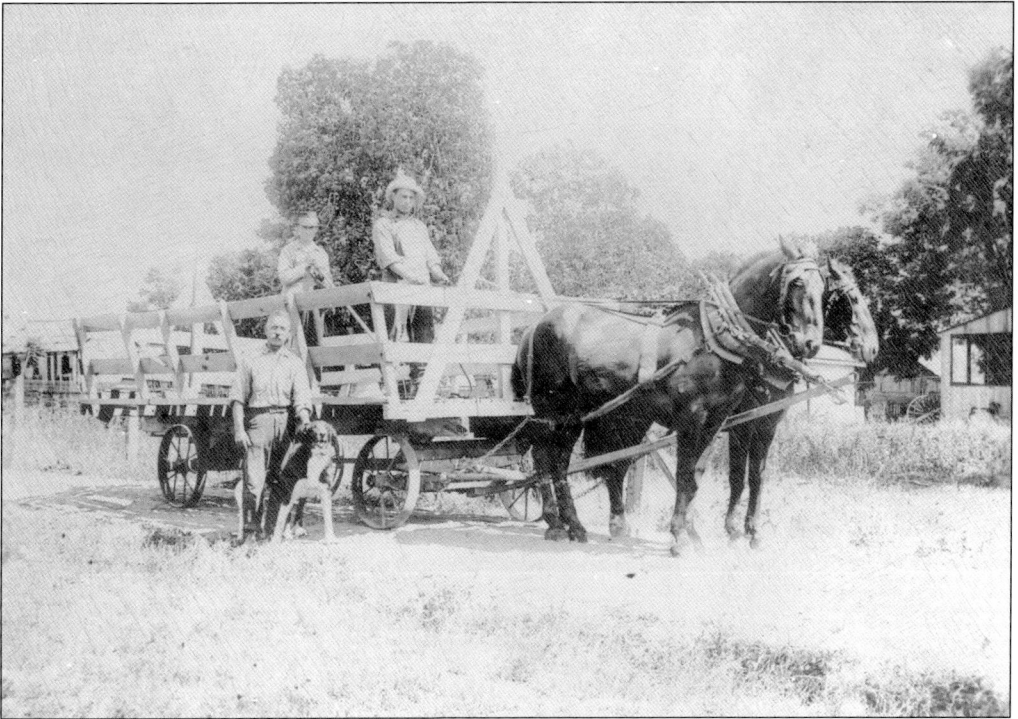

DALPORTO FARM. Nicodemo DalPorto (standing with dog) and his sons Emil (left) and Virgil work on their farm on Sharps Lane (later Airport Way) near Stockton. In this image, they have either just finished unloading hay or are preparing to load the wagon. In addition to farming, Virgil worked at Holt Brothers as a machinist; Emil had the same job at an unknown company. (Courtesy of the DalPorto/Galli family.)

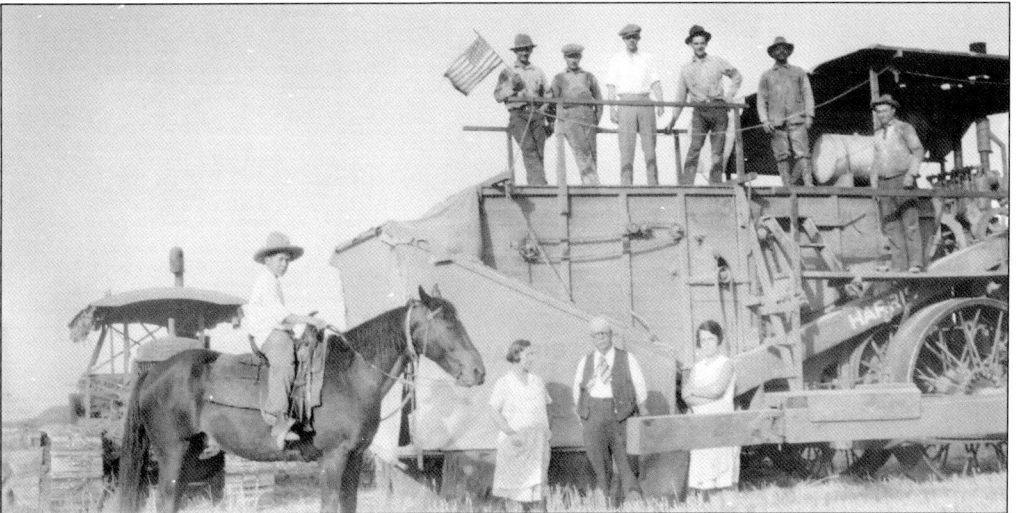

GRAIN HARVEST, LATE 1920S. Paul S. Sanguinetti rides his horse as the Harris combine works the Minahen Ranch harvesting grain, the staple crop of the county at that time. On the ground are Paul's mother, Aurelia Sanguinetti (left); Albert T. Minahen; and an unidentified woman. Those identified on top of the combine are Aurelia's brother John Cavagnaro (holding flag) and Amelio Barrera (far right). (Courtesy of the Sanguinetti/Prato family.)

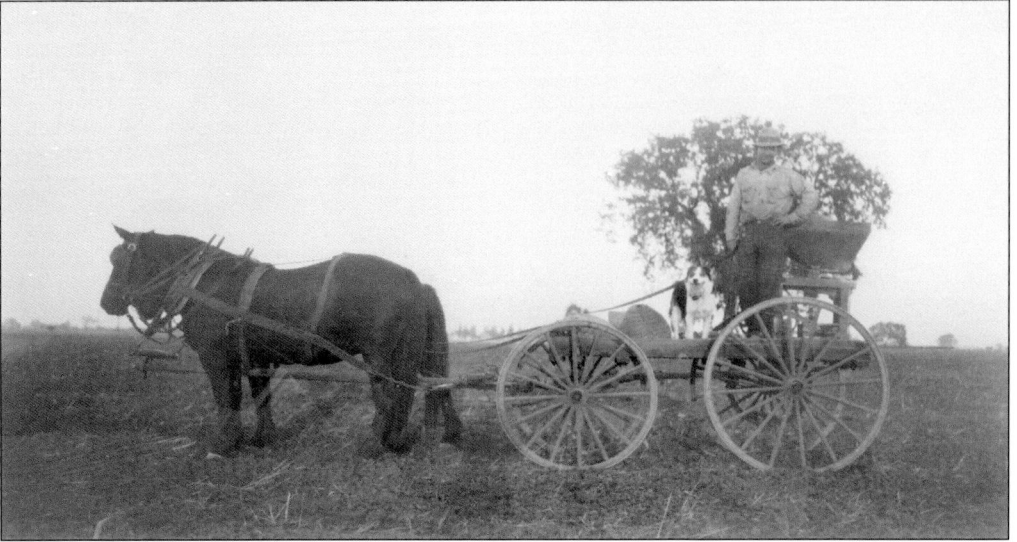

SOWING SEED. Francis John Sanguinetti rides with his dog and trusts his reliable horses to help him sow either grain or hay on his area ranch in the 1930s. In the days before mechanization, once the horses got the routine down, all the operator had to do was keep the seed hopper full. (Courtesy of the Sanguinetti/Prato family.)

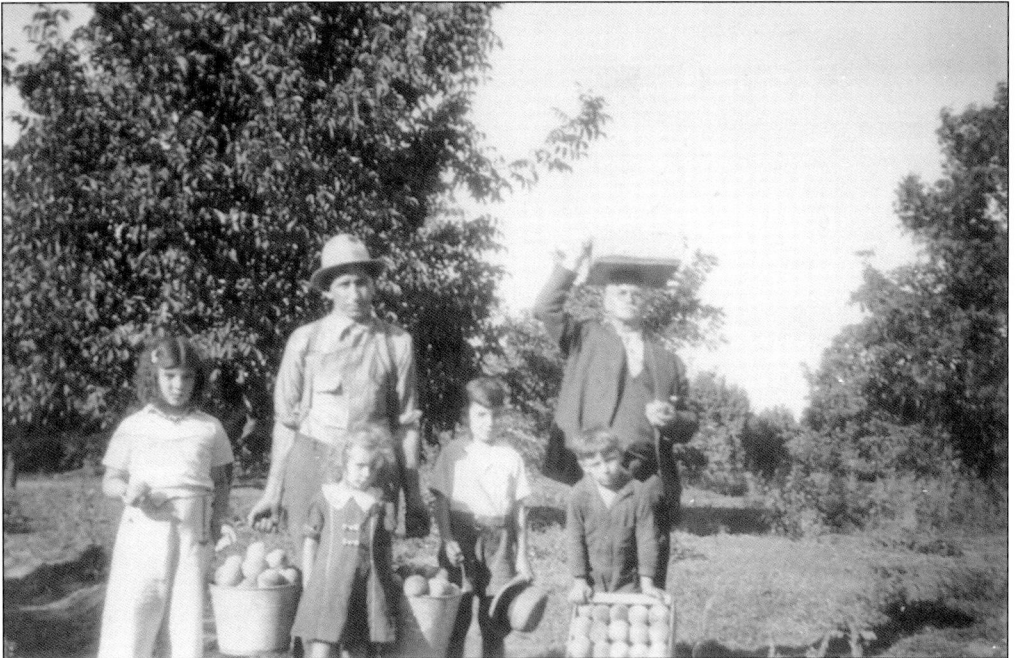

DEMARTINI FAMILY FARM. Cesare Demartini came from Lorsica, Italy, to America in 1910 and worked in Chicago and San Francisco before purchasing a farm in Linden in 1922. Here, cousins from San Francisco gather peaches around August 1936 or 1937. They are, from left to right, Flora Demartini, Cesare Demartini, Josephine Demartini Gerlomes, Walter Demartini, John Demartini (front), and Giuseppe Demartini. (Courtesy of the late Cesare & Maria [Masilia] Demartini.)

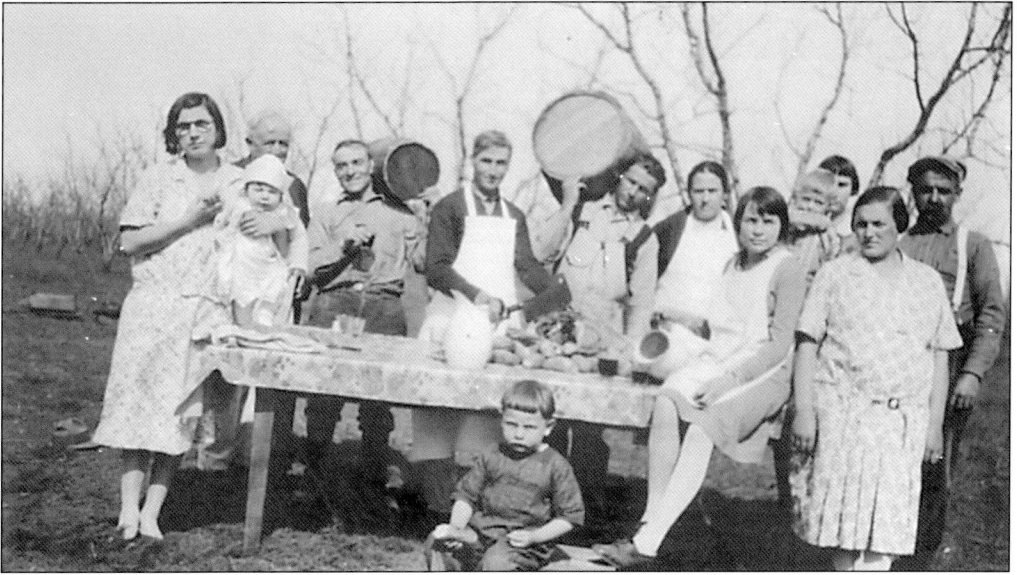

BASALTO RANCH CELEBRATION. Friends and family celebrate on the Basaltos ranch around late 1929 or 1930. Tony Basalto, wearing the apron in the center of the picture, owned one of the first gasoline-powered trucks in Linden. His wife, Giulia, stands on the far right. On the far left is Tony's sister Louisa Podesta, holding an unidentified child; her youngest son, Mario, sits on the crate. The two young women pictured are Louisa's daughters Eda and Alice. The man hoisting the large barrel is Davide Descalzo, and holding the smaller barrel is his brother Giovanni Battista Descalzo. Below, John rests in front of the windmill water tank on Duncan Road in 1948. Many times, their mother made the nightly minestrone with *vino di tavola* (table wine) when water was not available. (Both, courtesy of the Basalto family.)

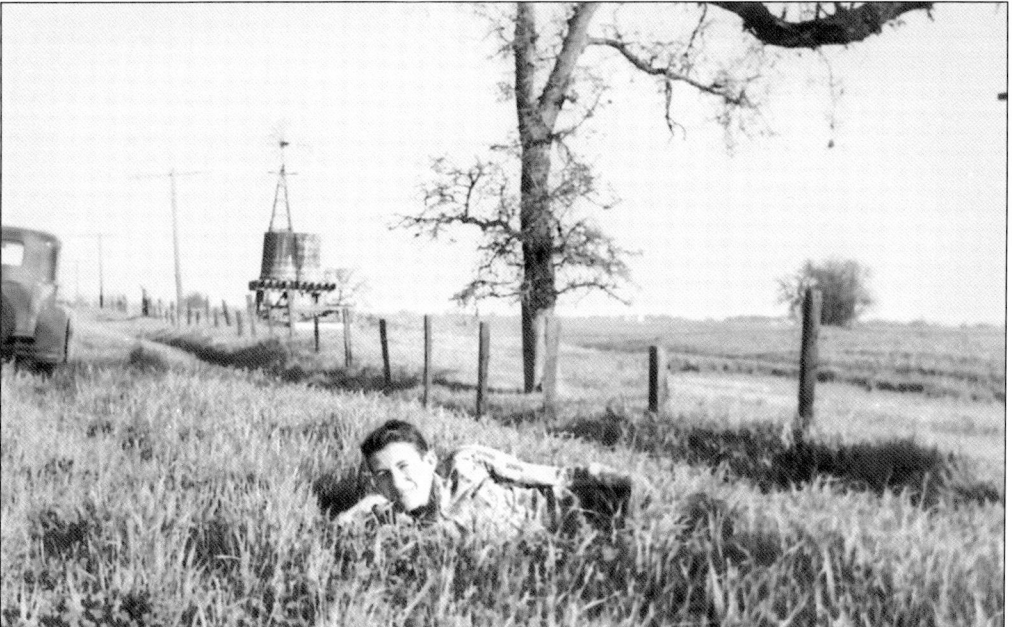

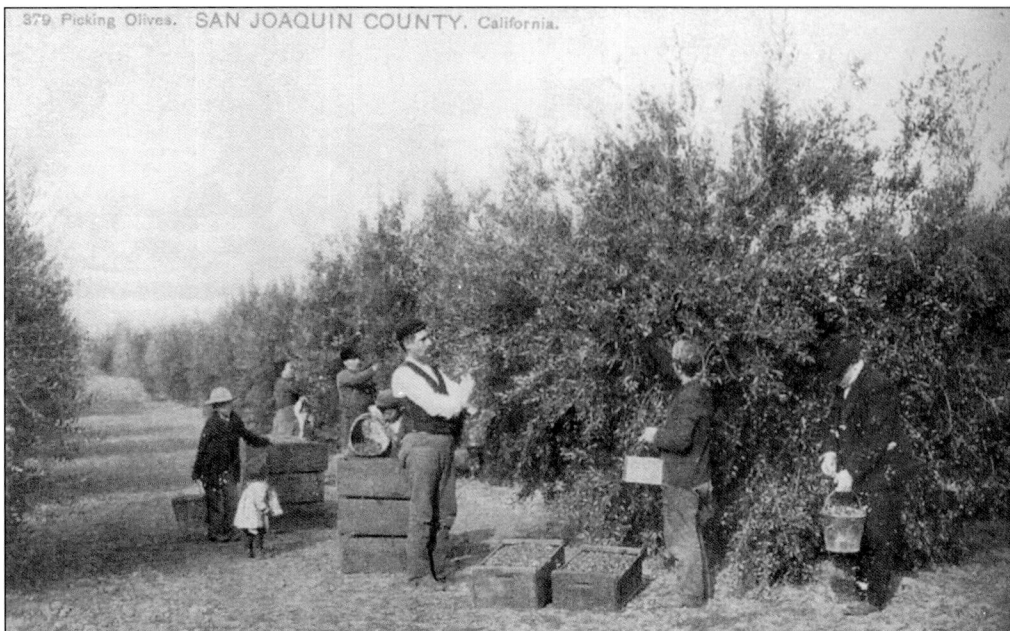

379 Picking Olives. SAN JOAQUIN COUNTY. California.

OLIVE HARVEST. An unidentified Italian family harvests olives in this postcard from the early 1900s. Olive oil has always been important to Italian cooking, and immigrants led the way in the cultivation of olives in San Joaquin County. It is estimated that in 1905, around the time of this photograph, 1,700 acres were planted to olives. (Author's collection.)

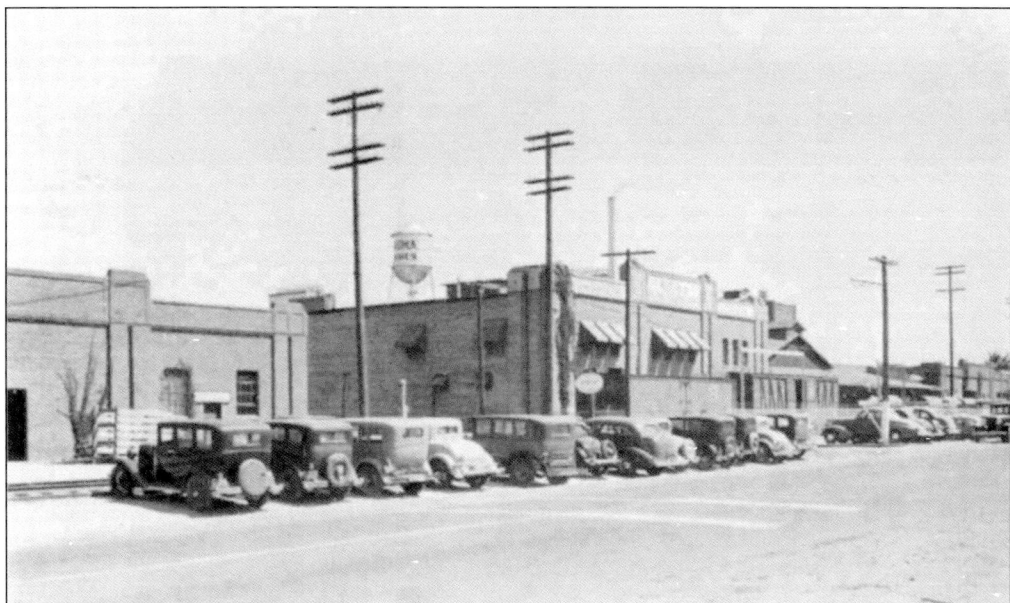

ROMA WINERY, LODI. This historic winery was constructed around 1915 on 320 acres along Victor Road in Lodi. The Cella brothers, Battista and Lorenzo (children of immigrants from the village of Bardi, near Parma), brought the Italian-style wines to prominence and sold the successful brand to Schenley Industries in 1942. (Courtesy of the Bank of Stockton Historical Photograph Collection.)

CANCLINI ORCHARD. After he had finally brought his family over from Piatta, Italy, Giacomo Canclini and his wife, Anna (on box), purchased 50 acres on Highway 26 and Archerdale Road in Linden in the late 1920s and became fruit and nut producers. Everyone worked the family farm, including sons Dave (on ladder) and Luca, seen here sometime in the 1930s during the peach harvest. (Courtesy of the Canclini family.)

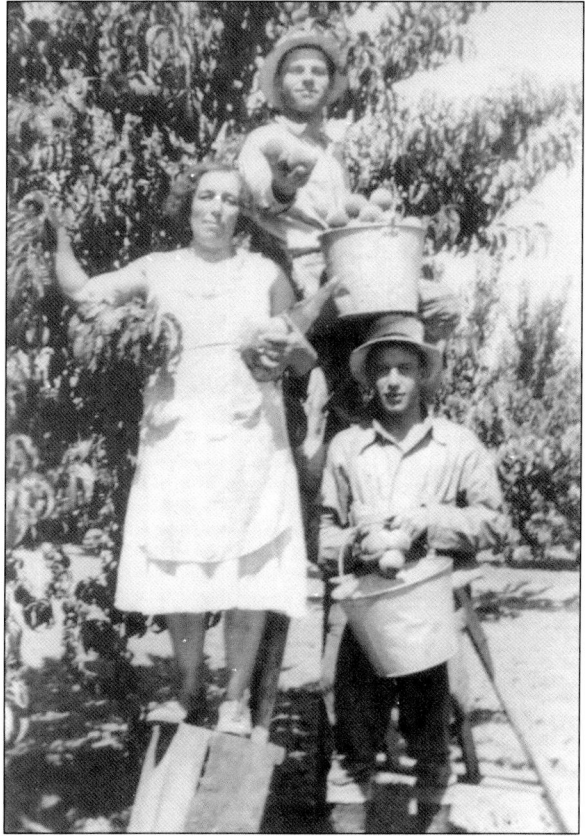

WORKING THE FARM. Taken in the 1930s, this photograph shows Regina Canclini (a daughter of Giacomo and Anna Canclini) working the farm with some heavy machinery. She would later marry Narciso Giovacchini and they would start a dairy in Manteca and raise four children. (Courtesy of the Canclini family.)

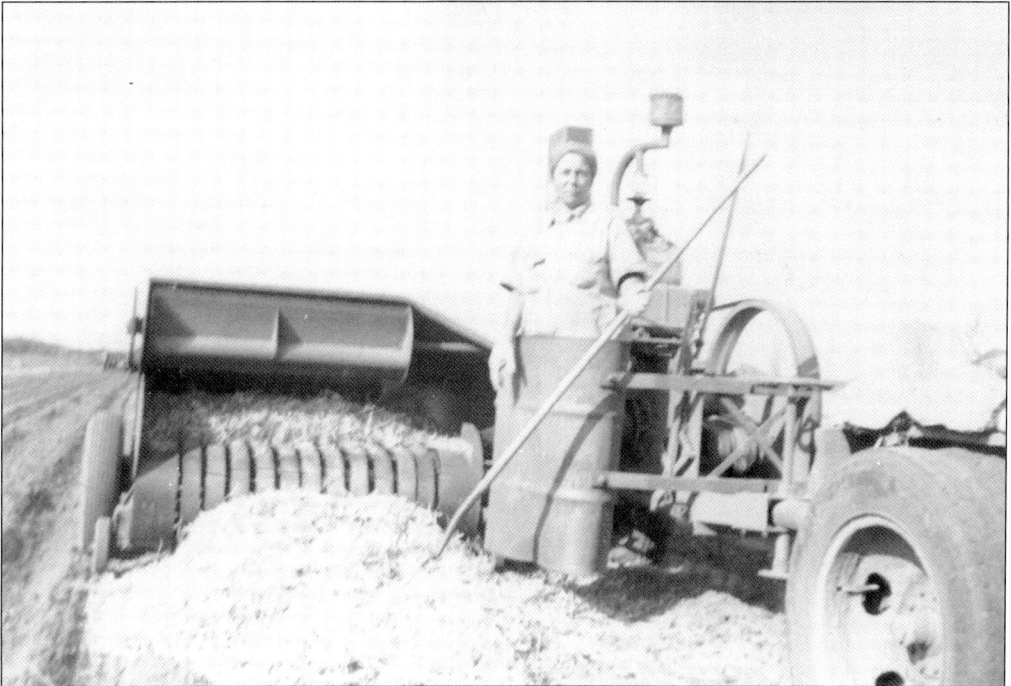

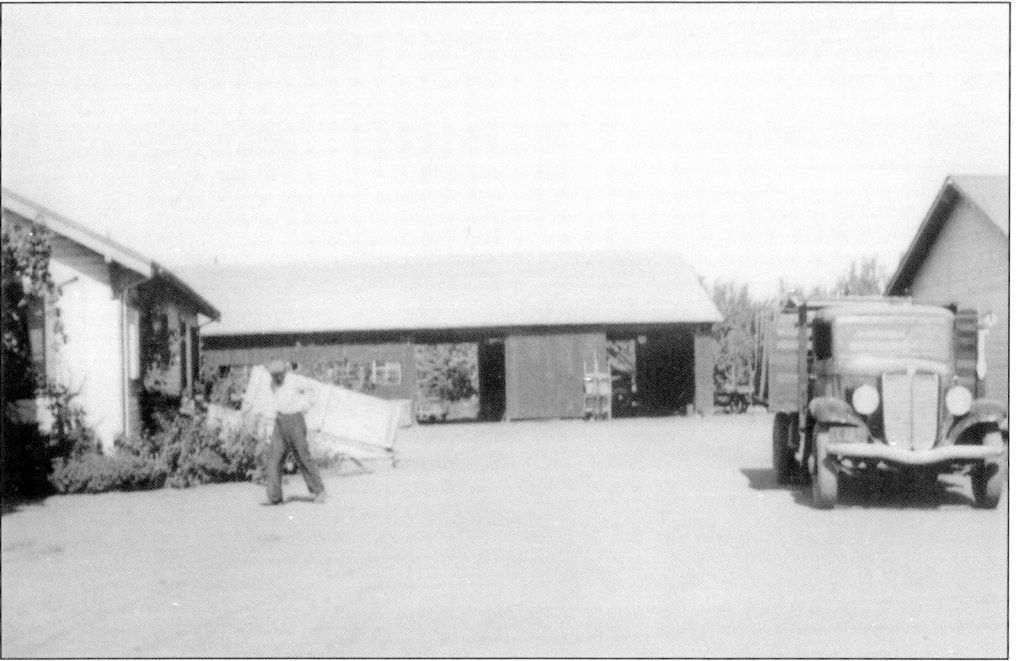

THE LUCKY RANCH. In partnership with financial backers Luigi and Giorgio Rugani, Amerigo and Vittorio Cortopassi and two other Italian partners cleared oaks off of a large tract of agricultural land on Eight Mile Road that became known as Lucky Ranch. After clearing land and planting orchards and vineyards, Lucky Ranch (seen above) had to weather 10 years of the Great Depression. The ranch, complete with a bunkhouse (on the left) and main ranch house (on the right), was well known in the local immigrant community. In 1937, Amerigo and Teresa Cortopassi had their first son while living on the ranch. The venturesome young Dino (below, at about age one and a half) would learn valuable lessons from his immigrant parents about the necessity of working hard to achieve goals. (Both, courtesy of Dino and Joan Cortopassi.)

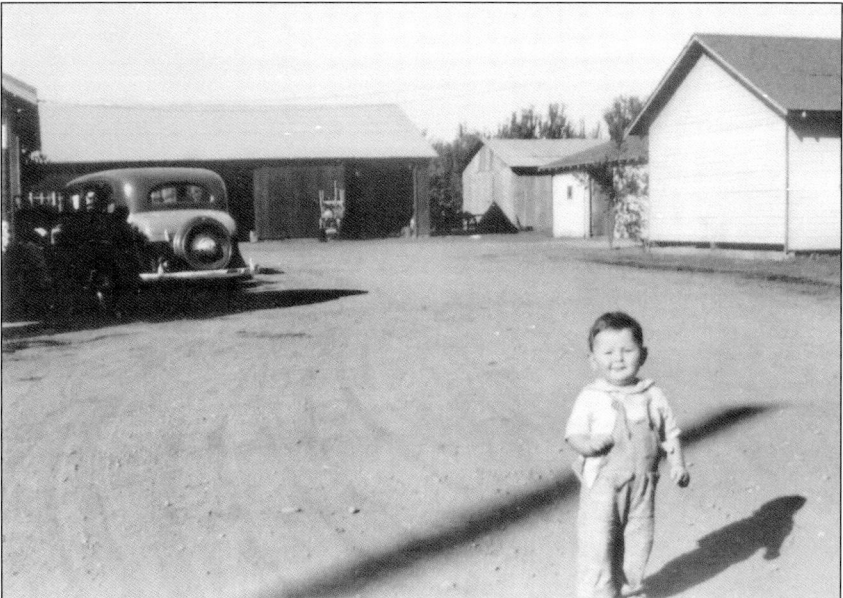

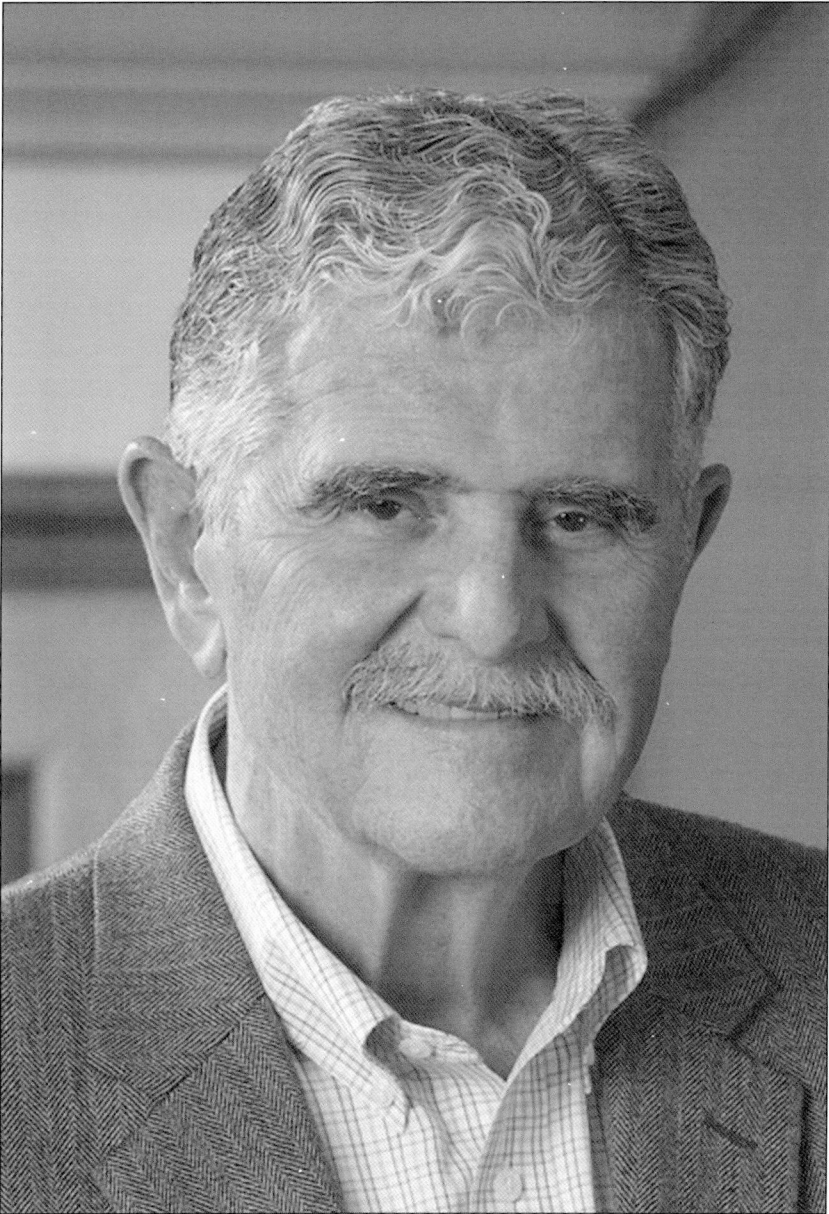

DEAN "DINO" ALBERT CORTOPASSI. Cortopassi grew up the son of an immigrant farming family in the Stockton area, and his father was adamant that Dino not follow his footsteps. He attended the University of California, Davis, graduating in 1958, one year after his father leased the family farm to a neighbor for a 15-year term. Looking for other work, he took a job as a grain buyer/trader with the Pillsbury Company, where he was exposed to the mentoring that would be helpful to an agribusiness career. In 1960, Dino and his brother Alvin started farming part-time on 65 acres of leased land. Over the ensuing 50 years, Cortopassi Farms Incorporated grew to the present 7,000-acre size. In 1978, Cortopassi formed a partnership to purchase Stanislaus Food Products, and in 1986, he bought out the other partners. Dino currently acts as chief executive officer of San Tomo Group, Cortopassi Partners, and the Cortopassi Family Foundation. (Courtesy of Dino and Joan Cortopassi.)

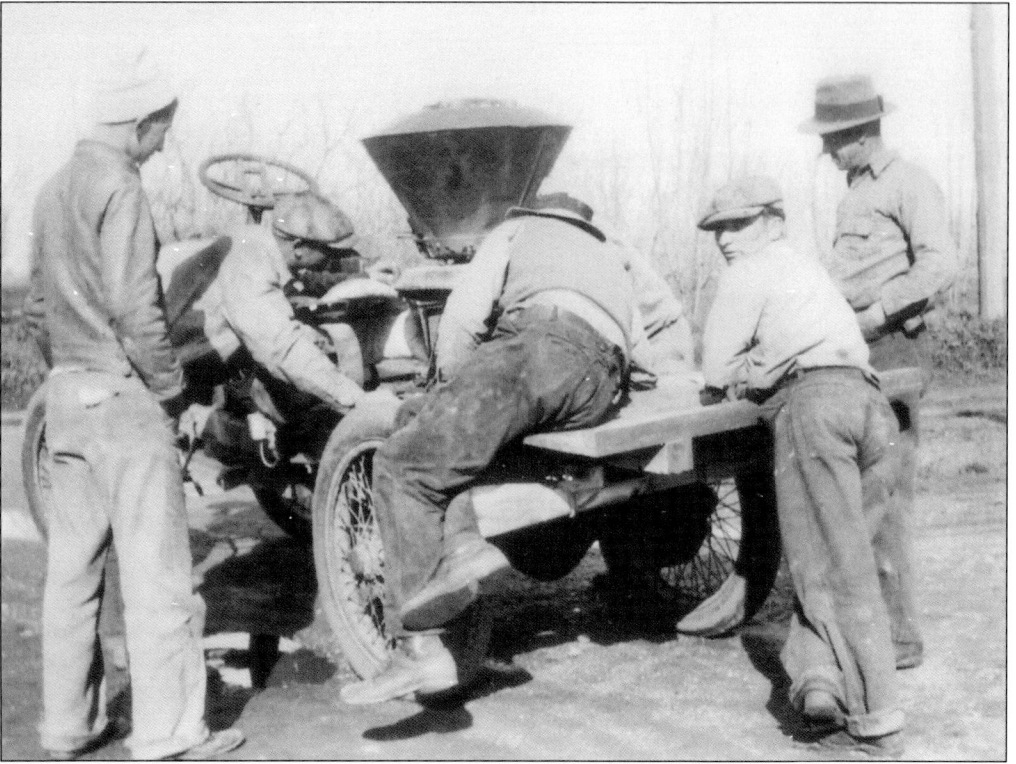

MACHINE INGENUITY. Ranch hands work intently on a malfunctioning grape duster at the Lucky Ranch on Eight Mile Road (Amerigo Cortopassi is the second from the left). The Lucky Ranch was famous for hiring crews of men to work on the large acreage, and they provided meals and steady work for many bachelors during the Depression. (Courtesy of Dino and Joan Cortopassi.)

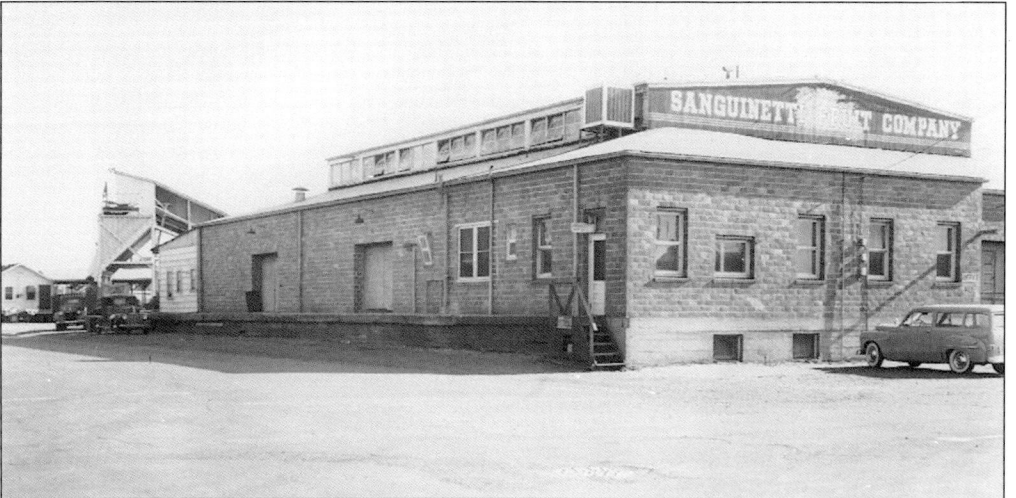

THE SANGUINETTI COMPANY. Stephen Sanguinetti came to California during the Gold Rush. He moved to Stockton in the 1860s and worked in an Italian garden making $15 a month. He became successful and farmed on a larger scale. Stephen married Geronima Lagomarsino and had seven children. His son Louis R. built the Sanguinetti Fruit Company warehouse seen here. (Courtesy of the Bank of Stockton Historical Photograph Collection.)

AVANSINO WALNUT SHAKER. This photograph, taken in September 1950, shows John Avansino with his belt-driven walnut shaker. Designed and built in Linden, the shaker was one of the earliest tree shakers to be patented. It greatly reduced the time required for the walnut harvest. (Courtesy of Joe Avansino.)

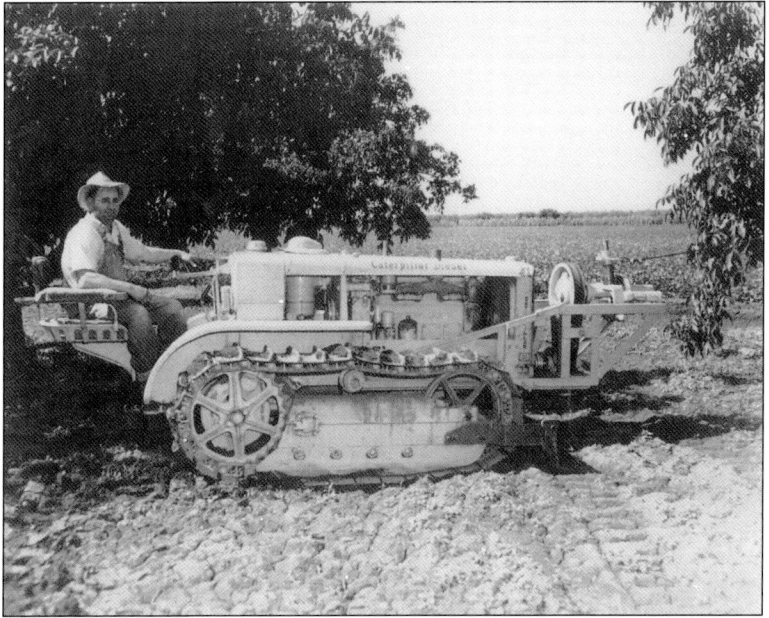

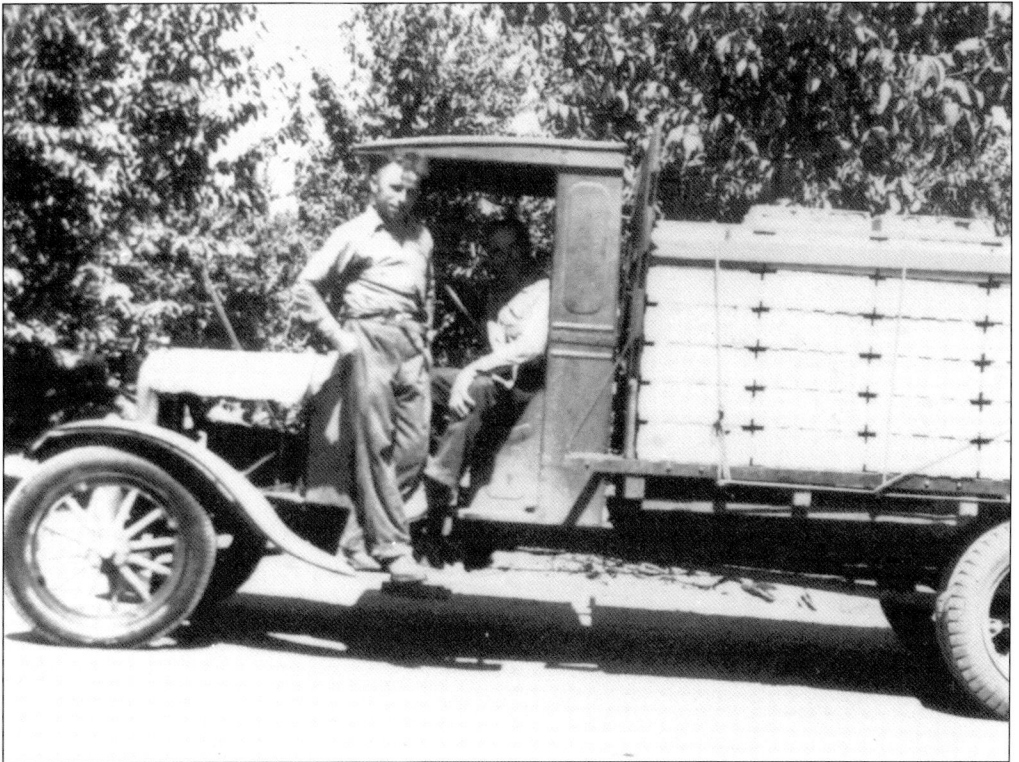

PODESTA PEACH ORCHARD. Early agriculture in San Joaquin County was centered on large-scale wheat and grain farming on large tracts of land. Italians farmers were instrumental in the transition from grain to the row and orchard crops that are the staples of the county's agriculture today. Here, Giacomo Podesta stands on the running board of his delivery truck in his peach orchard in 1938. (Courtesy of the Haggin Museum.)

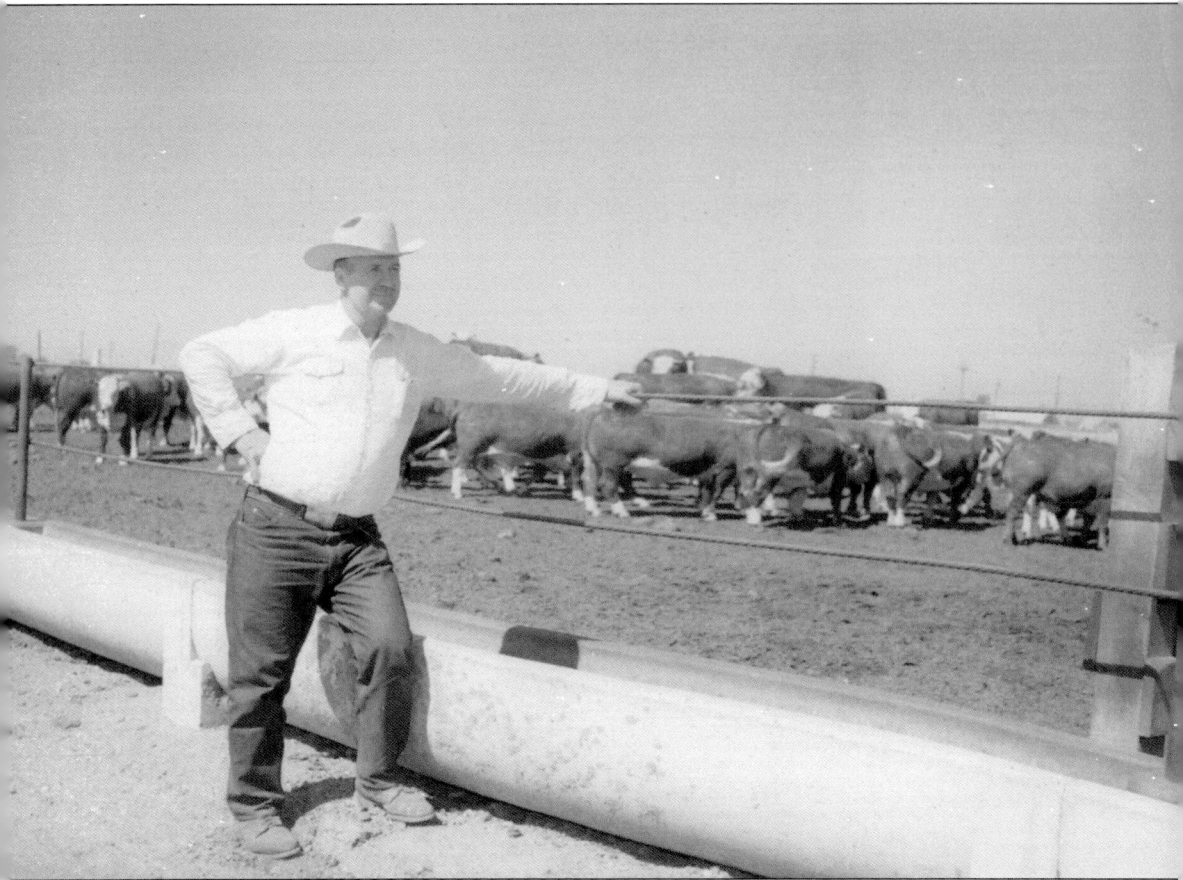

CATTLEMAN OF THE YEAR. Paul Sylvester Sanguinetti (1919–1992) grew rice, grain, and hay and also raised livestock on his area ranch. The Sanguinetti family has pioneer roots in California, with Paul's mother's family coming to Calaveras County during the Gold Rush and raising beef, vegetables, and grapes and making wine that they sold to the miners in the gold camps. His father's family settled in San Joaquin County in the 1860s and raised grain and cattle. In the fall of 1973, Paul earned the Outstanding Cattleman of the Year award from the San Joaquin–Stanislaus Cattlemen's Association, for which this photograph was taken. He built his own feed mill and feed lot in 1955, feeding out 7,000 head of beef per year and using 3,000 tons of hay, 7,500 tons of grain, and 1,500 tons of almond hulls with molasses and minerals as supplements. In 1947, he married Elsie Prato; they raised five children, all of whom continue in the agricultural industry. (Courtesy of the Sanguinetti/Prato family.)

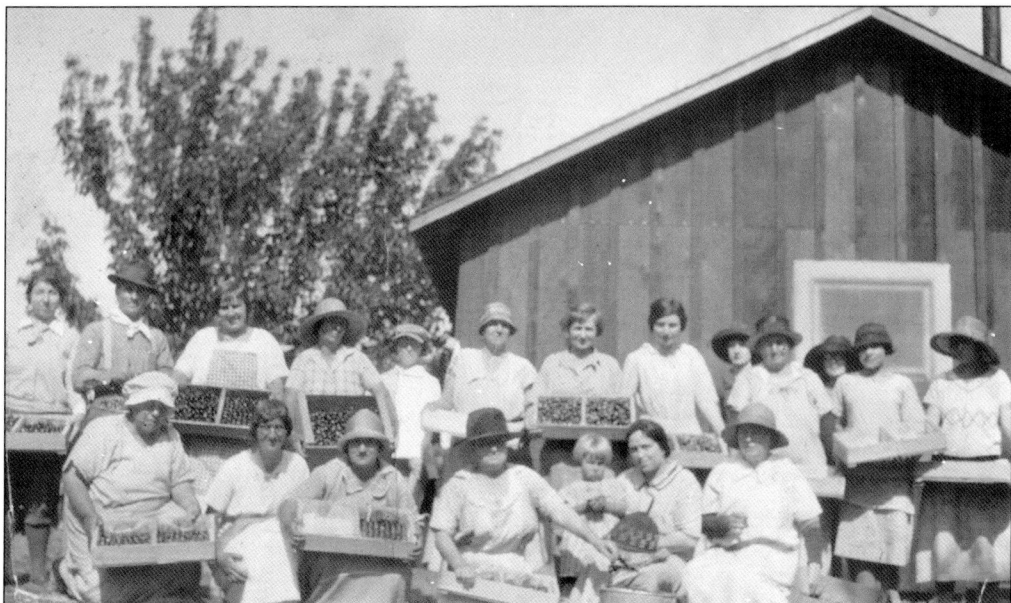

SANGUINETTI CREW. This photograph shows the Sanguinetti picking-and-packing crew with boxes of cherries on the Louis F. Sanguinetti place before the 1920s. Louis was born in Stockton, the youngest son of Angelo and Giovanna (Zignego). He owned 640 acres in the Peters district (west of Farmington) on which he also raised grain and livestock. (Courtesy of the Sanguinetti/Prato family.)

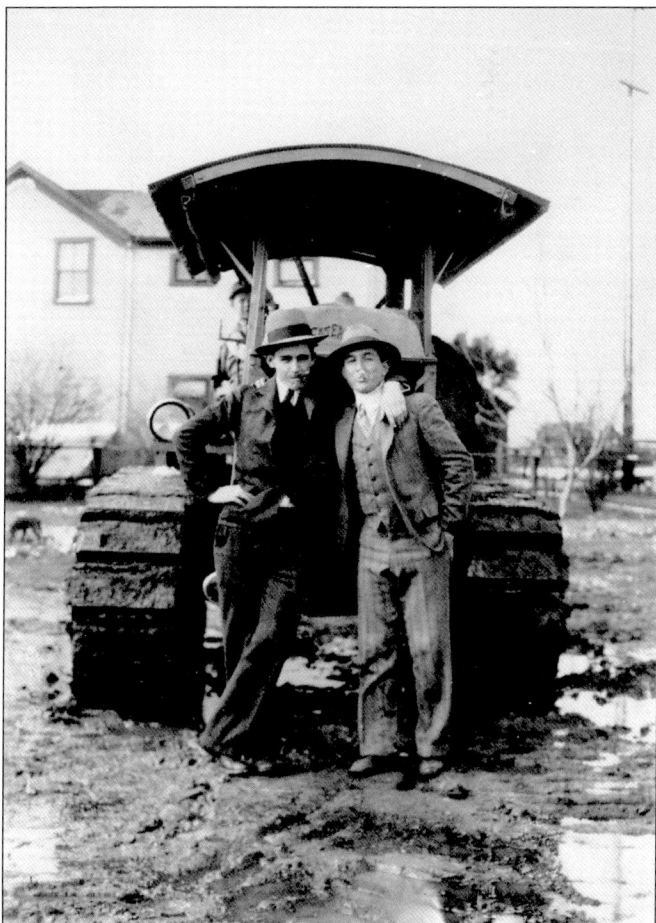

TRACTOR PRIDE, C. 1930S. Louis Cavagnaro (left) and his cousin Francis John Sanguinetti pose in their Sunday finest in front of John's new Caterpillar 60 tractor in the mud at Mariposa and Farmington Roads. John borrowed money for the tractor from his uncle Steve Sanguinetti, a prime example of family helping family. (Courtesy of the Sanguinetti/Prato family.)

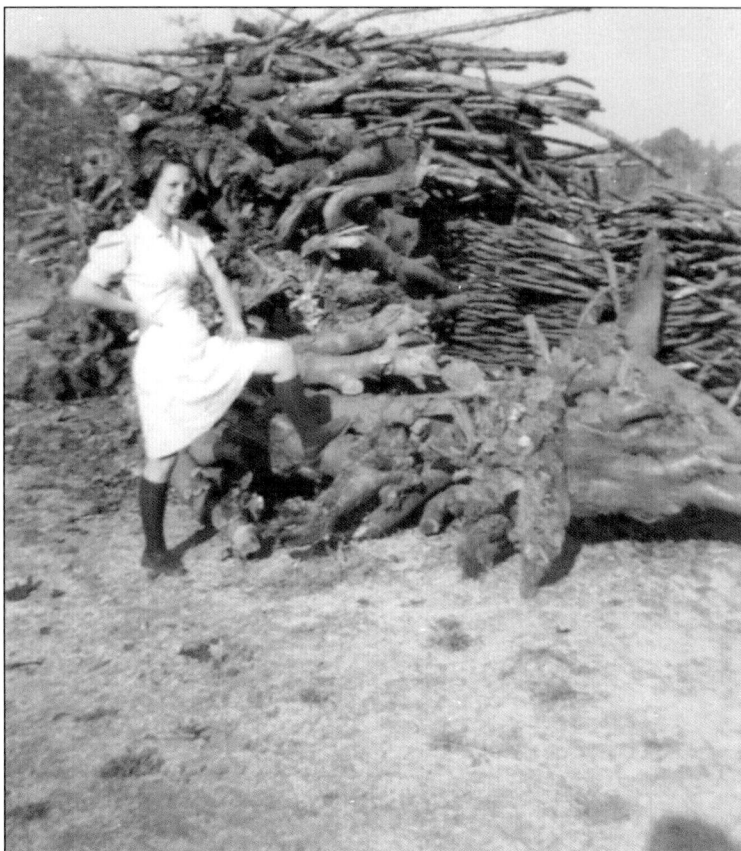

ORCHARD REMOVAL. In the early 1940s, the county experienced heavy rains that killed off many trees, including those of the Prato family orchard. Elsie Prato stands victorious over the remains of the family orchard in the photograph to the left. In the image below, an unidentified friend helps Benny Prato (standing on the truck) and his father, Bacci Prato (in front of truck), with the orchard removal on the family farm. Orchard removal was a labor-intensive task without the help of heavy modern equipment. (Both, courtesy of the Sanguinetti/Prato family.)

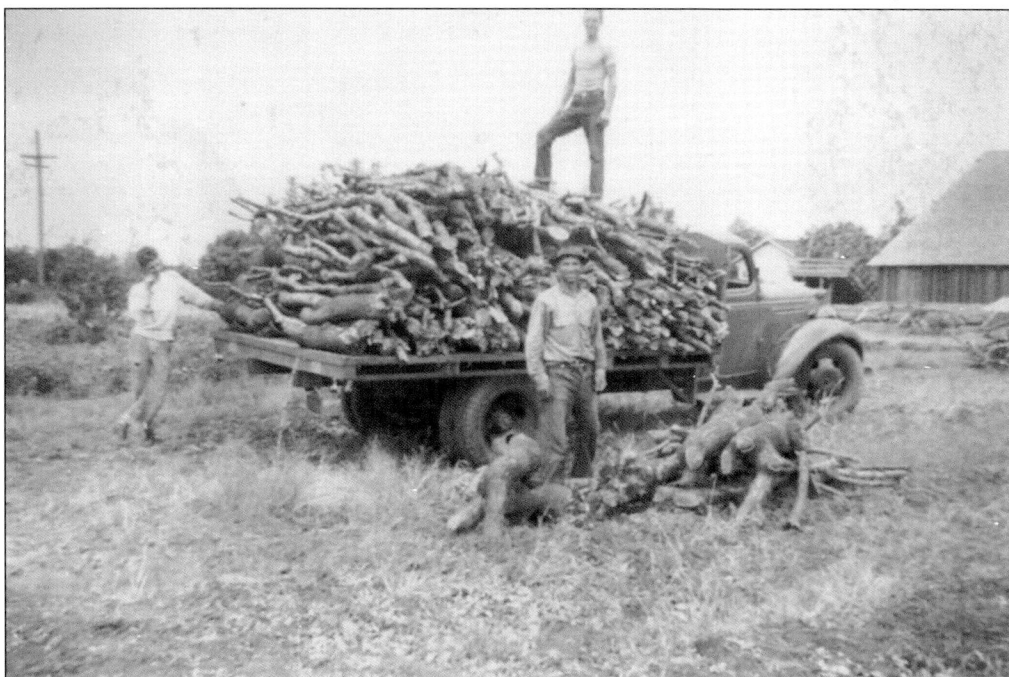

TENDING THE GARDEN, 1940s. A young George Prato works in the garden hoeing weeds at five or six years old. Family members would be put to work on the farm in some capacity at an early age. The Prato farm was located in a southeast corner of Stockton. Small gardens like this were the staple of Italian farming from the earliest days. (Courtesy of the Sanguinetti/Prato family.)

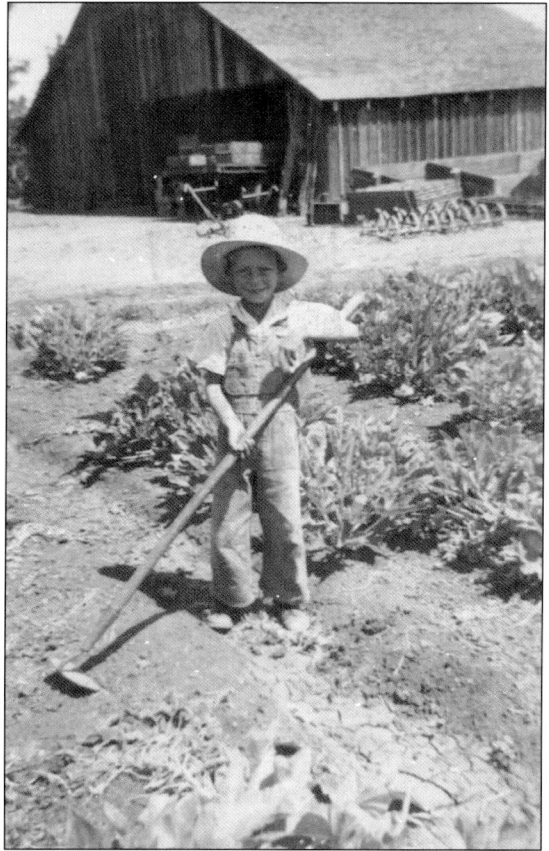

GETTING READY FOR MARKET. Giambatista "Maria" Prato readies some freshly picked peppers from the family farm for the market in this early-1940s photograph. Stacked lug boxes are filled, laid out, and organized for better presentation at the market. (Courtesy of the Sanguinetti/Prato family.)

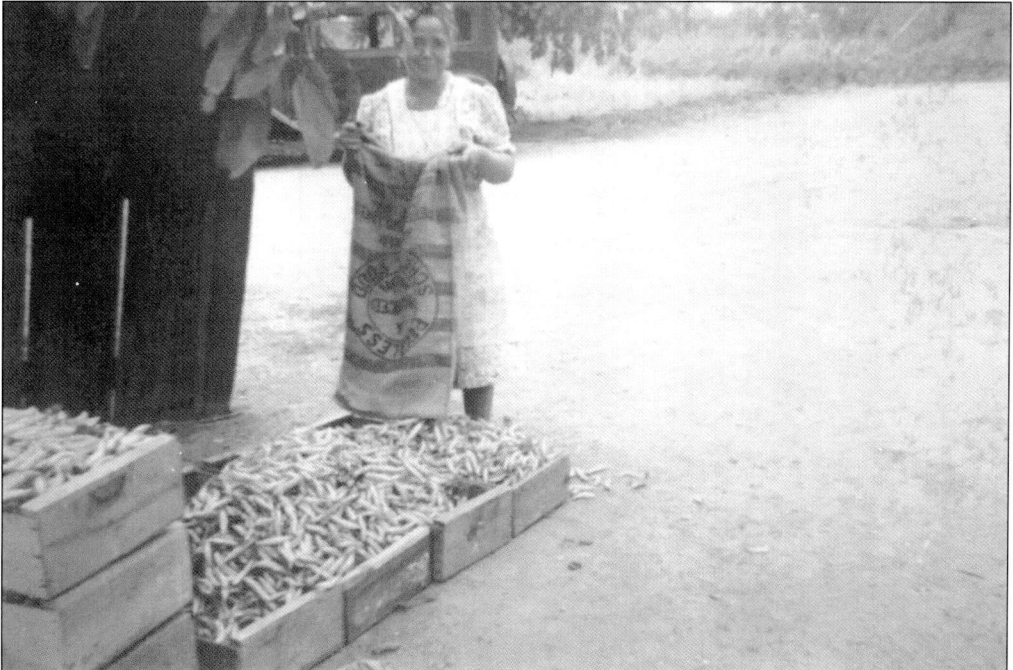

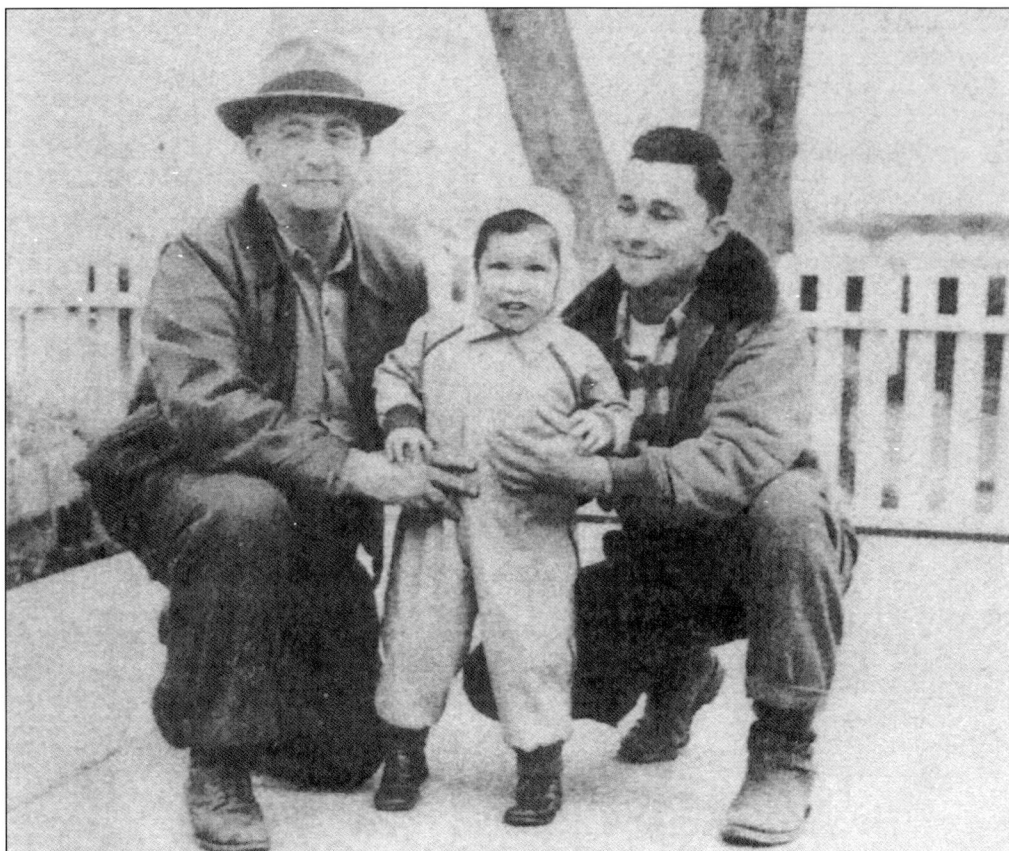

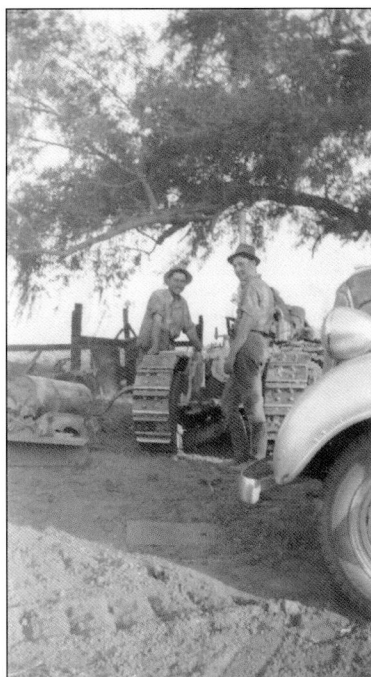

MARCO MARCHINI AND SONS. Above, Marco Marchini, his son Bruno (right), and grandson Vincent pose for a photograph in 1953. Marco came to America from Italy in 1913, farmed in several locations, and eventually ended up on Union Island north of Tracy. He was a pioneer in planting asparagus in the delta region and was the first man to haul asparagus to the San Francisco and Oakland markets by truck. Marco's sons Angelo (left) and Bruno joined their father in the farming operations and are pictured in the photograph to the left overhauling a Caterpillar 30 tractor during the early 1940s. (Both, courtesy of the Marco Marchini family.)

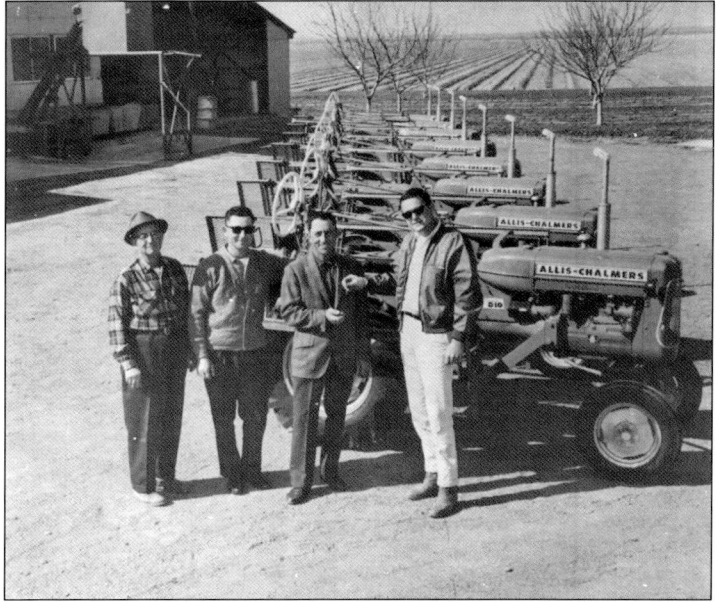

BUYING NEW TRACTORS. From left to right, Marco, Bruno, and Angelo Marchini receive keys to seven Allis-Chalmers D-10 tractors from salesman John West in a promotional photograph taken in 1961 at Sasser Tractor in Tracy. The tractors were equipped with special frames (built by the J. Milano Company of Stockton) to hold two sled boxes, one on each side, for collecting cut asparagus from the field. (Courtesy of the Marco Marchini family.)

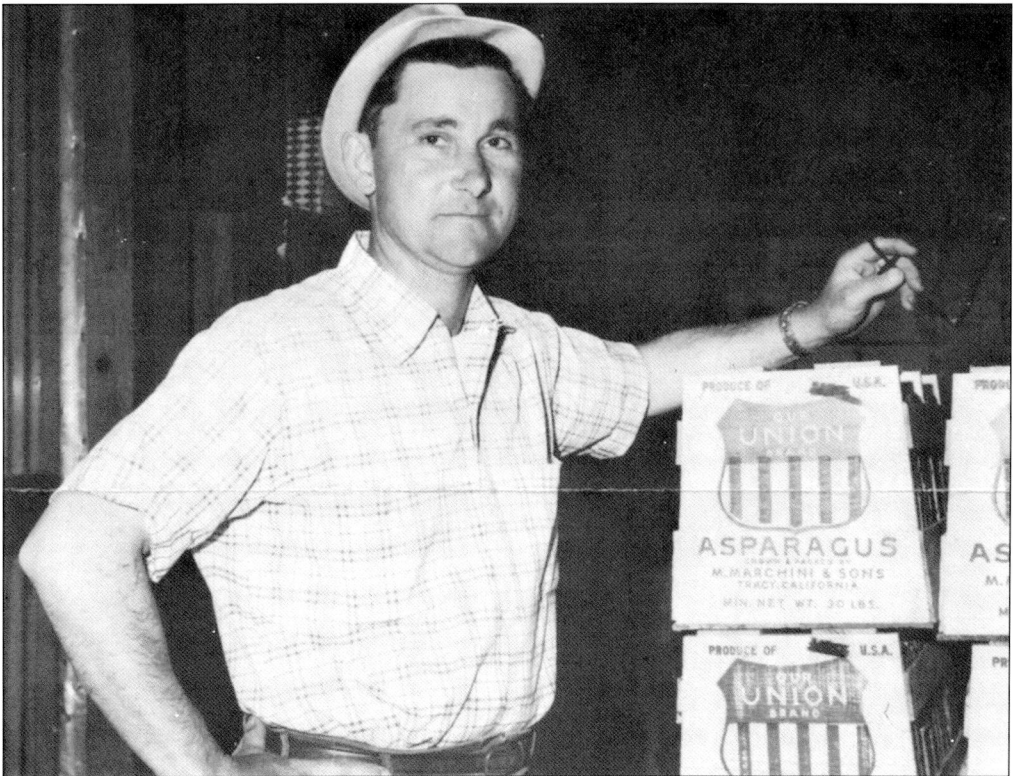

UNION ASPARAGUS CRATES. Bruno Marchini poses with the boxes in the packing shed for a photograph for the Stockton Box Company shortly before entering the Army around 1941. This label was purchased by Angelo and Bruno Marchini from another Union Island asparagus farming company (Jones & Pettigrew) for $1 the same year. (Courtesy of the Marco Marchini family.)

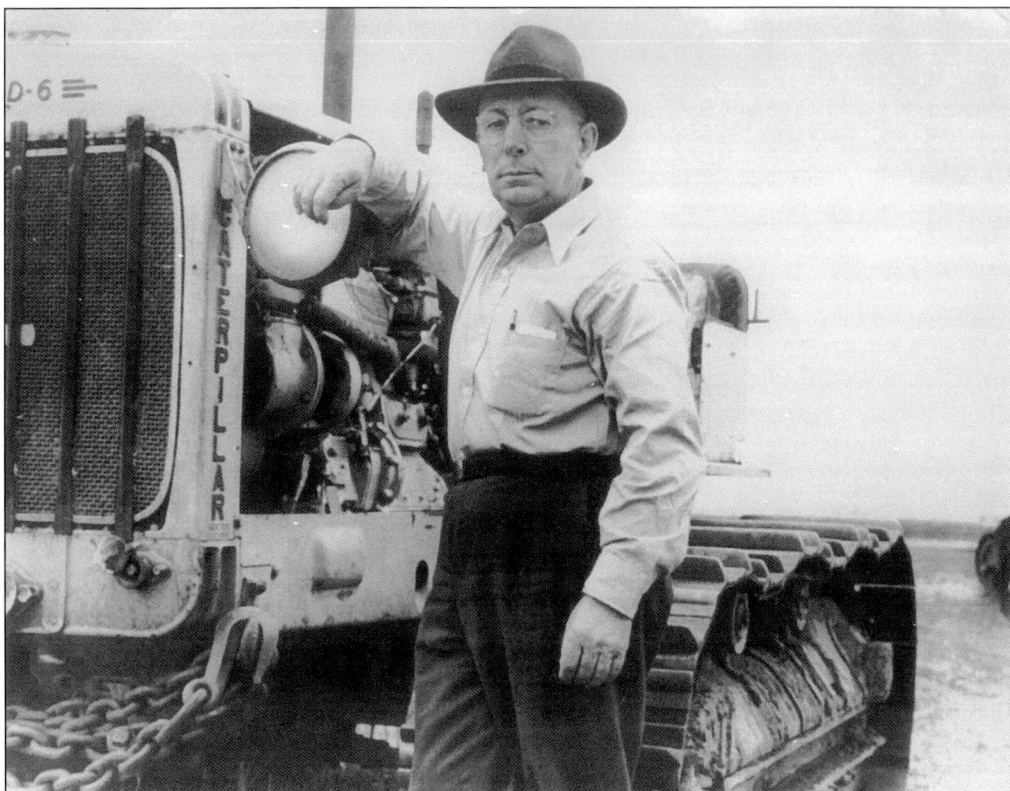

J.G. BALDOCCHI AND SONS. Joseph Baldocchi, an Italian immigrant from the Tuscany area, was one of the early asparagus farmers in California. He and his sons Armando, Guido, and Nello farmed in both San Joaquin and Contra Costa Counties. At the time of his death in 1958, Joseph was farming over 5,000 acres of asparagus and other crops. In the 1942 photograph above, he stands next to an RD-6 Caterpillar, which was used for working open ground to get ready for planting asparagus. Below, the Farmall tractor, with Joseph's grandson George Baldocchi sitting on it, was used to work the ground for row crops. This picture was probably taken in the early 1940s on one of the Baldocchi ranches. (Both, courtesy of the Armando Baldocchi family.)

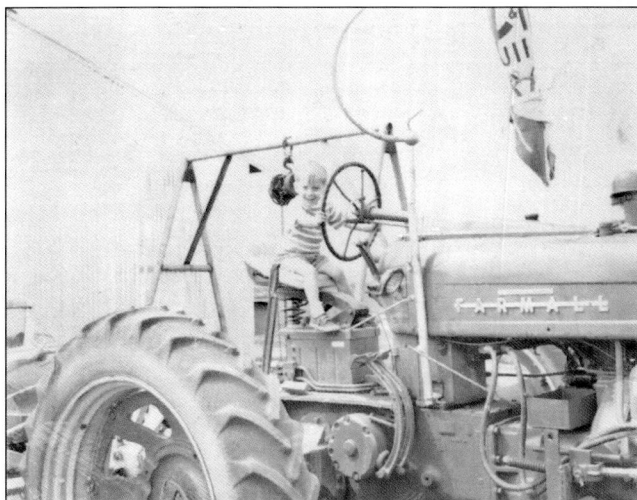

ARMANDO BALDOCCHI. Armando was posthumously inducted into the San Joaquin County Agricultural Hall of Fame in 2007. The Baldocchi family pioneered the raising of asparagus for fresh markets and the canneries. In 1958, Armando expanded operations to include row crops and grain. After his passing in 1998, family and friends established a scholarship for Tracy High School seniors continuing agriculture education in college. (Courtesy of the Armando Baldocchi family.)

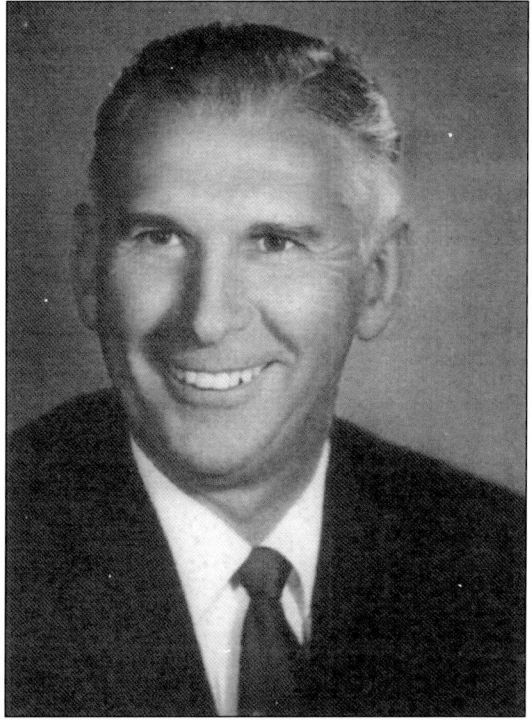

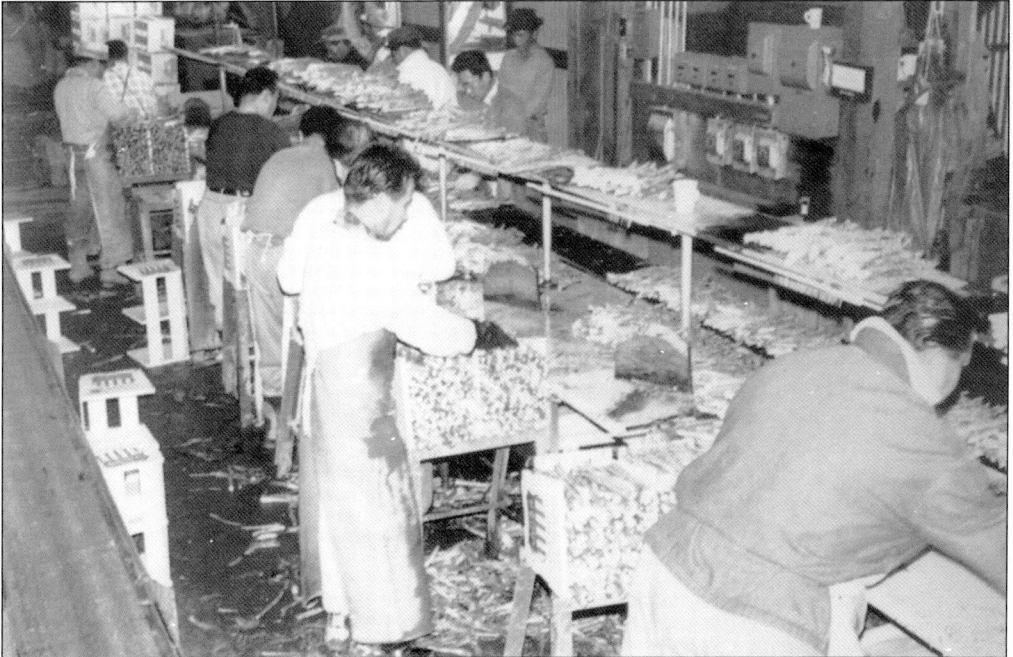

FRESH MARKET PACKING. Workers sort the asparagus according to size for the fresh market. Those on the opposite side would take the asparagus and pack it into wooden crates stamped with the farm's label at the Marchini packing shed. This photograph shows Filipino immigrants working in the new Marchini packing shed on Howard Road during the 1960s. (Courtesy of the Marco Marchini family.)

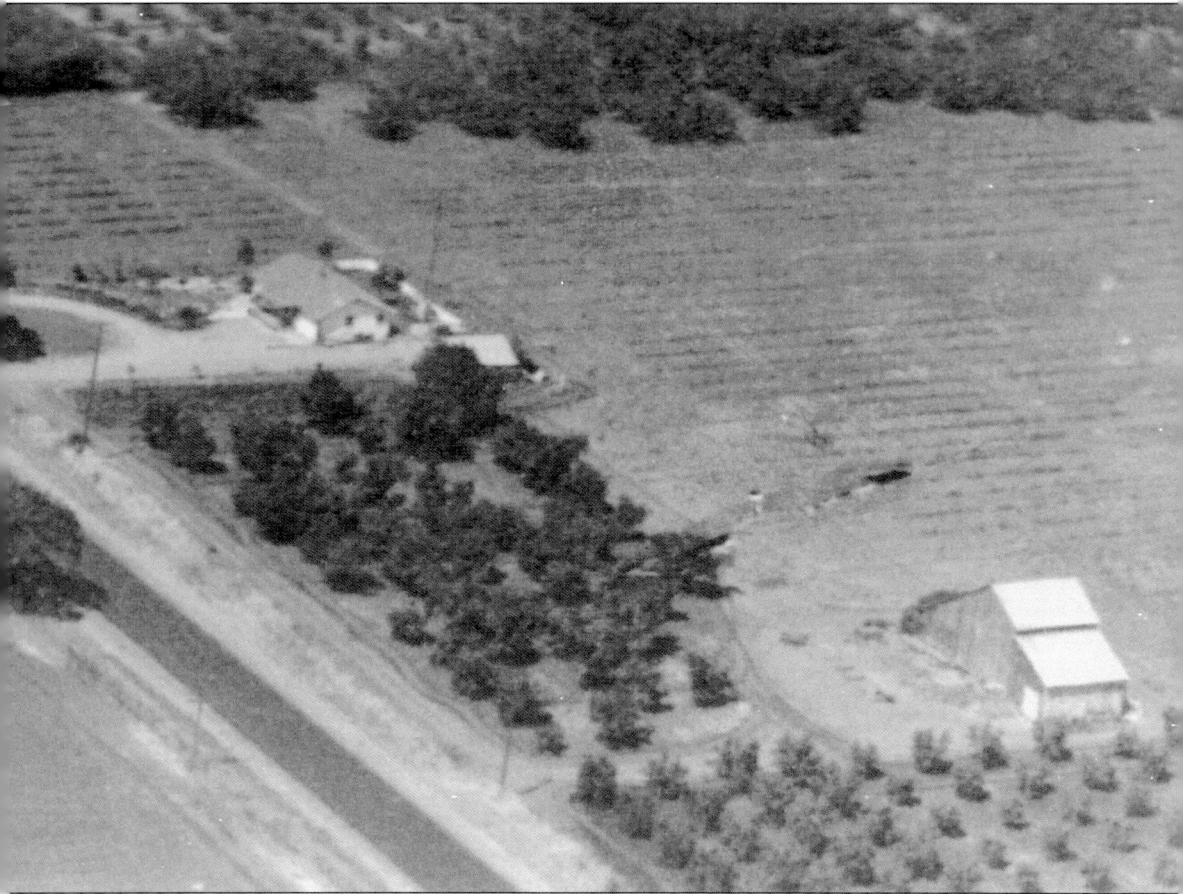

WATERLOO OR BUST. Starting at the age of 16, Frank Lucchetti worked for Pacific Gas and Electric for 16 years before he felt the call for something different. Stockton was growing and expanding rapidly, so Frank and his wife, Ina (see page 44), liked to get away on the weekends to spend time with friends and family in the Waterloo area, east of Stockton. St. Michael's Church, known as the "Italian Church," drew them deeper into the surrounding community. In 1944, Frank quit his job to work the fields east of Stockton. After he had spent a time working and learning with his bother-in-law Sylvio Scuitti, an opportunity arose that would change the family's life forever. Frank purchased 33 acres (seen here in this c. late-1950s aerial view) from Bernardo Sanguinetti, who wanted to retire and move to the city. Family friends Gaetano and Carmela Risso helped with a loan for the down payment on the ranch, and in December 1945, the details were finalized, and Frank and Ina became farmers. (Courtesy of the Lucchetti family.)

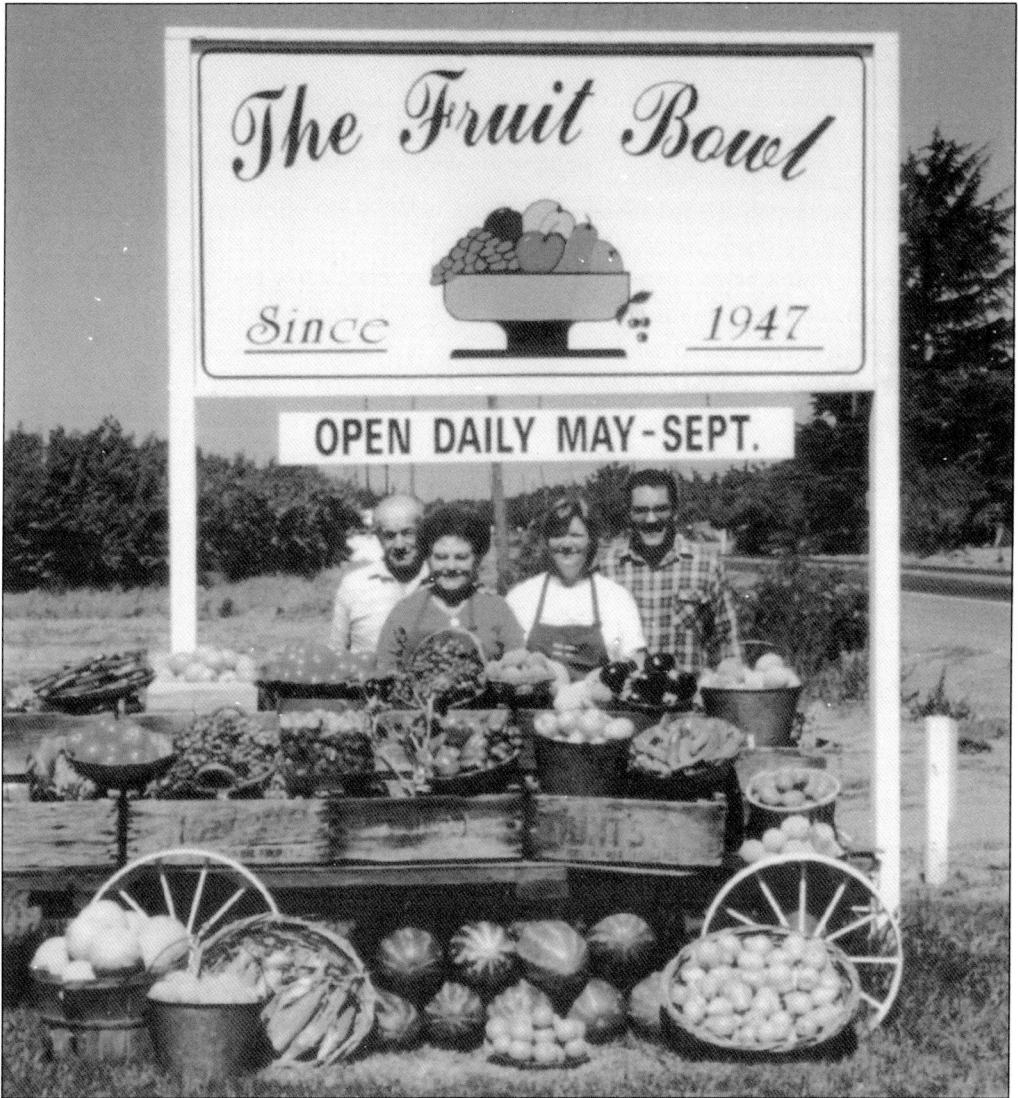

THE FRUIT BOWL. The Lucchettis moved into a two-story house on the property that had been built in 1860. After they had fixed it up and lived there briefly, a dramatic fire destroyed the structure. With the help of the church community, they rebuilt and persevered. In the summer, their first peach harvest was ready around the Fourth of July weekend, but unfortunately, the markets in San Francisco were closing, causing a dilemma. Trying something new, Frank set up a table and made signs with his children's crayons. At the end of the day, Ina counted $180, and the Fruit Bowl was born. The original stand grew into a 3,000-square-foot building and a popular roadside stop. Youngest son Ralph and his wife, Denene (seen here along with Frank and Ina), now run the stand and were inducted into the San Joaquin County Agricultural Hall of Fame in October 2011. The year 2014 marks the Fruit Bowl's 67th season of growing and selling fresh produce at the family fruit stand on East Waterloo Road. (Courtesy of the Lucchetti family.)

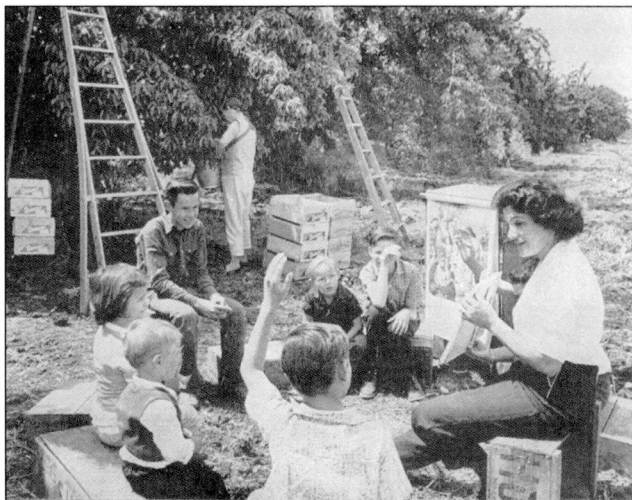

ORCHARD BIBLE SCHOOL, C. 1964. Ina Lucchetti's passion for teaching extended to the children of the migrant farmworkers who helped harvest the cherries, peaches, apricots, and walnuts on the Lucchetti ranch. In addition to teaching the children about God, she would also try to teach them history, geography, and other subjects. Ina's teaching was so popular that parents would bring their children back to where "the lady tells them about God." (Courtesy of the Lucchetti family.)

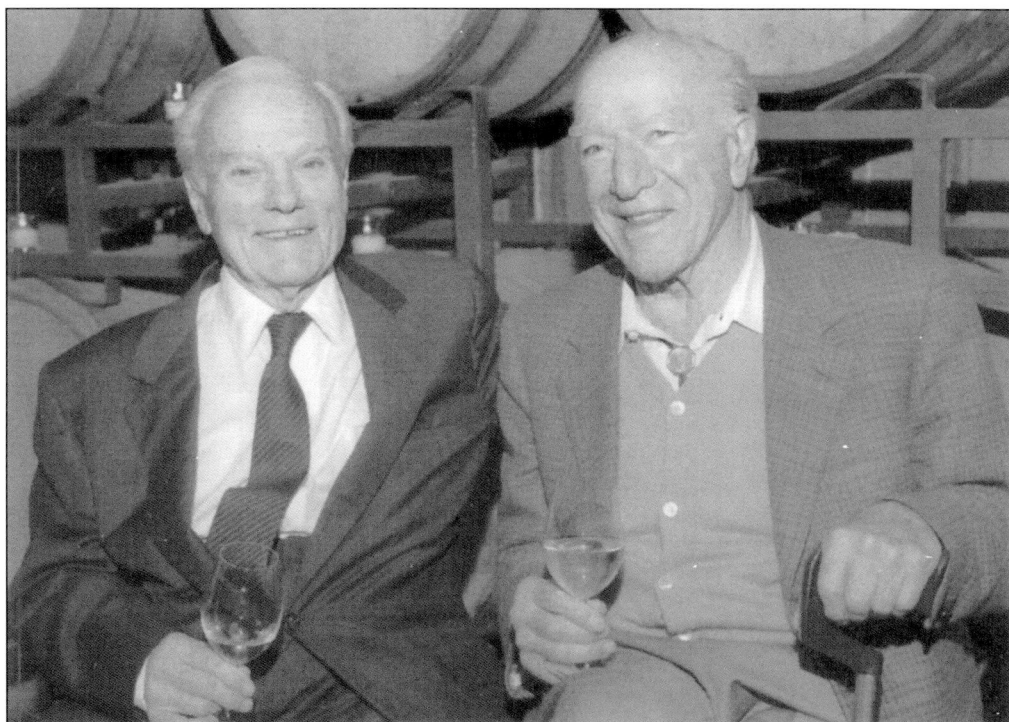

MONDAVI BROTHERS. The Mondavi family eventually moved to Lodi and entered the grape industry as shippers and then as winery owners. With the purchase of the Charles Krug Winery in Napa in 1943, the Mondavi family quickly became innovators and pioneers in the California wine industry. Peter (left) and Robert, seen here in 2004, helped put the California wine industry on the world map. (Author's collection.)

Six

THE ITALIAN SCHOOL

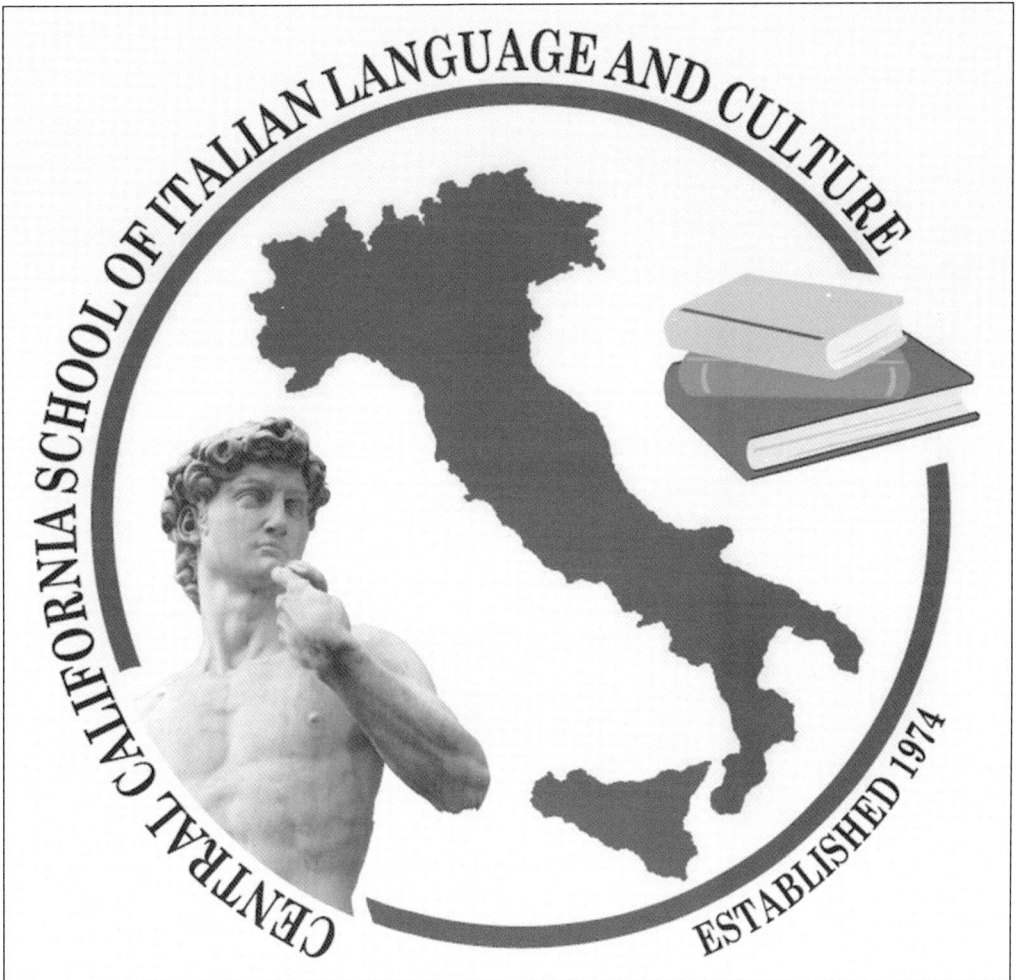

LEARNING CULTURE AND LANGUAGE. The Central California School of Italian Language and Culture (known affectionately as the Italian School) began informally in the 1950s with classes for children taught by Maria Marchesi and held after school in the homes of community members. This informal school laid the foundation for the formation of an official school. (Courtesy of the Italian School.)

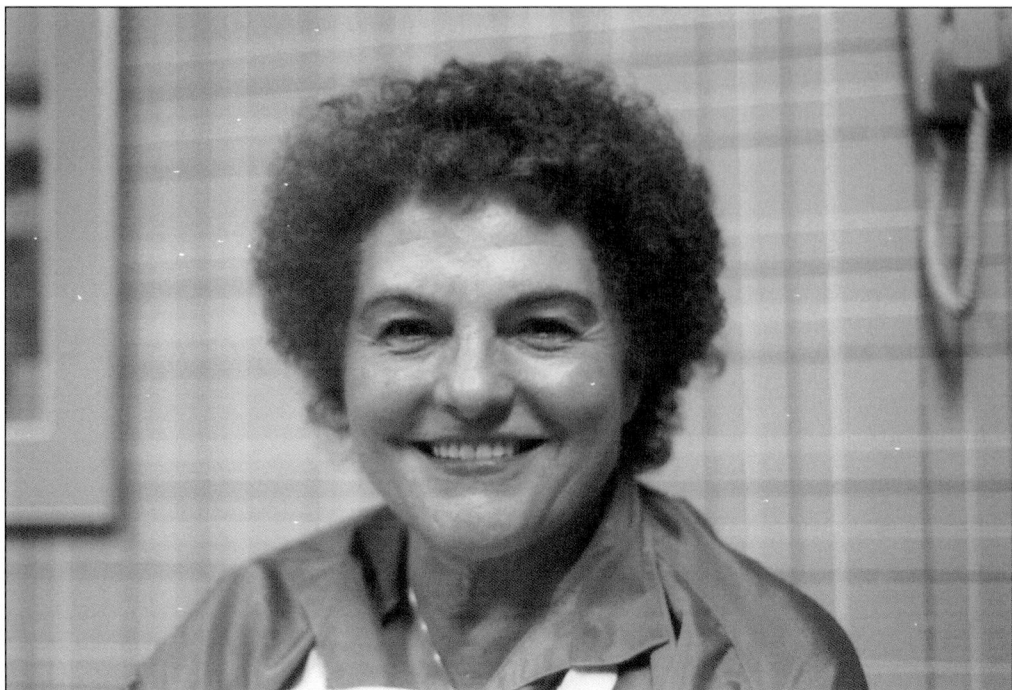

OFFICIAL SCHOOL BEGINS. Under the leadership of Cristina "Ina" Lucchetti (above) the first official classes were held in 1974, and later in the year, a board of directors was established with the help of the Italian vice consul of Stockton, Faliero "Luke" Lucaccini. Pictured below are some of the first board members: from left to right, (first row) Guiseppe Nepote, Rino Bertini (vice president), and Luigi Gherardi (a school teacher); (second row) Ina Lucchetti (president), Domenic George, Luke Lucaccini (treasurer), Elyse Sciutti (secretary), and Bill Lina (school principal). Board members not pictured include Alma Maccini, Paul Mariani, and John Muzio. (Above, courtesy of the Lucchetti family; below, courtesy of the Italian School.)

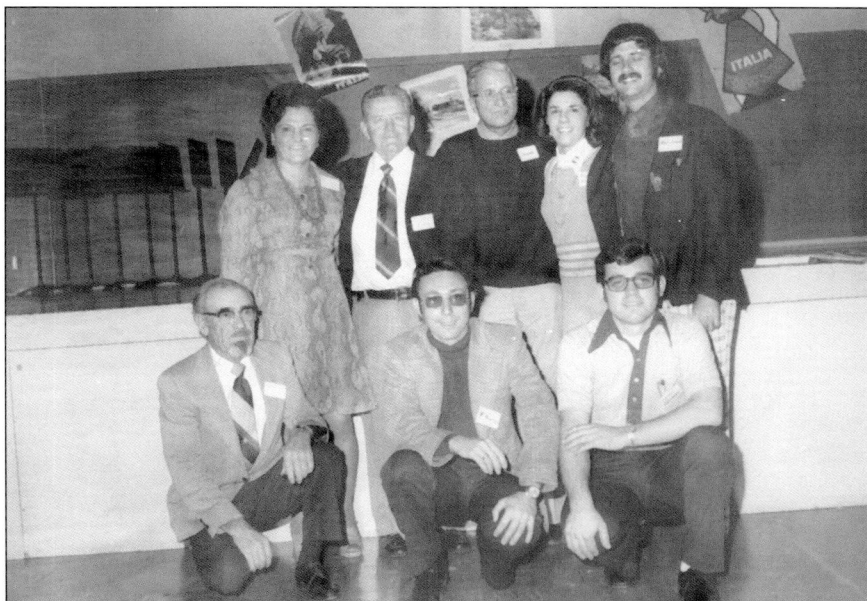

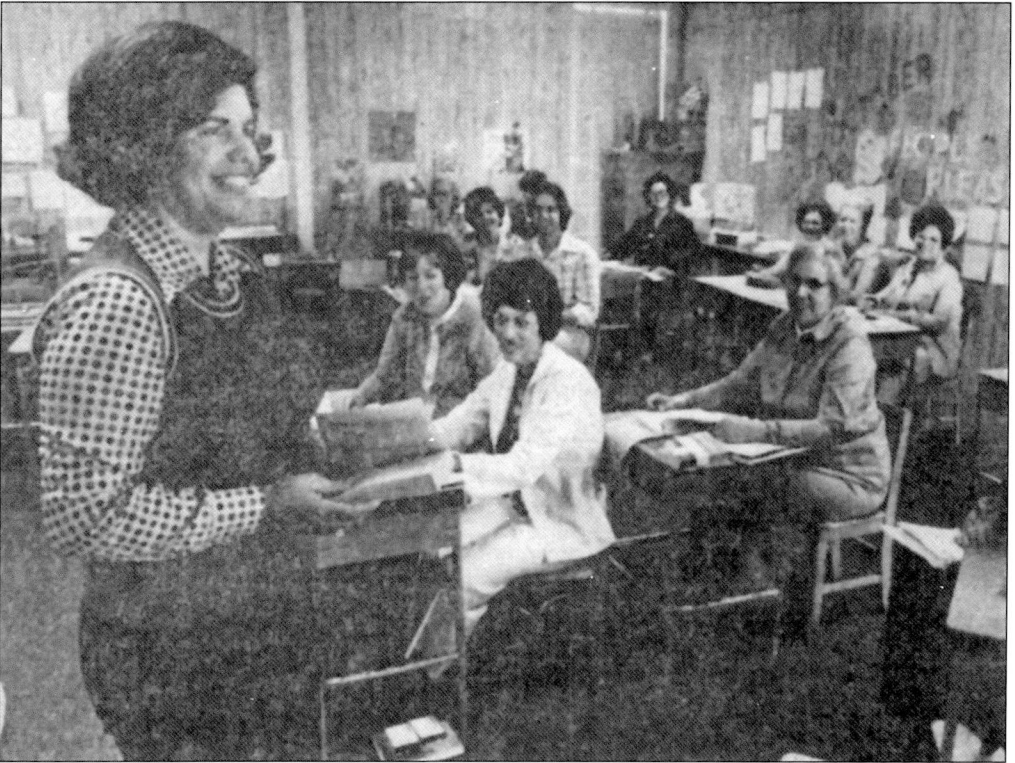

CLASSROOM STUDY. The first classes were held at Hoover Elementary in Stockton. Cathy (Canepa) Manassero (above) teaches the adult classes at the Italian School, while Susan Giambastini (below) teaches the children's class. Other original teachers were Vanda Cutwright, Luigi Gherardi, Antonella Tambollini, Sandy Tei, Flora Van Stecklenburg, and Nancy Volpi. During the first year, 209 students enrolled (101 adults and 108 children), and classes were held from November through May. Both the adult and children's classes are a part of the current school curriculum. (Both, courtesy of the Italian School.)

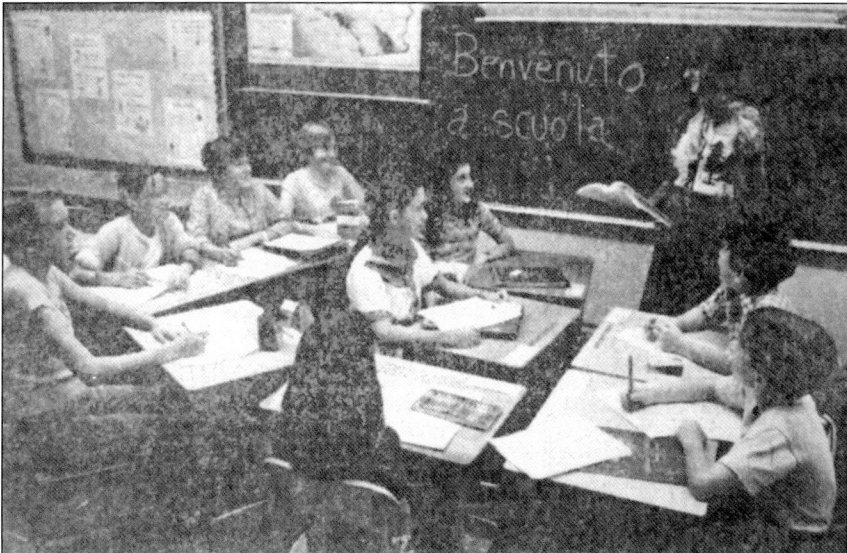

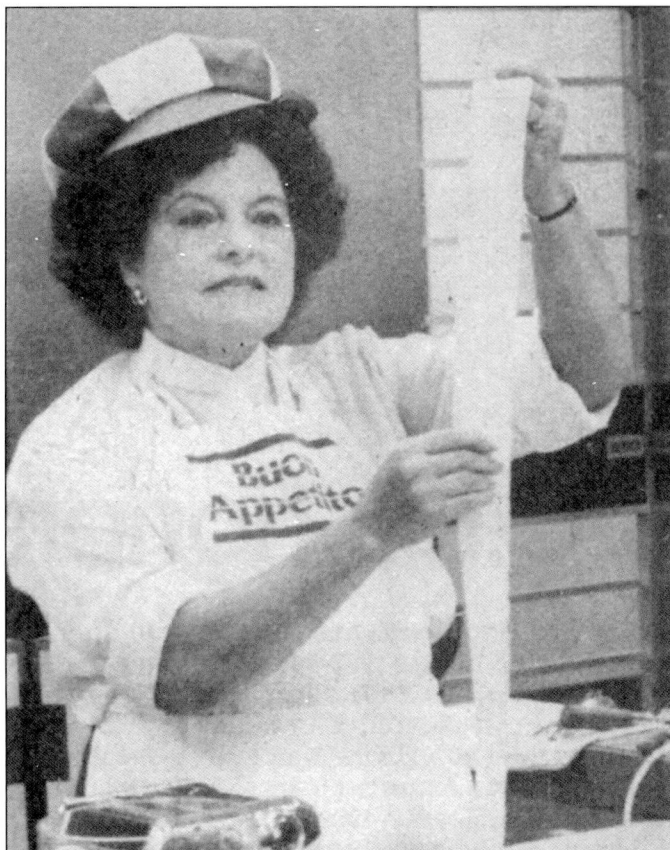

CULTURAL LEARNING. Ina Lucchetti demonstrates the fine points of making pasta at a promotional event. In the beginning, the school struggled financially, but a substantial contribution by Mr. and Mrs. Joe Marchesotti helped the school add more events in addition to its language classes. The curriculum includes a popular class for those interested in travel to Italy. The school also offers various programs, such as raffles, cooking classes, dinners (like *bagna calda*—a hot dip served in the autumn and winter months—and polenta feasts), fashion shows, benefit lunches, and scholarships. (Both, courtesy of the Lucchetti family.)

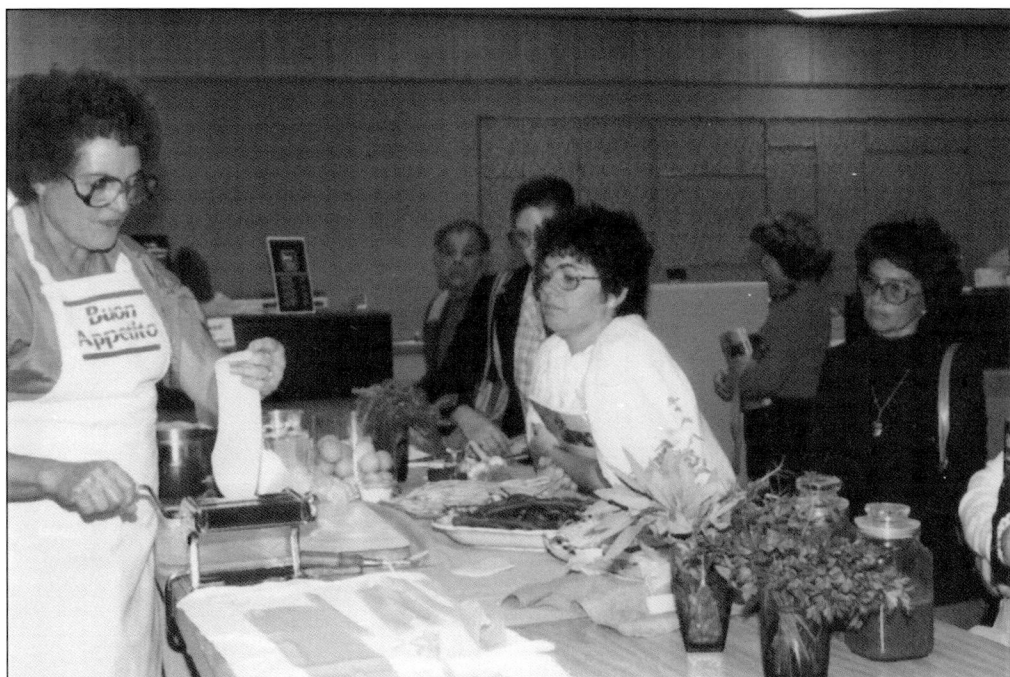

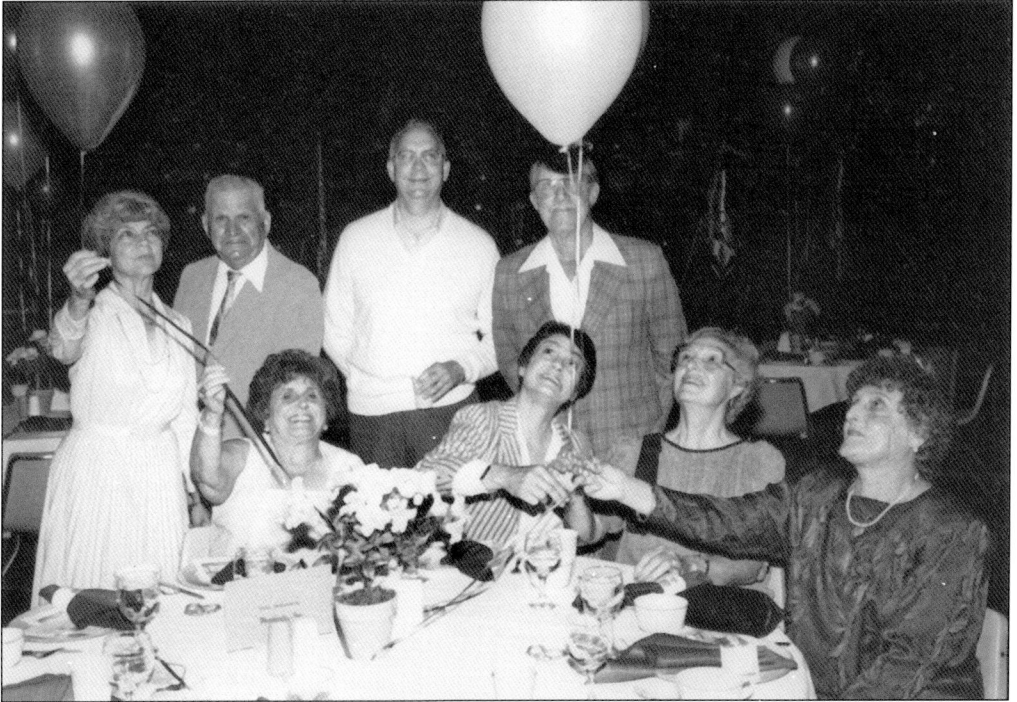

PRIMAVERA IN ITALIA. Primavera in Italia ("springtime in Italy") was a popular dinner-and-dance event held every April by the Italian School from 1975 to 1993. Open to the public, it served as a fundraiser for the school and was a highlight of the year. Pictured above from left to right, (first row, seated) Helen Rinauro, Jo Anna French, Jo Ish, and Margaret Tuso; (second row, standing) Angie Costa, Paul Rinauro, Joe French, and Charles Ish enjoy the balloons and decor at the 1985 event at the A.G. Spanos Center on the University of the Pacific campus. At right, Elyse Sciutti, the event's general chairman, and Luigi Gherardi, cochairman, wear traditional costumes to advertise the second annual dinner and dance in 1976. (Both, courtesy of the Italian School.)

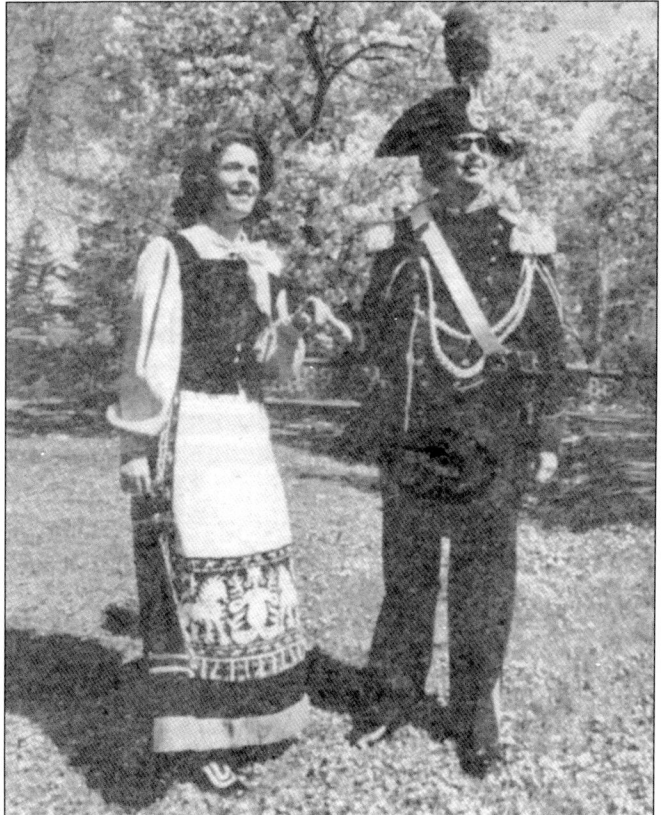

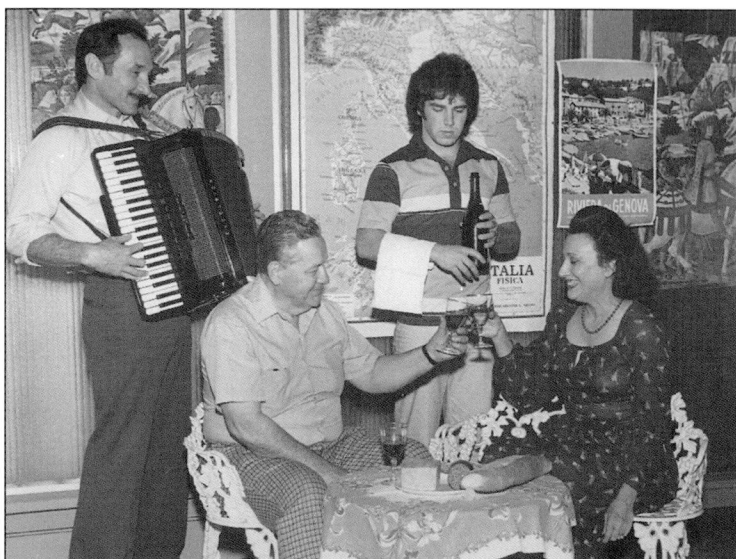

MUSIC AND WINE. Don Garibaldi plays accordion while Kevin Craig pours wine for Domenic George and Alma Maccini as they plan for the sixth annual Primavera event in 1980, held at the Civic Auditorium. Today, a polenta dinner has taken the Primavera's place as the main fundraiser. (Courtesy of the Bank of Stockton Historical Photograph Collection.)

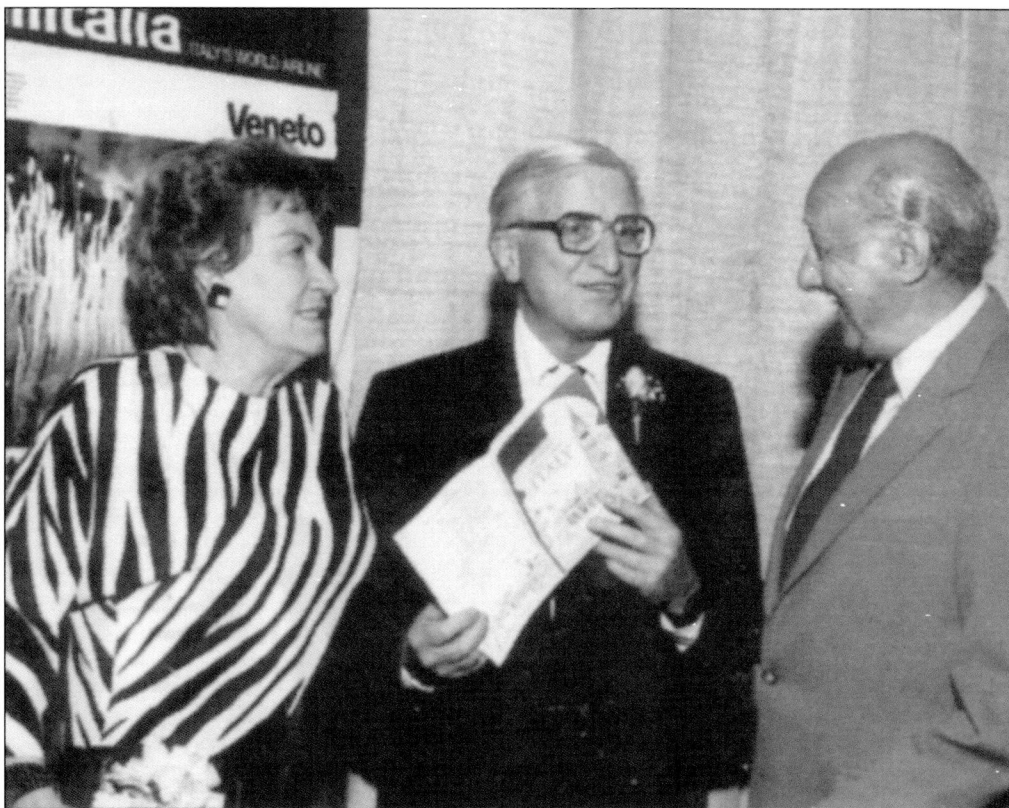

THE LEGACY CONTINUES. Luke Lucaccini stands between Irene and Frank Garavano at the 10th annual Primavera in Italia in 1984. The present-day classes are held at St. Mary's High School in Stockton. In 2014, the school marked 40 years of language and cultural-awareness instruction in the community. (Courtesy of the Italian School.)

Seven

ITALIAN GARDENERS SOCIETY

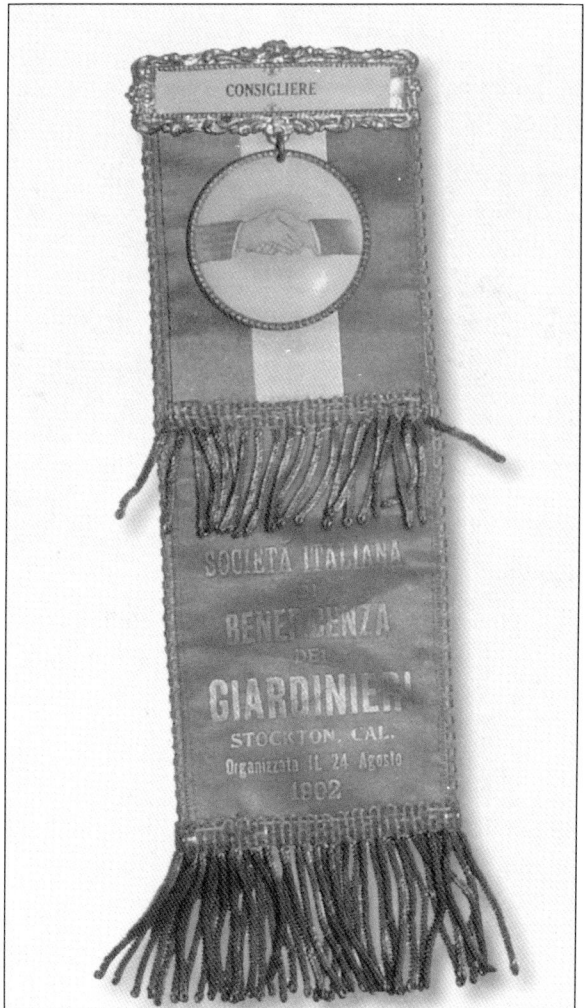

ITALIAN GARDENERS SOCIETY. This founder's badge denotes membership in one of the oldest and most unique Italian groups in the county. Officially known as La Società Italiana di Beneficenza dei Giardinieri di Stockton (the Italian Gardener Benefit Society of Stockton), it was formed as a way to support Italian farmers in times of distress and financial need. (Courtesy of the Haggin Museum.)

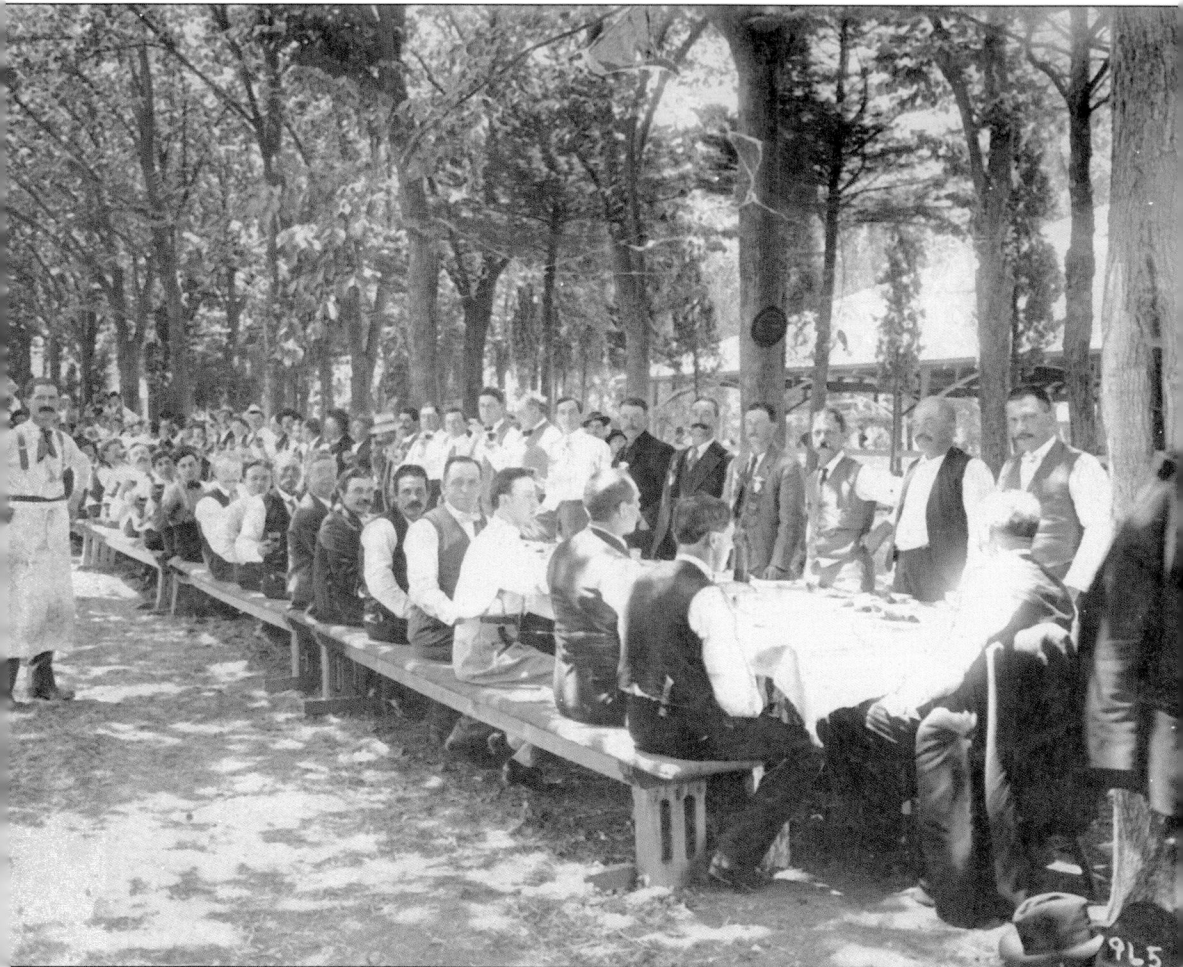

ITALIAN GARDENERS PICNIC, 1911. In 1902, several Italian growers who sold produce from wagons and trucks along the Weber Avenue waterfront and at Hunter Square began to contemplate creation of an organization for the benefit of immigrant Italian farmers who had settled in the Stockton area. The group met on Wednesday, August 24, 1902, and officially formed the organization. The cost of membership was set at $1, and by Sunday, 191 members had paid. However, there were some competing interests amongst members as a minority felt that a market should be established to set uniform prices and others only wanted to form a benevolent organization. Of the 191 members, 53 withdrew after the vote. A summer picnic for members (later involving the public) was started and became an important event for the Italian community. This photograph shows the ninth annual picnic in Bide-A-Wee Park, located at Wilson Way and Main Street. Giuseppe Tassano headed the organization that year, and Emilio Fontana (far left, wearing apron) served as cook. (Courtesy of historian Bennie Filippini, Italian Gardeners Society.)

PICNIC IN THE GROVE, 1973. Originally held for male members (until 1936), the annual picnic began to include families and friends and then opened to the wider public. It grew yearly, moving from its original location in Bide-A-Wee Park to Oak Park, and then, in 1923, to the new Growers Market. In 1928, it found its current home in Micke Grove. (Courtesy of the San Joaquin County Historical Society.)

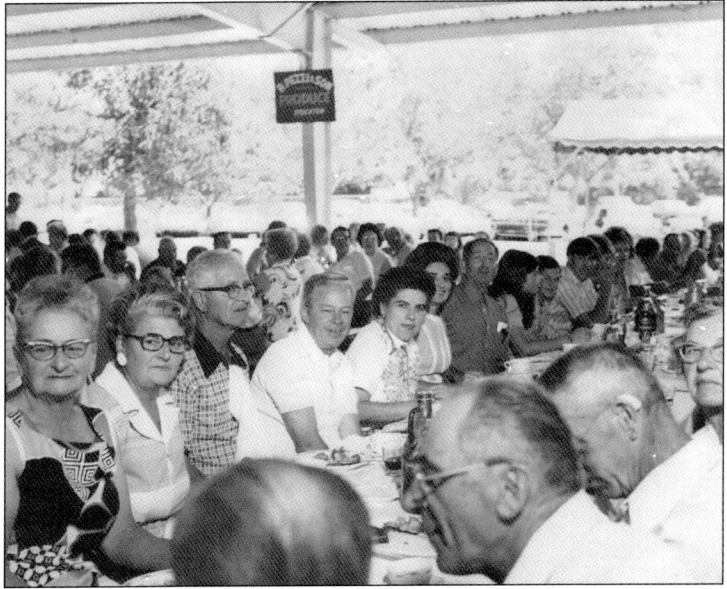

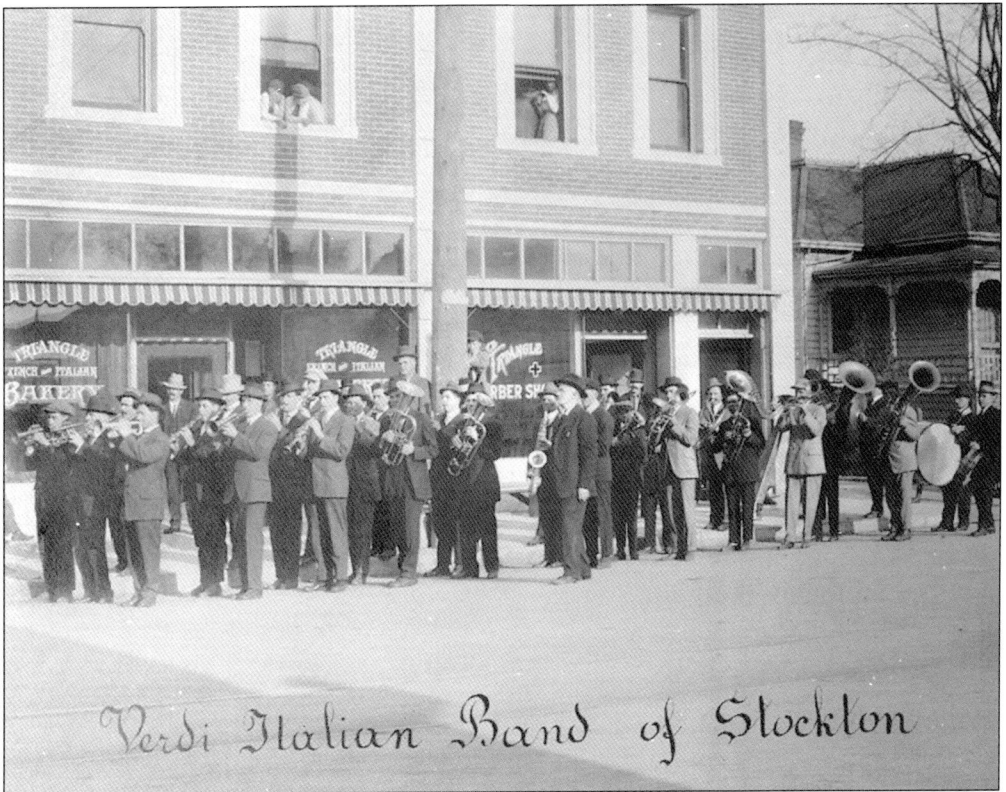

Verdi Italian Band of Stockton

VERDI ITALIAN BAND. One of the most popular bands of its day, the Verdi Band of Stockton marched at the head of the processional at the 21st anniversary of the society and the opening of the new Growers Market that the Italian Gardeners had built in 1923. Maestro F. Pellegrini led the band and gave a concert. (Courtesy of the Bank of Stockton Historical Photograph Collection.)

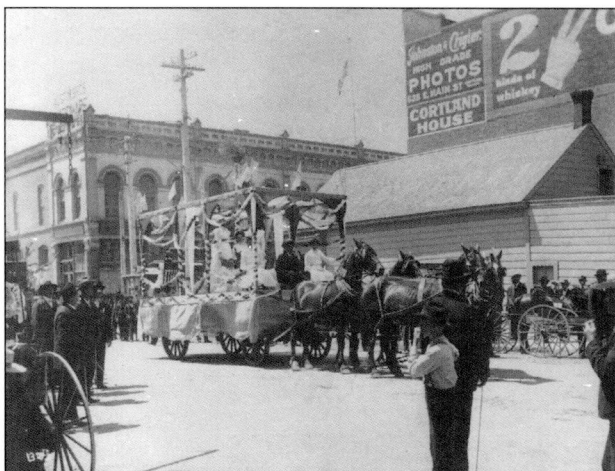

PARADE FLOATS. Following the band were several floats that displayed all of the finest products of the Italian gardens and orchards. These were followed by automobiles carrying parade officials like grand marshal Giacomo Tassano and other prominent Italians. After traveling through the business district of Stockton, the parade stopped at the San Joaquin Marketing Association on East Street. (Courtesy of the San Joaquin County Historical Society.)

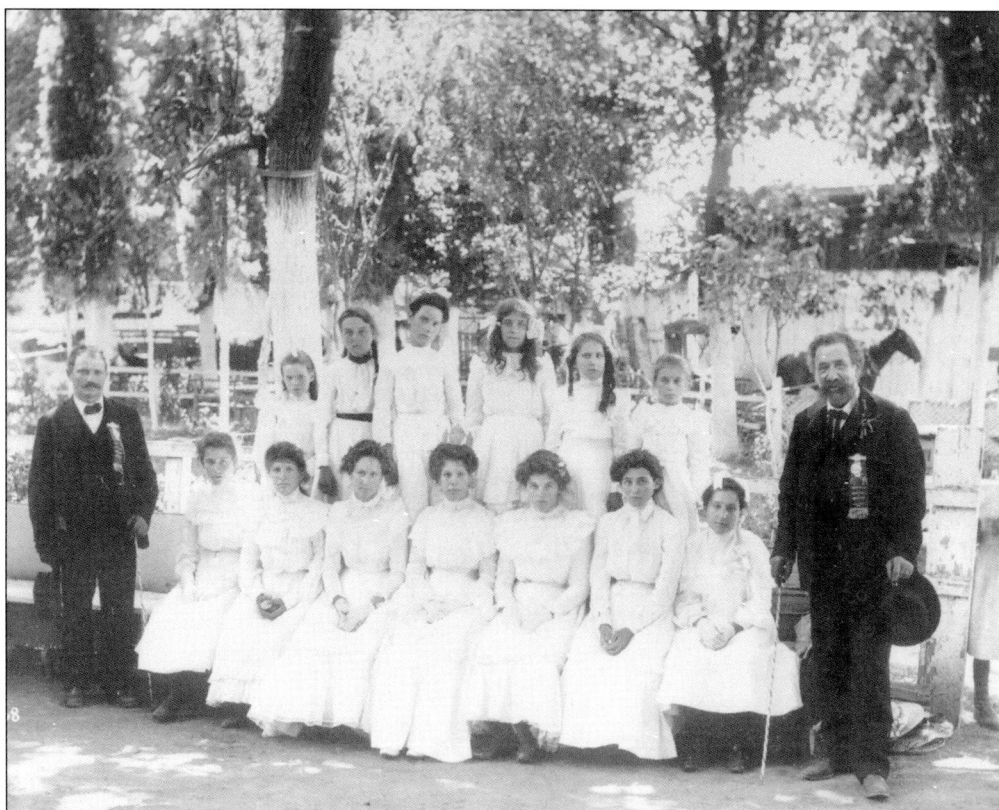

GARDENER COURT. Members' daughters competed in a beauty pageant to reign over the celebration. Pictured here, the court of possibly 1904 or 1905 includes officials Alberto Sacco (far right), an unidentified man (far left), and, from left to right, (first row) two unidentified young ladies, Kate Prato, Louise Campodonico, Anne Campodonico, unidentified, and Mary Zignego; (second row) two unidentified young ladies, Mary Capurro, Mary Piccardo, Virginia Zignego, and unidentified. (Courtesy of historian Bennie Filippini, Italian Gardeners Society.)

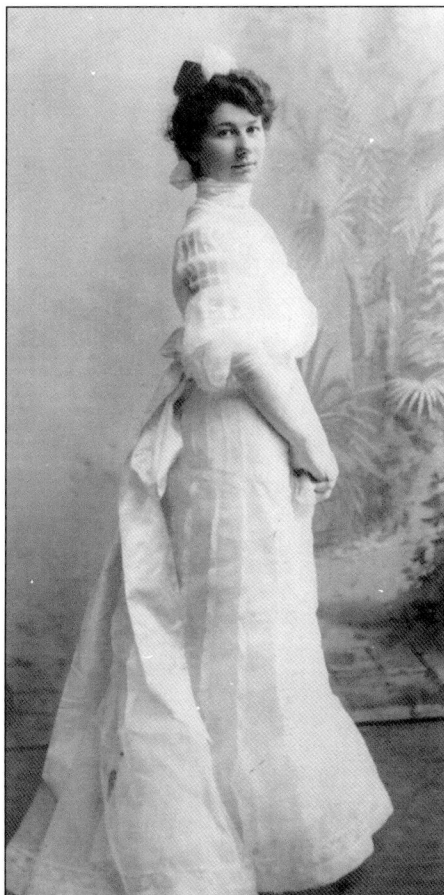

PAGEANT TRADITIONS. Seen at right, Grace Sacco poses in her royal dress after her coronation. A daughter of charter member Alberto Sacco, the 17-year-old had the honor of serving as the very first queen of the Italian Gardeners Society picnic in 1904. After the 25th anniversary in 1927, the pageant became a thing of the past, but in 1977, at the 75th anniversary, the tradition was temporarily revived, with the last named court and queen serving honorarily once again, as seen below. The royal ladies pictured are, from left to right, Theresa Avansino Cortopassi, Mary DeMattei Busalacchi, Edna Leonardini Filippi (queen), Marie Schenone Cima, and Linda Basso Angerini. (Right, courtesy of the San Joaquin County Historical Society; below, courtesy of historian Bennie Filippini, Italian Gardeners Society.)

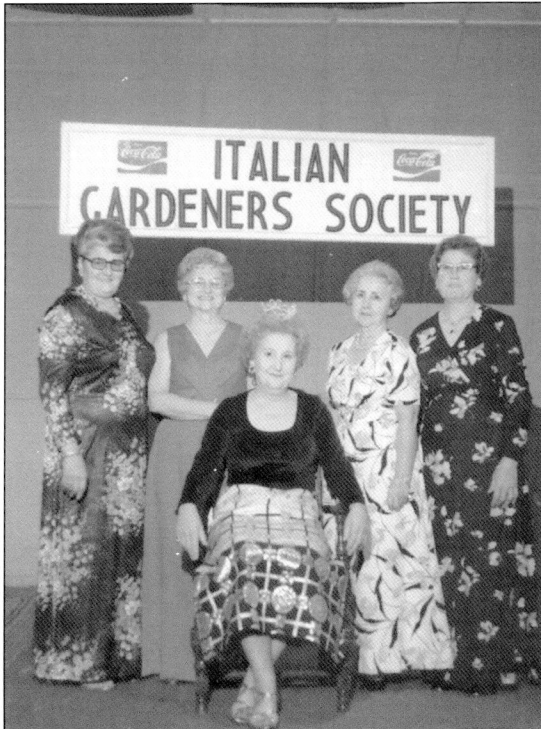

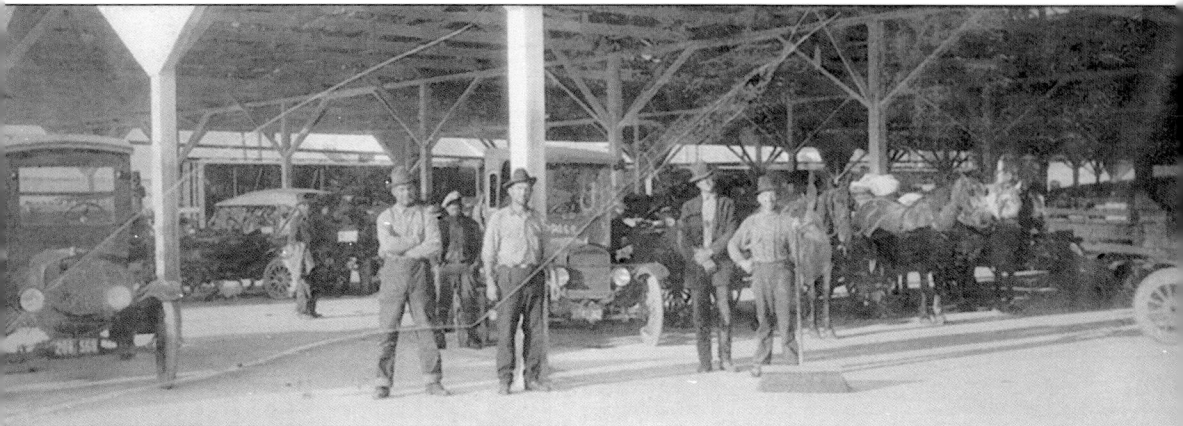

A New Market. On December 5, 1922, Stockton City Council unanimously passed Ordinance No. 811—which outlawed the practice of selling farm products from wagons, vehicles, or portable stands on public streets—to take effect in 30 days. This was a serious threat to the growers whose business relied on this type of marketplace. At a special meeting, the society immediately made plans to start a new organization and build the Growers Hall, with Giacomo Tassano spearheading the operation. Ironically, this was the very issue that had divided growers at the founding in 1902. The new group named itself the San Joaquin Marketing Association, and 500 shares of stock would be issued at $200 apiece, with no one able to take more than five shares. A 13-acre site was selected on East Street (now Wilson Way) between Channel Street and a local railroad spur. On December 18, the city rejected a time-extension request to continue street selling, so the marketing association secured permission from every resident near the new site to continue business. (Courtesy of historian Bennie Filippini, Italian Gardeners Society.)

FRUITFUL ADVICE. Noted pioneer and merchant Gaetano Alegretti was approached to provide assistance to the gardeners in the official formation of their association. He also served as secretary at its very first meeting in Bersaglieri Hall, and minutes from that meeting survive. The society honored his part in its establishment at the 58th anniversary picnic in 1960. (Courtesy of the San Joaquin County Historical Society.)

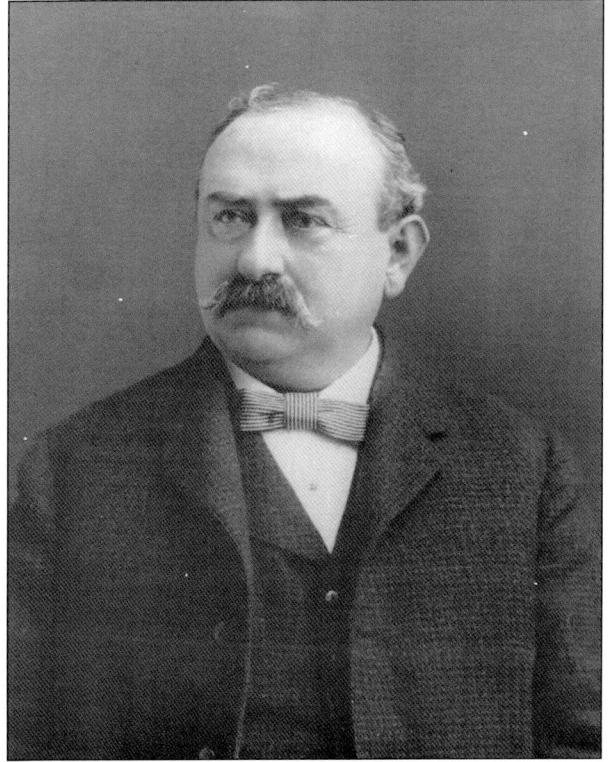

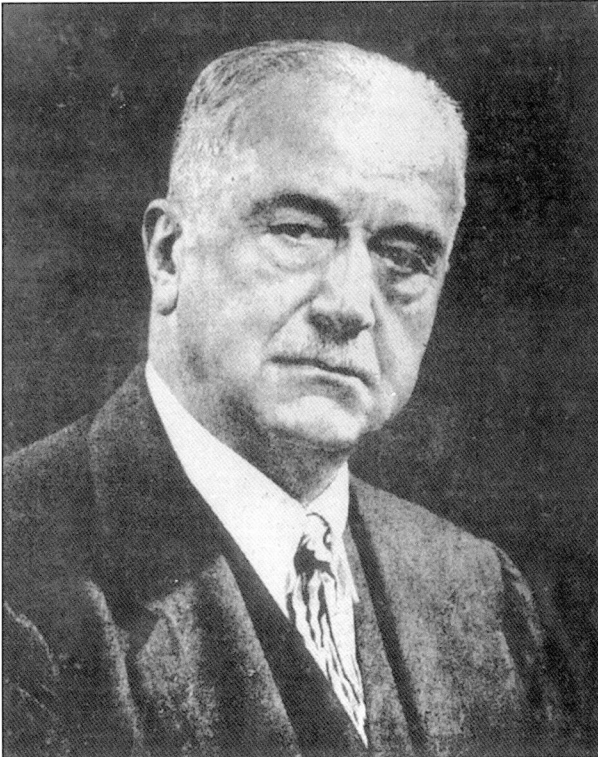

AMADEO GIANNINI. Even though 260 growers had invested $70,000 by December 1922, it was not enough capital. The society then secured a loan of $300,000 from Amadeo Giannini, the founder of the Bank of Italy, in January 1923. It purchased a seven-acre site and the hall was under construction by March; the facilities were opened to the public on April 30. (Courtesy of historian Bennie Filippini, Italian Gardeners Society.)

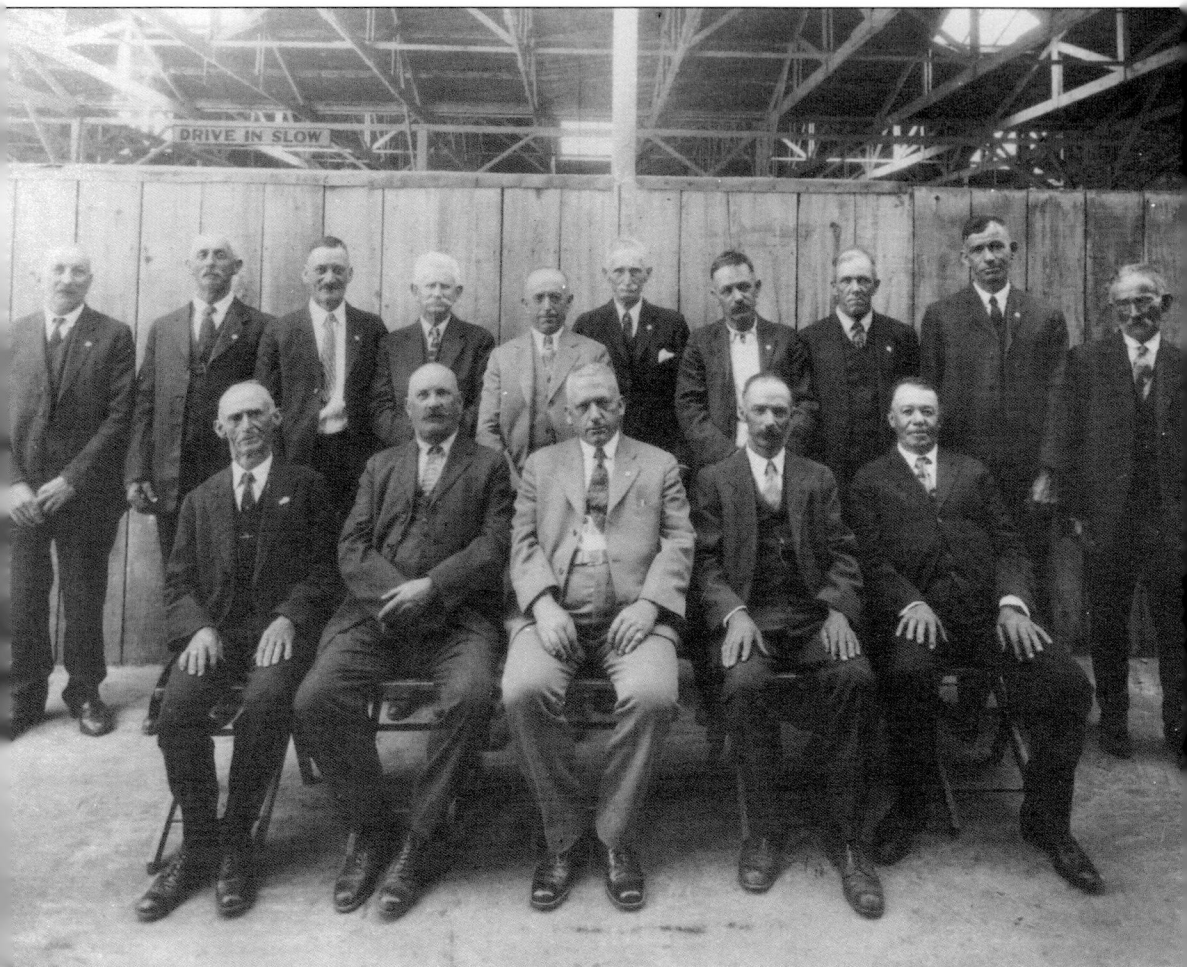

ITALIAN GARDENER OFFICERS. The officers of 1927 pose in their new building only four years after its construction. A shed with 656 stalls was built along with a structure containing street-level stores with Wilson Way frontage. A large hall above the shops could be used for business and social events, accommodating up to 750 people. It contained stalls for members, with each stall being large enough for a grower's truck. Half of the stalls were under a covered roof, and the other half, in the open air. It was a success, with two markets held every day, and by 1926, an estimated $5 million in product passed through the market annually. The officers are, from left to right, (first row) Edwardo Ghiorzo, Giovani Barosso, Giacomo Tassano, Giacomo Camera, and Agostino Ventre; (second row) Domenico Lartora, Antonio Pisacco, Vic Boggiano, Giuseppe Armanino, Pete Leonardini, Pete Partigiano, Frank Capurro, Luigi Grondona, Giuseppe Frugone, and Vincenzo Rossi. (Courtesy of historian Bennie Filippini, Italian Gardeners Society.)

Eight

THE PACIFIC
ITALIAN ALLIANCE

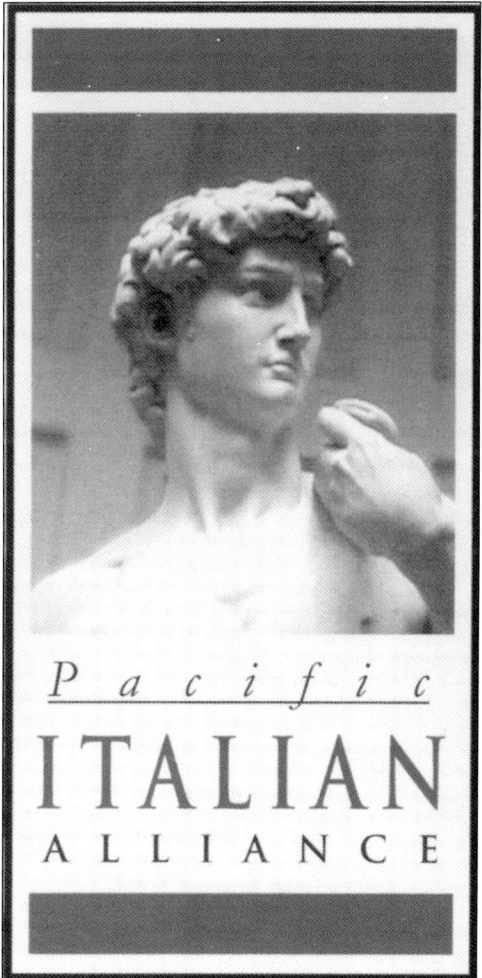

PACIFIC ITALIAN ALLIANCE. The Pacific Italian Alliance (PIA) is a unique organization dedicated to celebrating the wonders of Italy and bringing the Italian American community together to celebrate and promote a common heritage. Founded in 1991, the PIA marked its 20-year anniversary in 2011 and remains a driving force in the community of San Joaquin County. Membership is open to everyone with a love of Italy, its traditions, and its culture. (Courtesy of the Pacific Italian Alliance.)

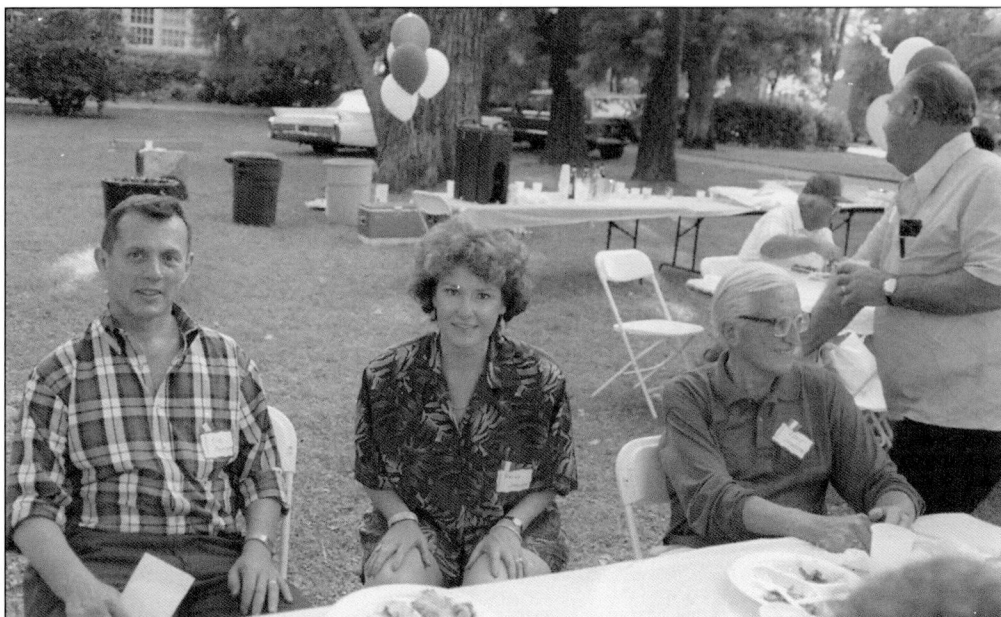

FIRST PIA PICNIC. The first Pacific Italian Alliance picnic was held in 1991, with Dr. Robert Benedetti, PhD (left), president Kathleen Lagorio Janssen, and F.M. "Luke" Luccacini. The picnic was conceived as a family-friendly event in partnership with the University of the Pacific's Italian Club to bring all generations together. (Courtesy of Dean Janssen.)

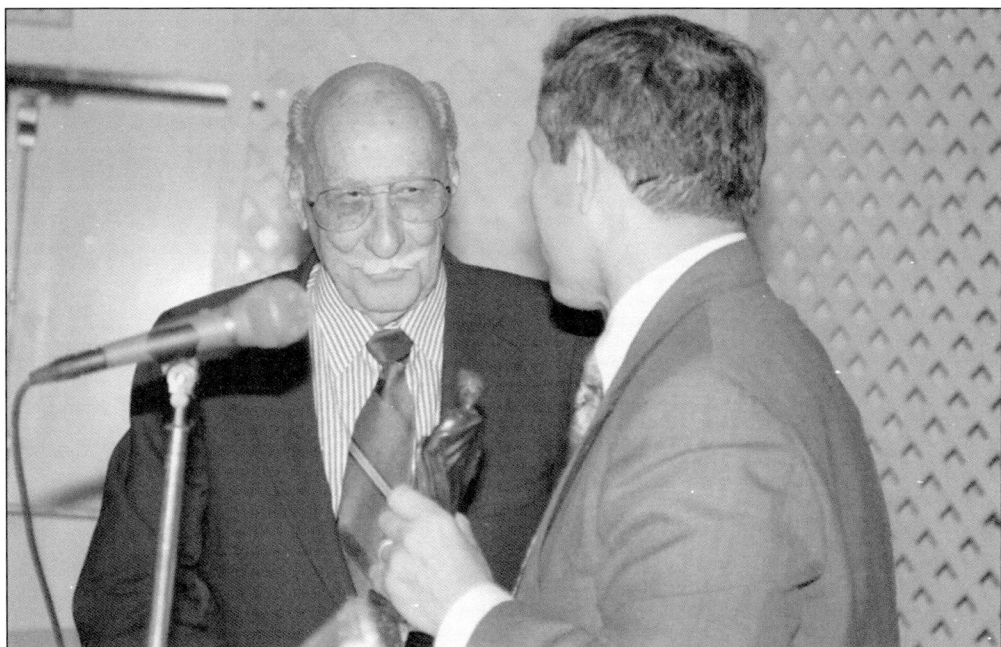

LUKE AWARDS. Here, Frank Garavano receives one of the very first Luke Awards. The Luke Award is named in memory of F.M. "Luke" Lucaccini, a longtime friend to many and a great crusader for the preservation of Italian culture and heritage. The statue of St. George is a replica of a work sculpted by Donatello and is hand cast in solid bronze by Frilli Gallery in Florence, Italy. (Courtesy of Dean Janssen.)

PASSPORT DINNER. Passport Dinners, annual banquets for members of the PIA, were often held at Capecchio Ovest, the beautiful Mediterranean-style estate of Dino and Joan Cortopassi. Each Passport Dinner celebrates a specific region of Italy with both decor and menu. Here, Amanda Podesta greets guests at the Passport to Palermo dinner. (Courtesy of Claudia Pruett.)

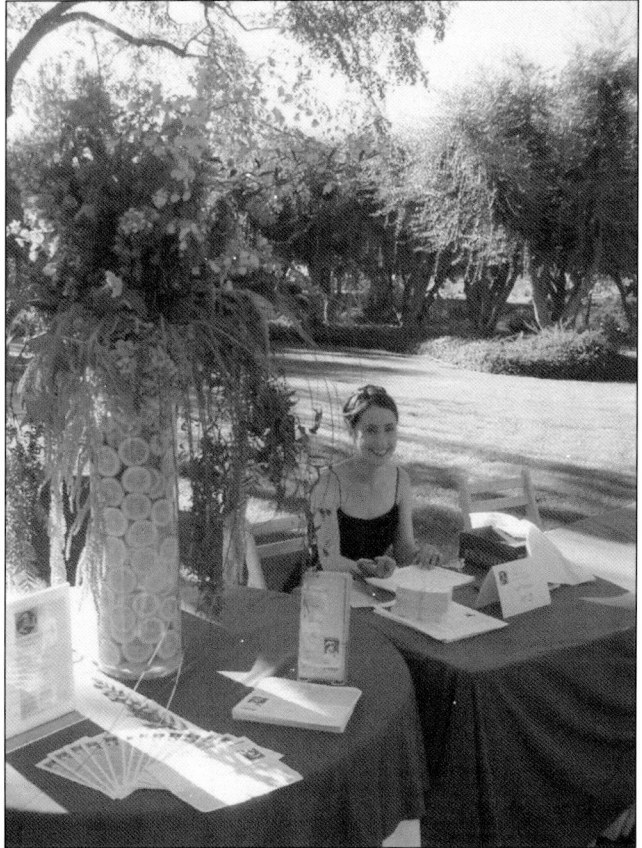

FESTA ITALIANA. In 2012, the PIA partnered with the Liguri Nel Mondo to bring an Italian festival to the area. At the conclusion of the 2012 Picnic Italiano, the PIA decided to host a larger event and enlisted the Italian School to hold Festa Italiana at the Waterloo Gun & Bocce Club. The 2013 Festa was attended by more than 2,000 Italians and friends in the community. (Courtesy of Ulmer Photography.)

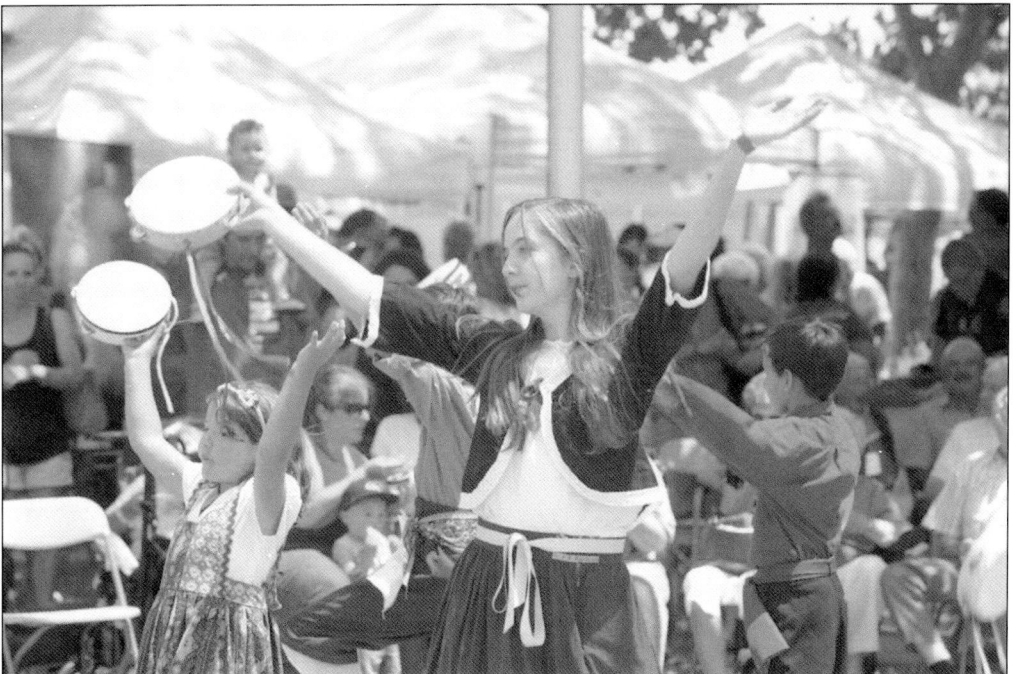

INDEX

ABOUT THE
ORGANIZATIONS

The Pacific Italian Alliance was organized in 1991 and is dedicated to celebrating the wonders of Italy and bringing the Italian American community together to honor and promote its common heritage. Membership is open to all with a love of Italy and comes with many benefits. Find out more at www.PacificItalianAlliance.com.

The Central California School of Italian Language and Culture was founded in 1974 and continues to offer quality education in the language, traditions, and culture of Italy for both children and adults. Classes are ongoing and available to all. For more information, please visit www.ItalianSchoolofStockton.com.

The Italian Gardeners Society, founded in 1902, continues today in its historical mission to promote the Italian American community. Membership is no longer restricted to gardeners or agriculturalists but is open to anyone with any Italian heritage. For any questions or more membership information, please contact society historian Bennie Filippini at benellen@aol.com or 209-931-2322.

Founded in 1928, the Haggin Museum is one of San Joaquin County's finest cultural institutions. An excellent art and history museum, the Haggin is located at 1201 North Pershing Avenue in Stockton. More information is available at www.HagginMuseum.org.

The San Joaquin County Historical Society and Museum started in 1966 to collect artifacts and information related to the development of San Joaquin County and is located inside the Micke Grove Park and Zoo complex at 11793 Micke Grove Road in Lodi. For more information, visit www.SanJoaquinHistory.org.

The Bank of Stockton started operation in 1867 and has served the community for over 145 years as a pioneering financial institution. In 1990, it acquired the collection of historian and photographer Leonard Covello, and its archives now contain more than 20,000 images. More information is available at www.BankofStockton.com.

DISCOVER THOUSANDS OF LOCAL HISTORY BOOKS
FEATURING MILLIONS OF VINTAGE IMAGES

Arcadia Publishing, the leading local history publisher in the United States, is committed to making history accessible and meaningful through publishing books that celebrate and preserve the heritage of America's people and places.

Find more books like this at
www.arcadiapublishing.com

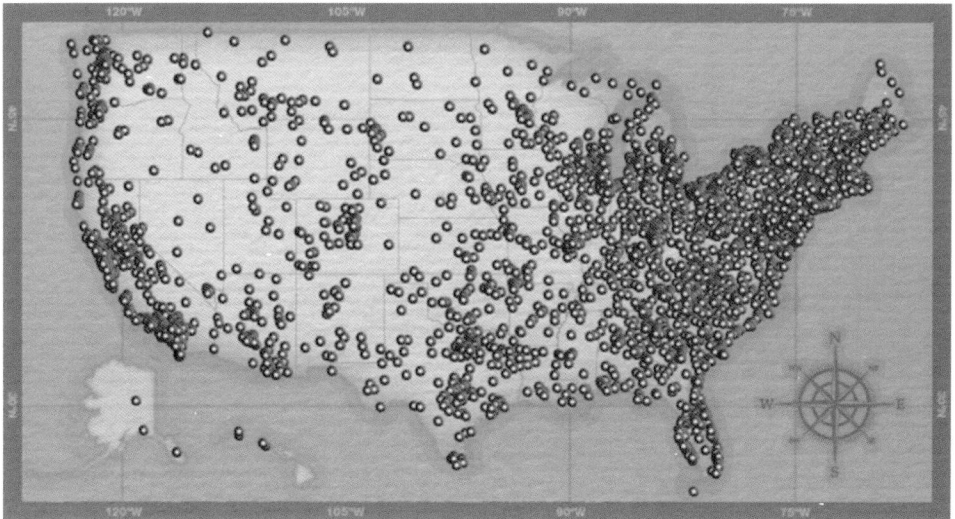

Search for your hometown history, your old stomping grounds, and even your favorite sports team.

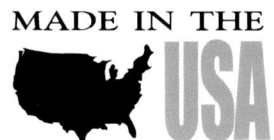